The Reminiscences

of

Captain Charles J. Merdinger

U. S. Navy (Retired)

U. S. Naval Institute
Annapolis, Maryland
1974

Preface

This volume consists of the transcript of five tape recorded interviews given by Captain Charles J. Merdinger, USN (Retired) and conducted by John T. Mason, Jr., for the U. S. Naval Institute in Annapolis, Maryland. These interviews were begun at the Institute in December 1971 and were concluded in March, 1972.

Captain Merdinger reviewed the original transcript and made a few corrections. Otherwise the manuscript stands essentially as it was spoken.

A subject index has been added to facilitate use of the material.

Captain Merdinger's career as a Civil Engineer Corps Officer in the U. S. Navy has many points of interest for the historian. In yet another sense it is of particular interest for it indicates clearly how higher education and a Rhodes scholarship have influenced the development and the direction of this naval career.

DECLARATION OF TRUST

The undersigned does hereby appoint and designate as his (her) Trustee herein, the Secretary-Treasurer and Publisher of the United States Naval Institute to perform and discharge the following duties, powers, and privileges in connection with the possession and use of a certain taped interview between the undersigned and the Oral History Department of the United States Naval Institute.

1. Classification of Transcript.

(✓)a. If classified OPEN, the transcript(s) may be read or the recording(s) audited by the qualified personnel upon presentation of proper credentials, as determined by the Secretary-Treasurer of the U. S. Naval Institute.

( )b. If classified PERMISSION REQUIRED TO CITE OR QUOTE, the user will be required to obtain permission in writing from the interviewee prior to quoting or citing from either the transcript(s) or the recording(s).

( )c. If classified PERMISSION REQUIRED, permission must be obtained in writing from the interviewee before the transcribed interview(s) can be examined or the tape recording(s) audited.

( )d. If classified CLOSED, the transcribed interview(s) and the tape recording(s) will be sealed until a time specified by the interviewee. This may be until the death of the interviewee or for any specified number of years.

2. It is expressly understood that in giving this authorization, I am in no way precluded from placing such restrictions as I may desire upon use of the interview at any time during my lifetime, nor does this authorization in any way affect my rights to the copyright of my literary expressions that may be contained in the interview.

Witness my hand and seal this ___4___ day of ___AUGUST___ 19_72_.

Charles L. Merdinger
Captain, U.S.N. (retired)

I hereby accept and consent to the foregoing Declaration of Trust and the powers therein conferred upon me as Trustee:

OFFICER BIOGRAPHY SHEET

NAVPERS 979 (REV. 12-56)

This form is to be completed in triplicate and submitted in accordance with current BuPers directives.

DATE: 11 April 1969

NAME (Surname) (First) (Middle)	GRADE	DATE RANK	FILE NUMBER & DESIGNATOR
MERDINGER, Charles John	CAPT	7/1/59	100153/5100

HOME TOWN ADDRESS FOR PUBLICITY PURPOSES	DATE OF BIRTH	PLACE OF BIRTH
1252 Fairlands Vista Way, La Jolla, Calif (Brother's add.)	4/20/18	Chicago, Ill.

FATHER'S NAME AND ADDRESS	MOTHER'S MAIDEN NAME AND ADDRESS
Walter F. Merdinger (deceased)	Catherine G. Phelan (deceased)

PRESENT RESIDENCE OF WIFE OR NOK	OFFICIAL (PERMANENT) ADDRESS OF OFFICER
Quarters A, U.S. Navy, San Bruno, Calif 94066	Chicago, Ill.

DATE AND PLACE OF MARRIAGE	MAIDEN NAME AND FORMER HOME OF WIFE
10/21/44 - Cambridge, Mass.	Mary F. McKellaget, Cambridge, Mass.

NAMES OF CHILDREN	DATE OF BIRTH	SPECIAL CIVILIAN ACHIEVEMENTS, SOCIETIES, CLUBS, ATHLETICS, HOBBIES
Anne MERDINGER	10/29/46	College letters in football, soccer, basketball and lacrosse. All American (English) lacrosse; Mbr: ASCE, SAME, NSPE, RSP, ACEC, SigmaXi, TauBetaPi, ChiEpsilon, Phalanx, Eagle Scout, Listed in Who's Who, Am. Men of Science, etc.
Joan MERDINGER	5/24/48	
Susan MERDINGER	11/12/50	
Jane MERDINGER	6/24/52	

SCHOOLS OR COLLEGES ATTENDED PRIOR TO ENTERING NAVY	DEGREES
Marquette University (Civil Engineering) '35-'37	

AS APPLICABLE: USNA CLASS—MIDSHIPMEN SCHOOL AND CLASS—NROTC SCHOOL AND CLASS—OCS CLASS	DATE BEGAN NAVAL SERV.
U. S. Naval Academy - Class of '41 (Bachelor of Science)	6/12/37

DATE COMMISSIONED	GRADE COMMISSIONED IN	SPECIAL NAVY DESIGNATIONS AND DATES (AVIATOR, SUBMARINER, EDO, AEDO, LDO, SDO)
7 Feb 1941	ENS, USN	CEC - 1945

SPECIAL NAVY ACHIEVEMENTS, ADVANCED NAVY SCHOOLING.

Rensselaer Polytechnic Institute, Troy, N.Y. '44-'46 Degrees: Bachelor and Master of Civil Engineering

Brasenose College, Oxford University, England '47-'49 Degree: Doctor of Philosophy

BRIEF BIOGRAPHY OF CAREER: Include information relative to—

(a) Occupation and outstanding experiences in civilian life.

Registered Professional Engineer - State of Wisconsin
Rhodes Scholar (Wisconsin and Brasenose '47)

(b) Newsworthy data on personal life, such as "Wife was former Wave," "Son at Naval Academy," "Escaped from Corregidor," etc.

In charge of building Navy's first Jet Air Station, Miramar 1954-'57
Toulmin Medal awarded by Society of American Military Engineers 1952, 1957 and 1961 (for best published engineering article of year)

(c) Unusual war experiences, campaigns, operations.

Sunk at Pearl Harbor aboard USS NEVADA 7 Dec 1941
Served aboard USS ALABAMA on "Murmansk Run" 1943
In charge of Seabees at Adak in Aleutians 1953-'54
In charge of Navy's largest Public Works organization (Seabees & Multinational Force), DaNang, Viet Nam 1967-'68

(d) List decorations (M of H, Navy Cross, etc., PUC + NUC with units, include stars + devices).

LEGION OF MERIT for service in Viet Nam
NAVY UNIT COMMENDATION for service in Viet Nam

(e) List campaign and service medals, with stars, clasps, etc.

1-American Defense Service Medal with Fleet Clasp
2-Asiatic-Pacific Area with 2 battle stars
3-American Area
4-European-African-Middle Eastern Area
5-World War II Victory
6-National Emergency Service with 1 star
7-Viet Nam Service Medal with 3 stars
8-Republic of Viet Nam Campaign with device

(f) Outline chronologically all Armed Forces service (include enlisted service, reserve activity, PUC or NUC awards): (Estimate dates, if unknown)

FROM MO.-YR.	TO MO.-YR.	SHIP--UNIT--STATION	PRIMARY DUTIES	REMARKS (and noteworthy collateral duties, etc.)
Nov 35	Jun 37	Btry"D", 121st F.A.	Fire Control Party	Enlisted (PFC Sp.6/c)
Jun 37	Feb 41	U.S.Naval Academy	Midshipman	Cruises:USS NewYork,Claxton,Texas
Feb 41	Jun 42	USS NEVADA P.H.	Fire Control	Pacific Fleet
Jun 42	Dec 43	USS ALABAMA MURMANSK	Turret Officer(16")	Atlantic and Pacific
Jan 44	Apr 46	RPI Troy N.Y.	PG student	Transferred to CEC
Apr 46	Jun 46	CECOS Davisville	Student Officer	
Jun 46	Jun 47	15ND HQ Balboa, Panama Canal Zone	ROICC and Base Maint.Officer	In chg of CPFF Contract building roads, houses, etc.
Aug 47	Aug 49	Oxford University	Rhodes Scholar	Asst to Naval Attache, London
Sep 49	Mar 51	BUDOCKS Washn DC	Engineering-Design	Res.Ofcr in chg of A&E contracts
Apr 51	Jan 53	Puget Sound NavShipYd	Asst Pub Wks Ofcr	Base Basketball Coach 13ND Champs
Jan 53	Mar 54	Adak, Alaska	Pub Wks Officer	Primarily Seabee Org.(old 124 NCB)
Apr 54	Oct 56	NAS Miramar Calif	Pub Wks Officer	ROICC ($17,000,000 maximum)
Oct 56	Aug 59	Naval Civil Engr Lab Pt Hueneme Calif	Commanding Officer and Director	Engaged in Research & Development
Sep 59	Jul 62	Fleet Activities, Yokosuka, Japan	Pub Wks Officer	Base Basketball Coach
Aug 62	Jul 65	U.S.Naval Academy	Head of English History & Govt Dept	Off.Rep. of Lacrosse Member of Academic Board
Aug 65	Jan 67	BUDOCKS WashingtonDC	Asst Chief for Operations & Maintenance	
Mar 67	Mar 68	Public Works, NSA DaNang, Viet Nam	Pub Wks Officer	Seabees,Vietnamese,Koreans,Filipinos,Chinese (4500 men)
Jul 68	present	Western Division, NAVFACENGCOM San Bruno Calif	Commanding Officer & Dist Civil Engr, 12ND	

(g) List all promotions with effective date of rank.

```
ENS       7 Feb 1941
LTJG      Jun 42
LT        1 Dec 42
LCDR      20 Jul 45
CDR       1 Jan 51
CAPT      1 Jul 59
```

(h) Has photograph been submitted in accordance with current BuPers directives? [X] YES [ ] NO

(i) I authorize the release of the foregoing in official releases for publicity purposes.

DATE SUBMITTED 11 April 1969

Interview No. 1 with Captain (Dr.) Charles Merdinger

Place: U. S. Naval Institute, Annapolis, Maryland

Date: 28 December 1971

Subject: Biography

By: John T. Mason, Jr.

Q: Captain, I've really been looking forward to this series with you. You've had a very distinguished naval career but you've also had a very distinguished academic career in which you're still involved, so the combination should make for a very readable oral biography, once it's transcribed. Will you begin, Sir, in the proper way for a biography. Tell me where you were born, the date of your birth, and something about your family background.

Captain Merdinger: I was born in Chicago, April 20, 1918, went through the public schools in Chicago through my junior year in high school at which time we moved to Milwaukee. Then I went one final year to Sherwood High School in a suburb of Milwaukee. My father was in the Kran-Mer Corporation, ultimately became its president. This was at the time, I guess, the largest wholesale dye house in the United States and possibly the world. So he was one of these rugged Middle West businessmen who in a sense fought his way up from the bottom, with a great distaste for unions and all that that implied; and that was mainly the reason that we moved from Chicago. The racketeers of the Capone era and even later had forced their way into what was called the cleaning and dyeing business, although as I mentioned, he was in the wholesale part of it. In other words, he was not concerned with direct contact with customers. All these places that call themselves cleaning dyeing places do the cleaning there, but they send their dyeing into a central dye house. Actually Kran-Mer took in business all over the country. It was a mail order business as well. They had so much trouble with unions - Chicago and things connected with them that they decided to move to Milwaukee.

Now, most of the people they had in the plant, the artisans, were dyers, old timers who'd come over from Germany, so Milwaukee seemed a natural place for them to move. That's how we happened to go up there.

Q: Was there any more protection found in Milwaukee?

Merdinger: Generally speaking, yes, although ultimately the unions came to the point where they were at least trying to picket the plant because it wasn't union labor. Ultimately the company agreed to pay all the union dues for its employees with the understanding that the union wouldn't bother them. This was satisfactory to the emplyees. They didn't want to belong to the union, and the management wasn't particularly eager for them to belong either, so this was the compromise that was finally reached.

Q: Was this satisfactory to the union leaders?

Merdinger: Apparently so. They had the money, which was the important thing, as I gather, following Dad's views on the subject.

Q: That's somewhat disillusioning, isn't it?

Merdinger: That's right, and that's where I got some of my first experience. I worked in the plant in Milwaukee, in the summer time as a student, making the princely sum of $12 a week. That played a big part in helping me go on to Marquette University for a couple of years. I lived at home. The first year, I went into the liberal arts school with the thought that I would try to win an appointment to West Point; I wanted to be an Army engineer. This was my great ambition.

Q: What was the source of this ambition?

Merdinger: Well, it's kind of hard to say. I don't really know, except that from the time I was a very small boy I was always interested in war stories. The military itself rather fascinated me. I read the books on "Dick Prescott at West Point" and "Dave Daren, at Annapolis," so I think this was a kind of an inspirational thing that spurred me on. I'm not quite sure where the engineering came from except that something in me wanted to be a builder of some sort.

Q: Did your father aid this ambition?

Merdinger: Well, he didn't stifle it. Put it this way, I think that he ultimately expected me to come into the business.

Q: Were you the only son?

Merdinger #1 - 4

Merdinger: No, I had a brother. I think both of us got a little turned off, much like youth today - I guess perhaps we thought there was more materializm in it than interested us. He went off and ultimately became a surgeon, and starved for a number of years as he went through various phases of medical school and postgraduate training, this, that and the other thing. The business of the plant really never interested either of us too much, apart from a summer job there.

At any rate, at Marquette I was in the liberal arts school, and I felt that I could get enough of the background to qualify for the exams at West Point, and in the course of taking these exams I found myself on a combined list of people who'd taken the exams for both West Point and Annapolis, and --

Q: This was a Congressional appointment?

Merdinger: Yes, this was a Congressional appointment, and interestingly enough, I stood higher than any of those who were going to Annapolis on this list. The trouble was, I hadn't signed up for Annapolis. So the first year went by and I was still at Marquette.

Q: Was that standing commensurate with what you had done in previous years in high school and were doing at Marquette, the fact that you were higher than the rest of them on the list?

Merdinger: Well, I'd been reasonably successful in high school, and so I guess that it wasn't too much of a surprise to realize I was fairly high on the list. But, of course, I wasn't high enough to get the appointment, which was the whole thing. You either win or lose on that one.

The following year then I determined to apply for both academies, although I didn't know anything about Annapolis at all. As a matter of fact, at the time I was also in the National Guard, so I was trying for a West Point appointment from that source.

As fate would have it, the next year I ended up winning both Senatorial and Congressional appointments to Annapolis, and I had the National Guard appointment to West Point. So I had in essence four principal appointments.

Q: Which one did you select, Senator Wiley's?

Merdinger: No, I selected the Congressman's, for some reason. His came in first; Congressman O'Malley was his name, I think it was the 5th Congressional district of Wisconsin but I'm not sure of that, but I had a kind of peculiar reason for choosing it. Among other things, I'd been to the CMTC camp, and had a lot to do with horses in the field artillery. I was in the field artillery in the National Guard as well, although we were not horse drawn. I reasoned that in the Army I was going to have to clean some more horses, and I knew they had horses at West Point. I didn't know what they had at Annapolis, but they didn't have horses. And I think that in the final analysis, I just finally decided that I had more appointments to Annapolis. I didn't know anything about the ocean but I thought I'd go there. So it was a kind of a funny choice, really.

Q: How did your family react to this?

Merdinger #1 - 6

Merdinger: Well, my dad was very surprised because he was under the impression that getting an appointment to the academy in those days was simply a matter of political influence, and we had none. He didn't know any Congressmen, Senators or anybody and I'd never made any attempt other than to take their competitive exams. Well, it turned out that every one of them was giving a competitive exam under civil service and since I'd won, it just seemed to me a very natural thing. I didn't realize that sometimes these things were as competitive as they turned out to be.

Q: He was the generation before.

Merdinger: Well, I think so. I think they were very pleased and proud and just generally happy that I'd got what I wanted. So off I went to the Academy.

Q: With two years of college behind you. This must have been a distinct advantage.

Merdinger: I think it was, although in looking over the statistics of my class, somewhere between 75 and 80 percent had gone to college or had done something before they came to the Academy beyond high school. There was a complete reversal of today's situation, where most of the midshipmen are coming directly out of high school now.

Q: Prior to that time that had been the case, had it not? Not many of them had college or schooling.

Merdinger: No, if I could generalize, and I don't have the statistics

Merdinger #1 - 7

at my fingertips, if I could generalize I would say that most of them did not come directly from high school in those days. There were some who were college graduates, as a matter of fact, who came in as plebes. I would say that the average age of our class on entry was over 19 years of age.

Q: What was the maximum permitted?

Merdinger: The maximum was 20 years of age and most of us were pressing the upper limit. There were some, I do recall one or two who were about 16 or 17, but the majority were above the average college entering age at that time.

Q: Tell me about the course of study at that time. It was in 1937, was it not?

Merdinger: Yes. We all took the same course with the exception of foreign language. We had a choice, I recall -- we could study French, Spanish, German and Portuguese, I believe. I took French simply because I'd studied it before and thought perhaps I'd be a little more at home in it. For some of us it made for an easy plebe year. For instance, if you'd had calculus before, which I had - and we even had the same textbook - it wasn't too great a strain. I think some who came in with that kind of advantage also suffered a disadvantage in that they got lulled into a false sense of security - that this place wasn't going to be as tough as it turned out to be. I don't know whether the course was so tough or even the instructors so good, but there was something about the place that really turned out some very good people, just speaking in the academic sense now. Most of them who went on to postgraduate school were very successful, no matter where they went. Regardless of where they stood in their classwork at the Naval Academy they did very well in postgraduate work. So I think it says something for the selection process perhaps that brought them in here. Maybe it says something for the course of instruction too. I'm not sure about that.

Q: Since in retrospect you've had a chance to compare their engineering courses with those of other institutions, how did they stack up?

Merdinger: Well, of course, you've got to appreciate the philosophy that was underlying the course here. I think the engineering that we were getting was really just a broad view, trying to give us a smattering of what engineering was like so that when we came up against it in the fleet as we must, the general approach to engineering problems wouldn't be completely foreign to us. Now, later on, when I went to Rensselaer Polytech, for my postgraduate work in civil engineering, it wasn't only civil engineering we studied. We went to graduation with the electrical engineers and the mechanical engineers as well, but since we were in the civil engineering program we got the degree in civil engineering. This was much more oriented to the civilian design engineer. In other words, we didn't have design courses at the Naval Academy, but as RPI there was a heavy emphasis on design.

So from the standpoint of learning good hard engineering, I felt that the RPI curriculum was far more complete, far better for turning out a good design engineer. In terms of turning out an engineering executive, I think you might be about to argue in some other directions. RPI was totally engineering and science, whereas at the Naval Academy we had this leavening of the humanities and other activities that I think would help turn out a broader person.

So you're comparing apples and oranges I think in a sense, because the Naval Academy was not an engineering school per se, but it was a school with a bias toward engineering, if you will, and I think it did a very good job for what it was attempting to do.

Q: Its primary objective was to turn out a naval officer.

Merdinger: That's right, and I think it did a very good job of that.

Q: How did it emphasize leadership in the courses?

Merdinger: Oh, I think the whole atmosphere of the place, the living in Bancroft Hall, the general military atmosphere of the place, the midshipman and officer system, the watch standing, going to sea — all these things, I think, played a part in giving us a background first in following, then in leading. I don't think anyone can lead very well unless he's had a good deal of following, and I think we had the opportunity to get both kinds of experience.

Q: One of the superintendents before your time told me once that his feeling was that they should turn out naval officers and gentlemen. Was that also an element in your education?

Merdinger: I would subscribe to that. I think it was there. I don't think people stressed every day that one would be a gentleman, but there was something in the air. There was something implicit in all that

Merdinger #1 - 10

we did.

The formal dances, the little bits of etiquette that we were brought face to face with -- to many of us it wasn't particularly new, to others perhaps it was. In the long run it gave a certain cast to the overall social environment of the place. I think that helped, a certain amount of leavening there that was valuable.

Q: Did you find the life of discipline very rigorous and confining?

Merdinger: If anything, I was a little disappointed that it wasn't stricter than it was. I think that I had been so brainwashed with the Dave Daren at Annapolis books and Dick Prescott at West Point that I expected the discipline to be much tougher. So in summation on that score, I never found it restrictive at all. I enjoyed the life. I enjoyed the four years there. Oh, not everything; obviously there are times when things don't go right and you don't like something, but in the rosy afterglow as I look at it after a span of years, my memories are essentially happy ones.

Q: You were quite an athlete, too?

Merdinger: Oh, I don't know that I was so much of an athlete, but I was on a team every year.

Q: What were your specialties?

Merdinger: The first year I played on the plebe football team, plebe basketball, then finally the plebe lacrosse team. I'd never seen lacrosse before I came there.

Q: It was largely confined to the East Coast, wasn't it?

Merdinger: Yes. I'd read about it, but I think the thing that brought me out for it was really the realization that so many people were going to get into the game. I went down and saw a few scrimmages, saw them carrying a lot of people off the field, and figured there would always be room for one more, whereas I'd played baseball before and that was pretty much of a nine man operation. But it looked as if there'd be great opportunity on the lacrosse field. So I went out and played on the plebe lacrosse team.

Q: Had you demonstrated an interest in athletics at Marquette?

Merdinger: Only on the intramural teams. I played on the liberal arts college basketball team and softball team, not in the varsity sports. I had played varsity sports in high school, but at Marquette, there were several factors. One, I probably wasn't good enough, for the varsity team. Two, I was working as janitor on the side, and I was also trying to get to the Academy and spending a lot of extra time studying for that, so everything added up, and I didn't get out to really participate except on these intramural teams. At the Naval Academy I had much more time and the system was much more geared to giving a fellow a chance to go out. So then, sophomore year, I ended up on the varsity soccer team. I'd been a place kicker in football, and really wasn't much good but I liked kicking the ball. Soccer seemed a natural outlet so I ended up on the varsity soccer team.

Then I went on to JV basketball, then varsity lacrosse, and

this pattern continued then through the rest of the years.

When I got to RPI, I hadn't used up all my eligibility, so I did play on the varsity football and varsity lacrosse teams there. It was at RPI, my third varsity year after two at Navy, that I made the All-American squad there, as a defense man.

Then subsequently when I went to Oxford, I played on the varsity basketball team and the varsity lacrosse team.

Q: They have lacrosse at Oxford?

Merdinger: Oh, yes. The Oxford-Cambridge game antedates the Army-Navy game. Most of the teams we played were club and not college teams. I was captain of the team over there. The captain is also the coach, by the way. They don't have very high-powered athletics. It's pretty much up to the players themselves to get organized and do these things.

Q: A different approach from ours.

Merdinger: Very different. Yes, our basketball team, for instance, traveled all over Europe. We played a good many of the Olympic teams, in Europe. This was prior to the '48 Olympics. Yet this was all student organized. There was nothing really that the university had done to put this tour together.

So I guess if you sum it all up, lacrosse then would have been the sport. You asked what did I concentrate on. I guess if you follow this progression through the years, you'll find that I played lacrosse as a varsity sport more than anything else.

Merdinger #1 - 13

Q: As a middlewestern landlubber of sorts, how did you take to the salt water, sailing, that sort of thing?

Merdinger: I loved the sailing. I found myself seasick, however, on the first destroyer cruise we took. The battleship cruise we took our youngster year was fine. No problems with mal de mere. But in our second class year, we went to sea on these old four stack destroyers. This happens to be one of the ones we gave away to Britain, as you may recall, in a 1939 trade for bases. I have never been so miserable in all my life, I think, as I was in that ship in a storm off Cape Hatteras. Most of the ship's company seemed to have the same problem. It wasn't any great comfort to know that the old chief petty officer who'd been in the Navy 26 years was about as sick as I was.

Q: It comes down to an individual matter —

Merdinger: Yes, it really does. I'm afraid that I didn't generate a great deal of enthusiasm for destroyer duty as a result of that particular cruise. But I enjoyed going to sea. I enjoyed being in battleships, where I served subsequently.

Q: Tell me about your cruises while you were at the Academy?

Merdinger: Well, we were midshipmen in every sense of the word. We lived amid ships and we were something midway between the enlisted men and the officers.

Q: This is in your youngster year.

Merdinger: Yes, particularly in the youngster year. We did all the things that the seamen did in a very menial way in those days. We shined the same dog in the morning, then we'd go back and shine it again in the afternoon. We got up at the crack of dawn and scrubbed the decks, holystoned them, scrubbed them down. This was a lot of fun in your bare feet and cold water. We slept in hammocks. That's disappeared from the Navy, lo, these many years.

Q: You were spared what some of your predecessors did, however, coaling a ship.

Merdinger: That's one thing we never had to do. And the cruises were -- well, they were so eye opening in so many ways. After all, everything had been theoretical at the Naval Academy. We'd get out and see the fleet in actual operations, talk to the sailors and the officers in their natural habitat - I think it was certainly great for us.

Q: The practical application.

Merdinger: Yes, the really practical application for these things that you'd been reading about. Or perhaps you'd been answering questions. After all, as plebes we had a lot of questions to answer about the Navy, and many of these were rote answers. I must confess that I didn't realize all the time just what the answer meant that I was giving. Well, here the thing came alive, on board ship, and the fact that we were all midshipmen together I think was a great advantage to us, because we could learn almost in classroom situations. We weren't an extra number in the way. Now, some subsequent midshipmen cruises have perhaps fallen a bit in that category, in that a few midshipmen have been assigned to some of these ships regularly engaged in fleet operations. For one reason or another some ship's companies just couldn't pay the attention to them that perhaps they needed, whereas in our case it was all for the midshipmen. That was the purpose of the cruise.

Q: Where did you go on the battleship?

Merdinger: In 1938 we went to Europe. Let's see, we went to France and Great Britain and Denmark. I recall the trips Cook's travel agency or somebody had generated for us, so we had an opportunity to see not only Paris but to get out in the countryside, see a bit of France, not only to London but see a bit of the countryside there.

Q: Did you get a feel for "the gathering storm," as Churchill put it?

Merdinger: I wish that I could say that I had, but to be perfectly honest with you, I missed it. I missed it entirely. A number of people asked me that, when I came back, and I made some broad statement to the effect that "everybody looked peaceful to me." I didn't really see this. No, I didn't.

Q: You were a wide-eyed tourist.

Merdinger: I was a wide-eyed tourist and I enjoyed it tremendously, and I'm afraid that it's a bug that got into me that I've never gotten over. I can't resist taking a trip some place. I like to go some place because it is there, and because I haven't seen it before. This manifested itself as late as last summer, when my wife and I took two of our daughters

Merdinger #1 - 16

and jumped on a space available plane out of McGuire Airport and we went to the first place it was going. We ended up in Spain. Then we hopped from there to Greece and other places. So it's just - I think it all goes back perhaps to that youngster year cruise, when I got excited about the business of foreign travel and I've never gotten over it.

To go on about the cruise itself. We learned something about gunnery, and I must confess that theoretical ordnance and gunnery was not one of my favorite subjects here at the Academy. Of course, we hadn't had that as plebes and I'm really skipping ahead to the next year or so, but I found practical gunnery much more interesting and absorbing. Strangely enough, I didn't particularly care for engineering. That is, I didn't care for shipboard engineering, and I think that had to do with being below decks. I like to be out in the salt air. I loved being on deck. Later on when I was an officer in the fleet, and I became a 16 inch turret officer, and I was an officer of the deck under wartime conditions of one watch in 3. To me that was one of life's great experiences - being an officer of the deck.

I wouldn't have traded it for going down in the engine room. That wouldn't have interested me at all, which is kind of peculiar I guess in the eyes of some, since ultimately I became a professional engineer and it's been much of my life's work. But shipboard engineering, as I say, did not appeal to me nearly as much as being out on the open deck.

Well, to sum up the youngster cruise, I think if anything it just gave me a great deal of love for the Navy.

Q: It solidified your determination to be a naval officer.

Merdinger: Well, yes. I went with all kinds of blue and gold and everything in my eyes anyway. I was prepared to be seduced, if you will, by the Navy and so it was an easy matter. It wasn't any great problem.

Q: Was this the prevailing attitude of your classmates as well?

Merdinger: That's kind of hard to say. I think that a good many of them did. Certainly the record would seem to indicate it, in that our resignation rate from the class, until we could retire 20 years later, was something around 13 percent who resigned. This, of course, is very low, in the light of today's figures at least.

Q: You came out with a world war after that.

Merdinger: Well, yes, we came out in February of '41. Of course it wasn't very much later before the war started. But on the other hand, when the war was over there were many compelling reasons to get out. I know my family pressed on me with the idea of getting out, "Who's going to stay in the Navy? You'll never get promoted again. The war's over and you'll stagnate for years and anybody who can do anything, who's worth anything, is getting out."

I heard this in a number of places and I think probably a number of my classmates were subjected to the same thing, yet relatively few did get out. I'd say that the majority of them did get out right at the close of World War II, and that was it, although resignations

Merdinger #1 - 18

continued on a sporadic basis until about 15 years out. The reason I know this is because some years ago I made a little study on the class, as to what happened.

Q: Were you one of the class officers?

Merdinger: I was the treasurer, I think, for a while, but I was never around enought to keep the money so it ended up in somebody else's lap. But no, I did it just out of a whim, as a matter of fact. I happened to be here on the faculty of the Academy, and we were asking ourselves what are the particulars of success in the naval profession? What do we do here at the Naval Academy that's important? Of course you know we've always thought in terms of athletics and academics, and stripes and this sort of thing. Well, are they important or aren't they? So I did a little study on the class after we'd made captain (but nobody had come up for flag rank yet). Less than 50 percent of the class did finally reach the rank of captain, but the interesting thing was that a majority had stayed in for over 20 years, so that's why I happen to know a few of these things.

Q: Tell me about some of the subsequent summer cruises.

Merdinger: The second class cruise aboard this four stack destroyer I was telling you about was simply up and down the East Coast of the United States. I do recall one pleasant part, where we went up to Poughkeepsie to watch the regatta up there, and we ended up at West Point for some sort of social occasion. I remember a social occasion down in the Norfolk area, and that was very pleasant, of course, for midship-

men to visit in those days. I found it, as I mentioned, very unpleasant in a storm off Cape Hatteras. I seem to recall that after we did some gunnery down south, maybe in Guantanamo Bay, but again that's a little vague in my mind --

Q: Why was this tour confined to the East Coast?

Merdinger: It was only six weeks, as I recall. Of course, they had to work all the second classmen through this experience, so some of us would be at the Academy while others were cruising, I guess, on the same ships.

Q: What did you do at the Academy when you exchanged like that? Aviation?

Merdinger: Well, we had a number of things. Part of the time we were studying ourselves. Part of it was second class summer aviation. We got exposed to the flying boats that they had here. Then, we also, a number of us, had details to take care of the incoming plebe class. That was traditionally a second class operations, to bring in the new plebes.

Q: Especially if you're athletically inclined?

Merdinger: I suppose that had something to do with it. I don't recall now, although I do remember teaching a number of plebes how to play lacrosse. But that was a pleasant part of the summer, I think, bringing in the new class this way. The studies, as I say, apart from the aviation, kind of faded from view. Now I'm not sure what it was that we studied. But I don't think that the task was very onerous. All in all, it was a very pleasant summer.

Merdinger #1 - 20

Then you go to first class cruise. This was in the summer of 1940, and I'm trying to recall where we went on that. We were originally scheduled to go to Europe, and -- let's see, I'd better check that......

We were going to Europe, but because of the hostilities we ended up taking the South Atlantic cruise, and I recall going down to the Virgin Islands and the northern tip of South America. We thought we were going to cross the Equator but we never quite managed that. However, we did get down to Venezuela. That was one of the ports of call. And there I was brought in contact the first time with Latin American temperament, there and in Panama.

I seem to recall being invited to a party that was supposed to start at 9 o'clock, and nobody showed up until about 11 except the midshipmen -- in the evening, this was, and we were scheduled to go back to the ship about 12. So as I say, I came in contact with the sort of manana attitude that one runs into in the tropics, and I think the same was true in Panama. I enjoyed that part of the trip.

From a professional standpoint, of course, now we were first classmen, and we were given responsibilities that were beginning to correspond to junior officer duties.

Q: Navigation?

Merdinger: We did some very serious navigation, and, of course, we were called upon to con the ship at times, take officer of the deck positions, in the gunnery drills and in engineering and so on we were in charge of the various watches and sections.

Merdinger #1 - 21

Q: What kind of ship was this?

Merdinger: This was a battleship, another battleship. In other words, the formula in those days used to be the youngster and first class cruise in the battleship and destroyer cruise for second classmen.

One interesting thing we ran into at that time. There was another battleship in the harbor, and I've forgotten where this was now -- probably Guantanamo Bay but I'm not sure - but we ran into a number of people who by our standards were rather seedy looking. They were in what passed for mishipman uniforms, but again they were kind of ill-fitting. They turned out to be the first group, I think, of what came to be called the "90 day wonders," the first reserve officers that were just coming into the Navy. Of course, we looked upon them as a group of sad sacks from our standpoint. But the funny thing was, when we got out in the fleet a few months later, they were senior to us because they'd been commissioned before we were. So the fellows we'd "looked down on" were now "looking down on" us, from their vantage point of seniority.

Q: And I suppose if you're like some other regular naval officers you came to appreciate the reservists a great deal.

Merdinger: Oh yes. Well, initially, of course, USN was very much of a snob thing. To be USNR was really rather low in our vocabulary, and it wasn't until we really got out and mixed with them that obviously we began to change our opinion. But we had a rather parochial view of it, and I must say that there was a pride that was developed here in being USN that simply transcended everything.

I recall, when my wife and I were married in '44, of course, the wedding announcements came out, and she had told them that it should be lieutenant in the United States Navy. And the woman said, "No, no, that's not it, it's United States Naval Reserve. We know. We do hundreds of them."

My wife had a fit trying to convince this lady that there was such a thing as a person who had United States Navy after his name.

So this continued, as I say, even on wedding announcements.

Oh, there's no question about it, after all, the regulars couldn't have fought the war. The reserves were obviously necessary and valuable. I think they infused a lot of values into the Navy that were necessary and desirable. On the other hand, I think that the regulars held the thing together. If it hadn't been for them you wouldn't have had that Navy. So it was a combination of the two I think that made up the great Navy that it was during the war.

I had a few reserve officers who served under me, when I was officer of the deck under way and things of that nature, who thought they were complimenting me by telling me that I was the closest thing to a reserve officer that they'd run into in the regular Navy. I wasn't particularly flattered by this.

Q: What characteristic made this possible?

Merdinger: I don't know, except that there were a number of these liberal arts graduates, and I'd always had an interest in the liberal arts side of things, so I was perhaps a little more versed in some of the latest books and political functions or something else than maybe some of my shipmates were. But I think that this was the thing - the sympathy, if you will, for the liberal arts graduate was perhaps more apparent.

Q: What was your class standing?

Merdinger: Oh, I was - well, I know I was in the first 15 percent. I think it was 51 but I'm not sure of that. My graduate number was 45. For some reason I remember that. In the Civil Engineer Corps, which I ultimately entered, I was the third senior in that group.

Q: The reason I ask is because standing seems to have such great importance at the Academy. It follows a man through his career. I wonder about the merits of that, in terms of late bloomers.

Merdinger: Well, I can say something in general about that on the basis of this study I made that I was talking about. I broke the class down academically into four quarters, and at the time that I made the study, all the class that were going to make captain had made it. Nobody had really seriously been considered for admiral. And since we only had this 13 percent resignation rate -- of course, we had 1 in 8 who were killed during the war -- that's a rather high percentage.

Q: What?

Merdinger: One in eight. Yes. I think it would be fair to say that success at this particular point was in achieving the rank of captain. I found that twice as many in the first quarter were selected as captain as in the fourth quarter, and the other two quarters were on a straight line in between. In other words, there was a direct correlation, if you will, between class standing as measured broadly by class quarters, right through to the end. I also found that those who had three stripes or better fared exceedingly well in this game, but that those who had worn the varsity N were somewhere between the 3rd and 4th quarter. That is, if you extracted them academically and put them in as a separate group among the four academic groups.

So to recap, I think that class standing in a general way is a predictor of success, but not completely so. In otherwords, the fact that a man stood say 20 or 70 wouldn't make a lot of difference. If he stood 20 or 500 probably would make a difference. But it's not the most absolute thing in the world, obviously.

I wrote a little article on this, and it came into the hands of the Bell Telephone personnel people. I got a letter from them and they said they were very interested in getting this because they'd made a study in their own company, I've forgotten, of 35,000 people, something like that, in executive slots, and they devided them into academic thirds for the colleges they came from, and they also arbitrarily divided the colleges into Ivy and Podunk and in-between. They found that anybody who came from the first third of Podunk would out-perform the third third of Ivy. However, those who both came from the same third then Ivy would probably out-perform Podunk. Their criterion of success was years with the company versus salary, and they said that they were interested in this study of mine which really encompassed about 25 years and was a rather controlled experiment, if you will, because you could define success - I hate to say define success because it means so many different things to different people, but at least in this case, in terms of rank, at least it was easily observable, and bears, as I say, in general this correlation.

Q: Where did your article appear?

Merdinger: It was in SHIPMATE MAGAZINE, December 1964, and then it was subsequently reprinted in a couple of other places. A midshipman publication reproduced it. It was translated into Italian and appeared in the Italian equivalent of our Naval Institute PROCEEDINGS, and I understand the Japanese translated it too.

Q: This subject of class rank, was it useful to you when you were an instructor here, when you were on the teaching staff?

Merdinger: Well, from this standpoint. One of the collateral duties I had was to stimulate interest in various post-doctoral scholarships, fellowships, Fulbrights, that sort of thing. And if you were going to sit down and determine who among the midshipmen you should concentrate on, who had the best chance, I think again these general class standings were useful guides. I wouldn't quibble about a hundred numbers or so, but when you got from one broad quarter to another, then it might make a difference.

So I would say this, for instance, on the Rhodes Scholar candidates, if they didn't stand in the first quarter of the class, we'd encourage them to try for something else. Obviously they weren't going to be seriously considered.

Q: I know in talking with various men who were naval constructors, I don't think they were even eligible for that graduate work unless they were in the first ten or something.

Merdinger #1 - 26

Merdinger: Well, yes, that may have been in earlier years. That's cutting it a little close. I could generalize this way. That with my class, to get into the engineering groups - and I'm speaking of a number of things I'm not only talking about what were the old naval constructors but I'm talking about civil engineers and even some of the more technically oriented post-graduate area - people tended to come from the upper quarter of the class. So the answer is, yes, class standing did have a bearing on the subsequent career from that standpoint; that is, those who were technically oriented.

I noted, too, that a number of those who stood further down the class were attracted to non-technically oriented areas - oh, this might be Marines or Supply Corps - something like that. The bulk of your line officers seemed to come from the middle two quarters. In other words, the engineers and technical specialists would come from the first quarter, the non-technical specialists from the fourth quarter, and the generalists in between. Again, this is over-simplifying it, because you find differences clear across the line.

Q: Were you at all tempted by naval aviation when you were in the Academy?

Merdinger: No, on the contrary, I think I was turned off from it.

Q: Was that the flying boats?

Merdinger: I think the flying boats did it. I didn't particularly like them. Perhaps there was too much enthusiasm. There was a bit of an oversell on this business. The fliers were trying to sell it a little too hard, and a number of midshipmen were accepting it, and I guess maybe there was just a perverse streak in me. I said, well, I'm not going to get sold on this. But then too, as I mentioned, I'd had that seasick experience on the destroyer, and there were times I felt a little woozy in the airplane too, so I think that could have had something to do with it too, although it wasn't that overriding. I think if I'd really had a real yen to fly, that I could have overcome that particular thing. I might add that in my later naval career, sometimes I think I logged more hours than the regular aviators did, because I was so involved in building the first master jet air station in the Navy and did a lot of flying. Then, of course, in Vietnam I did an awful lot of flying too, simply because that was the only way I could get to my troops. It wasn't safe to go through Indian country by jeep.

So I like to fly now as a means of pursuing my business because I get there fast, but I never was really one of these wild blue yonder boys who just seemingly had to fly. No, it didn't appeal to me. Submarines appealed to me. I might mention that. But, of course, in those days we couldn't get into subs right out of the Academy, and I don't really know why, again, why subs appealed to me so much.

Q: Did you have any particular experience with one during Academy days?

Merdinger: No. As I recall, we took one dive out in Chesapeake Bay in one. There's a certain fascination, I suppose, in the fact that perhaps you can get command earlier. But there was a lot an individual could do to influence the whole ship. The mere fact that as an individual you had a great impact on this thing because it was so small. Maybe that was another item. I don't know, it was just kind of a fascinating adventuresome thing to me. And why I didn't feel the same about flying, I'll never know, but I guess that's why we have some people in subs and some who fly.

Well, as it turned out I never had an opportunity to go into subs, because we went on to battleships or cruisers, for the most part, on graduation. A number went to destroyers. I just stayed on a battleship all during World War II until I got selected for Civil Engineer Corps.

Q: Tell me about your first battleship assignment - it was rather traumatic, wasn't it?

Merdinger: Yes. I went to the NEVADA. We reported to her in February of 1941, and I ended up in the plotting room. This, of course, was the heart and brains of controlling the big guns. A certain amount of mathematics connectied with it. The fire controlmen, who were the enlisted men there, tended to be among the better educated men on the ship. We always liked to think they were the sharpest people there. So it was a good group to work with. And, of course, these being close to the Depression years, I think the level of the enlisted men was generally higher anyway. We had really a good group.

So it was a fine enlisted crew then that was on the ship to begin with. I enjoyed the work tremendously. I liked the collateral duties of getting up on deck and being a junior officer of the deck under way and this sort of thing.

Merdinger #1 - 29

Q: Did you have a good set of officers as well? Who was the skipper?

Merdinger: Captain Rockwell was the skipper. He later became an admiral. A very fine officer. Of course, those were sort of relaxed days, even in February of '41, because my recollection is of going aboard ship on a weekend and finding that really there was nobody on board who cared whether I reported that day or not. It wasn't till about Monday that things got going.

Q: Sounds a little reminiscent of December 7.

Merdinger: Well, then I finally got to meet the executive officer and finally the commanding officer, and we had a fine group of officers aboard.

Q: That's important for your first tour.

Merdinger: There were four of my classmates and I who came aboard together, and there were a few - ultimately, a great many - reserve officers, also ensigns who came aboard about the same time. So we had quite a livly JO mess. We weren't stationed in the Long Beach area very long before we went out to Hawaii.

Q: You were part of the Pacific fleet.

Merdinger: Yes. And we stayed out there in Hawaii. Of course, that's where we were on Pearl Harbor Sunday.

Q: In the month immediately preceding Pearl Harbor, were you extra alert to the possibility of hostilities, that kind of thing.

Merdinger: Yes, I think we were. There was a lot of movement to upgrade quality of the fleet. We knew we were getting new anti-aircraft. This sort of thing. Certainly our maneuvers took on a great deal of meaning, when we went out. We tended to become very alert to the possibility of submarines; that is, submarines not our own lurking in nearby waters. I don't recall ever thinking much or hearing much from anybody else about a possible attack on Pearl Harbor. I think that most of us felt that if the Japanese should strike first - and I think there was concern that this was a great possibility - that in Hawaii it would take the form of sabotage and that the regular attacks would come in the Far East some place, the Philippines perhaps or somewhere even further south. But the thought of Pearl Harbor being attacked was a pretty remote one, really.

Now, as we went out on the town and saw all those people who looked Japanese, it was very easy to suppose that somebody might do a great job of sabotage. I think the kind of protection then that you would take against that threat would be far different from that you'd take if you expected it from the air. For instance, the business of putting all the planes together, as I understand they did at some of the airfields, was so they could be guarded better against sabotage, but it was certainly no way to protect them against air attack, obviously.

Q: What were the duties of the NEVADA as part of the battleship contingent?

Merdinger: Well, in those days, of course, we still had the philosophy that the battleship was the prime ship, and the idea was that the battle line would steam out and it would face the battle line of the enemy, and everything else was really auxiliary to that. That is the planes might fly off the carriers to attack the other battle line and so on. But at this particular period, that is before December 7th, in the regular fleet as I recall them, the carrier was certainly not the heart of the task force. The battleship was.

Now, all this changed, of course, as you know, very shortly thereafter.

Q: Practically overnight.

Merdinger: Overnight. I think we were forced into it. Whether this was the doctrine that had been long planned by our top strategists, of course, I don't know. I was an ensign, so I wasn't privy to much information along those lines. But it was a complete change that occurred in all of our fleet operations, which I observed as a relatively junior officer, from the time I went on the NEVADA to the subsequent time that I was aboard the ALABAMA. And again, I was on a battleship, but we were no longer the focal point.

Q: You think this represented Admiral King's philosophy?

Merdinger: Quite honestly, I have no way of knowing. I suspect that it's like so many of these other things, that in part it was the theory that some people had been working on, but the practicality of the situation forced us into it.

Merdinger #1 - 32

Q: Just reality.

Merdinger: I think so, but again I'm speaking with very little knowledge of what kind of plans we could have at that time.

Q: Were there any interesting incidents that occurred in the period from the time you went with the NEVADA until the December episode?

Merdinger: I don't recall anything in particular, except the last few days before December 7th.

Q: Tell me about them.

Merdinger: Well, we were out cruising and going through various maneuvers with a number of other ships, and my memory may be faulty now but my recollection is that we were scheduled to stay out at sea over that weekend. At least this was the rumor that we had down in the JO mess. Then there were some reported submarine contracts, so it was decided that perhaps we'd do better to go back into Pearl. Now, maybe we had been scheduled all along. Maybe this was just a junior officer mess rumor, I don't know. But it's intriguing to think that perhaps we got driven back into Pearl Harbor by these things when actually we should have stayed out and avoided what came on December 7th. But again, this is rumor, speculation, and it's 30 years ago.

The things I recall about life aboard the NEVADA in the pre-Pearl Harbor days - this was really the last of the old Navy. It was a pleasant way of life. "Rope-yard Sunday" was Wednesday afternoon, so at 1 o'clock, you went over the side and went swimming or played tennis or whatever it was that you wanted to do. Life was well ordered and regular

Merdinger #1 - 33

and pleasant. It was sort of a gentlemen's club, I suppose, in some ways - the junior officers' mess. I think it's something we never really returned to, probably never will see again. It's kind of hard to describe in words. It was an atmosphere that existed, and maybe didn't exist in the minds of everybody. There may have been some people in the same group who didn't even see it the same way, but this is the way I remember it.

Q: In retrospect, we've never had a period of calm and peace comparable, have we?

Merdinger: That's true. We've been really, essentially, continuously at war since that time. We certainly weren't at war then - although I think we were probably better prepared than a lot of people like to think we were. In other words, it's popular in some elements to say "totally unprepared," this, that and the other thing. This is not true, but certainly from the standpoint of being psychologically unprepared, I think many of us were. It was quite a surprise to wake up on December 7th and find we were at war.

Q: Tell be about that whole experience.

Merdinger: I can remember it very vividly. I'd gone ashore the night before and had bought an artificial Christmas tree, and I had all my presents that I was going to give everybody, and was feeling very much in the Christmas spirit, I guess. Some of my friends decided to stay ashore all night, but I went back to the ship, and I recall after we

Merdinger #1 - 34

got into this thing the next morning, I was beginning to wish I'd stayed with them.

The first thing that I became aware of was the alarm clanging. Well, this wasn't unusual because we were always being subjected to "man overboard" drill or "fire on the ARIZONA" or something else, at odd times, so I thought it was a drill when I first heard the alarm.

It was Sunday morning, and I was sleeping and intending to go to church about half an hour later, so this was going to be my late day for sleeping in. It was almost 8 o'clock.

Q: How large a complement was on board?

Merdinger: Gee, I'm very vague about that too, but it could have been anywhere from 1500 to 1800 men, something like that.

At any rate, I heard the alarm and started to get into my clothes. I always had everything hanging up ready. I had my dungarees there and cap and everything else. Well, I'd just put on one sock and was putting on the second sock, when all of a sudden I heard a boom and a ratatatat, and all of a sudden the whole place seemed to erupt, and a fellow ran outside my room and said, "It's the real thing. It's the Japs."

I stepped right through my sock in my hurry, put on my slippers and my dungarees and my officer's hat and I went to my battle station, which was about five decks below the main deck in the plotting room. That was the last I ever saw of my room, because subsequent to that a bomb hit it, and pretty much dispersed everything that was there. Ultimately we found my safe and my sword, several weeks later, when the ship was raised, and even some of my clothing was still around. But it wasn't in very good shape. Not only had a bomb landed in the room, but then the room was under water for several weeks.

Well, I went to my battle station. My roommate was Ensign Joe Taussig, by the way, and he was up on deck, had the watch up there, and as you may know, as a result of the wounds he suffered that day, ultimately lost his leg.

I went to my battle station. Normally I was the most junior officer there. There were two other officers more senior that I, but neither of them was aboard ship that morning, so this left me the senior officer in the plotting room.

Q: Was the Captain aboard?

Merdinger: The captain was not aboard. The most senior officer aboard was a reserve lieutenant commander. If memory serves me right, I think he was the damage control officer. But he was the one who took charge of the ship. We had, oh, a captain of Marines aboard, there may have been one or two Navy lieutenants, maybe a j.g. Everybody else was an ensign. In other words, this ship fought the battle of Pearl Harbor, got under way largely with ensigns and chiefs and petty officers and seamen. All the senior officers were ashore. This was natural. It was a peacetime effort and a lot of them had their families over there and they were with them.

I was in the plotting room with the group until about 3 o'clock that afternoon, during which time the ship sustained one torpedo and five bomb hits, so it not only listed but it ultimately sank, and I went

Merdinger #1 - 36

right down with it, as I say, five decks below the main deck.

Now, part way through the engagement I received a call from the people topside to send about half of my men topside to man the guns. We'd had a lot of people killed up there on the five inch guns and they needed men.

Q: From the bombs?

Merdinger: Yes. Well, it might have been -- heaven knows, there were machine guns shooting all over the place. Some of them might even have got hit by our own machine guns for all I know. But whatever it was, there was a lot of attrition up there.

So I picked out the men who were manning the phones that were really least useful to us. By this time, we weren't really directing the big guns. I mean, there was no need for that. But we were serving as communications center for the rest of the ship, because we were connected with the tops and the turrets and with a number of other sections of the ship. Well, those phones that were least important to us - those were the men I selected. "All right, Jones, Smith, and so on, you go topside."

This was a real Hobson's choice, because I know that those men who were singled out to go thought they were going to their deaths, and I know the ones who were staying thought they were staying to their deaths, because it looked as though we might get trapped down there. So this was one of these moments when you're faced with a life and death decision - but it had to be done in a split second. And after all, most of these people were older than I, they'd been in the Navy many more years, and yet there was never a murmur, "let's take a vote," or this, that or the other thing. People just "aye aye, sir" and they did it. I think again almost in the space of a very short time, I realized the value of the gold braid on the hat, the saluting, the differentiation that we make in military protocol. All these things, I think, pay off at a moment of crisis, because as I say by virtue of experience or age or anything else I certainly wasn't the senior man there. But nevertheless these people in essence went out to what they thought might be their death, or stayed, without any kind of conversation at all. This is the way it was and they were used to this kind of military discipline. I think what it might have been with a rabble down there that hadn't been subjected to this kind of background and discipline.

Well, as it turned out —

Q: — had you finally lifted anchor, or was she — ?

Merdinger: By this time I guess we had. I'm a little vague now as to the timing of these events, because we were the only battleship to get under way, as you probably know. We started to steam out, and then we were just getting lower in the water. I think this torpedo had really done us serious damage. And it was decided then to beach at Nevada Point, so we went over there, and I don't recall at what time. We could well have been over on the beach by this time, I don't know. As it was, we ultimately settled almost to the main deck. and I might repeat that we were about five decks below that point.

Well, there was another time when sombody undogged the door and came in, and he came in with a whiff of smoke, and he came in gasping

"Gas." We thought perhaps somehow we were the subject of gas attack by the Japanese. There were all kinds of rumors flying around - the Japanese are landing on the other side of Oahu, and so on - but again these were just pieces of information that somebody dreamed up somewhere. We were sitting down there and I was thinking, my golly I've left my pistol in my room in my safe, what a place, now that the war has started, for it to be up there - such little thoughts I suppose float through your head.

Well, in the course of all this, with the ship sinking and listing, I was getting reports from topside that the OKLAHOMA had just turned over. At this point we were canting maybe 12, 15 degrees, and it seemed a lot more than that down where we were, and to hear that the other ship had turned turtle didn't work for our peace of mind, of course.

Then a report that the ARIZONA had blown up. I was getting reports that there was a fire in one of the magazines very close to us and it was just about to blow and they couldn't get any water into it. So it seemed that everything that was happening to these other ships in some way seemed to be happening to us at the same time. Of course, your imagination will take you a good long way on something like that as well.

We were without fresh air for a good long time, and ultimately the main power failed. We shifted to auxiliary power, and developed this eerie green light. People took off their shirts, and ultimately it looked like one of these submarine pictures with people lying around, sweat on their bodies and this green light. But we were manning the phones and I think we were performing a useful function.

During the course of all these hours down there, certain thoughts ran through my head, little prayers, little thoughts, whatever, and the first was, as I recall, I hope that nothing happens to me, physically, personally, that I don't get wounded; and then secondly, again in this very personal frame of mind, well, if something does happen and I do get wounded, I hope it won't be a permanent loss, an arm or a leg, something like that. Finally, in the final stage, I thought perhaps we might just run out of time, and if I was going to go, I wanted to go like an officer and a gentleman. I steeled myself to go this way.

Well, fortunately I never really had to face up to the ultimate truth of it, but at least in mind's eye I faced it at that point.

I might add that some people in the other plotting rooms didn't make it out, so we were kind of lucky on that score.

Along about 3 o'clock, the water started coming in by the regular door by which we had entered this room.

Q: You were already sunk down.

Merdinger: We were already sunk. We knew we were sunk, and we knew we were under water pressure because it was beginning to drip through, the plates were beginning to go on top of us and the water was beginning to drip from the overhead, so we knew we were flooded above. In essence, we were in a big air bubble there.

Q: When and how could a command have come to you to abandon that plotting room?

Merdinger: We still were connected by phone to topside, to the commanding officer. By this time I guess the commanding officer had come aboard, and the executive officer and a number of senior officers were there. But then the water started coming in by this door by which we'd entered, and it was really coming in. The gaskets had given way. And now it was swishing around our ankles.

Q: That was the way you'd exit as well?

Merdinger: Well, there were two doors, one the regular door by which we'd entered, and this is the one that was giving way now, and the other one which went into central station, and we weren't quite sure what was over there. We did know, though, that the water was coming in this one.

I called up to the executive officer, and told him that it was impossible for us to hold this more than a few minutes longer, and we requested permission to secure it. He said yes, go ahead. So I gave the word. Everybody took off his phones and wrapped them up in the way that he always had done, and put them on the wall in the normal place that he always put them away - this with the water rushing past everybody's feet. Yet they were so trained that they did it exactly the way they'd done it a hundred times before, put those phones right back in their regular slot.

Then we opened the door to central station to go that way, and we didn't really know where we were going from there. Well, everybody filed in, and finally I closed the door behind us. This was a pretty smoke-filled place there. A few people were lying around. Going up from it was a communication tube that ran all the way up to the conning tower. This was just full of wires, and normally nobody ever went up this thing, but we all managed it that particular day.

So up everybody went, and about halfway up. --

Q: Were there steps?

Merdinger: Yes, there was a ladder there, but it was practically completely hidden by all those wires, because as I say it was not generally used at all. But as we got towards the top of the thing, I smelled fresh air for the first time in all those hours, and that was the greatest blessing. I just never felt anything so wonderful as that breath of fresh air.

Then we got out on the ship and looked around, and it seemed as if there were just dead bodies everywhere. So many people had just been burned up, they were all black --

Q: When you say we, how many were there making this escape?

Merdinger: Oh, there could have been ten of us, something like that, maybe less. But we got out and looked all over the harbor, and you've never seen anything like it. Nobody had ever seen anything like it in their lives. Just ships on fire everywhere you looked. Our own ship was on fire. Smoke coming out of every conceivable place. See, among other things, although these were metal ships we'd built up several inches of paint on them, and this paint just burned for days. This was true all over the harbor.

But the thing that remains with me to this day was the smell of diesel oil. It was all over the place, all over the water, as you

Merdinger #1 - 42

know. A number of people had to swim through burning oil to get to safety. To this day day when I smell it, I slip into Pearl Harbor.

I looked around. I might add that I'd gone to my battle station in my slippers and they were just soaked. I put them somewhere. They'd sort of rotted off me. And I hung up my dungarees to dry, and somebody walked off with those. So I ended up starting the war with just my hat. My room, of course, had disappeared. It was under water. But fortunately there was some kind of a small stores for Marines that was above the water line and we were issued new uniforms, so I got a Marine uniform out of that one.

Q: So there was a certain amount of order still on deck.

Merdinger: There still was. That was the amazing thing about it all. The ship had been completely lost below the water line, but here above the water line the guns were being manned. People were there. As a matter of fact, we continued on the ship through that night. All the wounded and dead were taken off, and we simply manned the guns and – it was just another gun platform there.

Unfortunately that was the night that the ENTERPRISE planes came in, and I never will forget that either. Somehow we knew that they were friendly, and yet somewhere in the harbor somebody started shooting at them, and the next thing you knew everybody was shooting. Even our own ship started to fire. It was kind of a horrible beauty to see this cone of fire just coming up, shooting down our own planes. We got a couple, as I recall. That was kind of a horrible aftermath of the whole thing.

I recall our gunnery officer telling people, "Don't shoot, stop shooting, they're friendly planes," but there was a kind of madness that seized everybody, and they just fired away.

Q: Sort of a psychotic state, I would think.

Merdinger: Yes. Well, it's hard to tell where the Japanese were. The intelligence by this time was sort of faulty, chaotic. There's one thing about the intelligence that I think is worth mentioning, and that is the business of radar. You know, so many people have talked about the fact that there were some radar operators on Oahu who spotted Japanese planes coming in, and somehow nothing ever happened. Well, radar, of course, would ultimately become a vital part of our gunnery operations, and in preparation for that a number of the enlisted men in my division had gone away to a radar school earlier in the year. All I knew was that they had gone to a school for training. They did not bring back the word radar. I'd never heard of it. They did not pass the word on, it was top secret. I don't know why you couldn't tell your own officers and other people; but at any rate, I did not know that there was such a thing as radar that existed. If somebody had told me that these people with this machine had spotted these planes coming in, I'd have said, "Don't kid me, there is no such machine." Theoretically, of course, our people thought this was a possibility, but we didn't know it existed.

Q: None of the ships were equipped with radar.

Merdinger: To my knowledge, nobody was equipped with radar. And, of course, radar soon got on the ships, as you know, but it was such a top secret that I as a fire control officer did not know that such a device existed, even though some of my men had been to school to get some early training in it. That's how top secret it was.

Q: What does that say about such a rigid policy?

Merdinger: Well, I must confess that through the years I've always railed a bit against the top secret. The secrecy has prevailed much of the time because it really didn't make much difference to anybody. We often thought that the other people knew it anyway, and the only people we were keeping the secret from was our own people.

I had subsequent experience with this secrecy business when I was on the ALABAMA. We were on the Murmansk run, and a roommate was assigned me from the British press. We were making a fake invasion of Norway at the time, to draw attention away from a feint at the underbody of Europe. This fellow was with us for a couple of weeks, and I was one of the officers of the deck. I never knew anything more than the ship's course and speed and who was in the formation. Didn't really know what we were doing or where we were going or anything else. I'm sure that the captain and the executive officer, perhaps some of the senior officers, knew. But below a certain level, nobody knew anything. And this poor correspondent was the most frustrated man in the world. Here we were miles from anywhere, and he didn't even know why we were there or what we were doing. And couldn't find out. When he left the ship, he was really mad as a wet hen, because he'd had a trip in Arctic waters where not only could he not see much of anything, but he never heard much of anything either. Except this. We were under continual

— so it seemed — attack by enemy submarines or threat of attack by enemy air and so on — most uncomfortable from that standpoint. But, as a matter of fact, we never got hit. Nothing ever really happened to us. We steamed around and then went back again.

Through the years I've seen so much over-classification of material, and I think that much of it has been useless. Now, obviously it hasn't always been so. There are some things that must for security be kept secret, but I think that we have just overdone it. Of course, all this business about the Ellsberg papers and so on has focused attention on the subject, and there's not much more I need say on that — not that I'm sympathetic with his point of view — but I think I am sympathetic with the idea of cutting out a lot of this classification.

Well, I got off a little from Pearl Harbor.

Q: You were talking about the radar and rumors of radar being in existence on the mainland.

Merdinger: Apparently some people knew of it, but those of us, at least at my echelon, knew nothing about it.

One part of the aftermath, the next day — I don't know whether it was because of the new issue, (I had the cleanest uniform) or what — but the captain decided to send me ashore as his emissary to comfort all the wives of those who had been aboard the ship. It turned out that none of these men had been there at the height of the action so none were wounded or killed. I didn't have the unpleasant task of making some kind of announcement about a tragedy. So it was a happy announcement, merely that everybody was safe and sound. I got a chance then to go into Honolulu

Merdinger #1 - 46

and go to a number of places up and down the beach to call on these various wives and tell them that their husbands were OK.

Q: What percentage of your personnel was lost? Those on board.

Merdinger: I don't know - the figures are available, I just don't know. It turned out, in my own division, who happened to be scattered all over the ship - we were in the tops, we were down at fire control, we were in all the turrets -- we didn't lose a man in our division. But other divisions did lose heavily, up in the five inch guns and so on. I'd rather not say because I never did have the statistics very well in mind.

Q: What about the emotional reaction to something like that?

Merdinger: There were a couple of emotional reactions. Some of the older officers were crying, "Oh, they've done us in" - it was sort of a cry of despair. My own reaction, as I recall it, was - well, first there was a selfish reaction: "I'm glad I made it, I got out alive." There there was the looking around, saying, by golly, these Japanese did a real professional job with this. In other words, they came to destroy our fleet and they really did the job. I think those were the thoughts that crossed my mind. But it ran the gamut - some people cried. They were really overtaken by the thing. Others were, as I say, kind of detached and viewed it a little more clinically. I think perhaps I was more on the clinical side than the emotional.

Q: As a younger man, younger officer, this was your first exposure to warfare, wasn't it?

Merdinger: Well yes, but it was the first exposure to warfare probably for almost everybody there. After all, nobody would have served before World War I, and naval engagements in World War I were not certainly very severe. I recall reading somebody's memoirs who mentioned a shell dropping 200 yards behind the ship, and mentioning this as the height of excitement - which, of course, in the light of our experience in World War II was nothing.

Q: Some people are tormented by the fact that there are certain men, certain officers especially, who are peacetime officers and there are others who can take it in wartime, but there is a sort of division of the sheep and the goats at this point. Would that be your observation as well?

Merdinger: I suppose it's possible in some specific instances, but I would not want to generalize along these lines. Rather, I would say the good man carries on regardless. As we get into the much more complicated world that we have today, there's a certain management aspect to all these things now that perhaps wasn't to the same degree in the simpler times. By that I mean, in peacetime you've got to be efficient in a paperwork sense, because the paper has to get through, the organization has to survive in a business atmosphere. It doesn't call for the same derring-do. It may call for a lot of moral courage to make certain decisions in peacetime - possibly a higher order of courage at times - but it's not the same thing as facing the shot and shell in battle. I think that at the combat end of the scale - those officers who have to fight the ship or run aground action, must be sustained by a certain physical courage. But as you get into the higher echelons of command, I think the shot and shell part of it fades, and the management part of it becomes much more important. So I guess the answer to your question is, it depends on the complexity of the kind of war you're fighting and it depends on the echelon of command you're talking about.

Q: At your level of command in Pearl Harbor, was there any feeling that we should have been more alert to this possibility?

Merdinger: No, I don't recall ever discussing this with anybody. I don't recall feeling it myself. As I mentioned before, I think that most of us felt if there were any difficulties they would come more through the route of sabotage. No, if anything, sometimes we felt we were overtrained. We spent so much time at sea, we were dead tired, and that we didn't get enough rest, perhaps, because these tours at sea were not just pleasure cruises. We were up a good part of the night for battle exercises of one sort or another, firing or simulating firing or something.

Q: Perhaps you had feelings of sympathy toward Admiral Kimmel, who was removed so abruptly.

Merdinger: Oh, yes, I think most of us there felt he was simply a scapegoat for the thing. I can't say that he was the most popular man with the junior officers, because we always attributed to him the fact that when we went ashore on liberty we had to wear coats and ties and hats, and this was a little uncomfortable in Hawaii. You could always tell a naval officer because he had one of these hats that he'd rolled in his pocket and he was carrying his coat over his arm. But that was the rule and as I say, on a very petty basis, I can't say that we had much sympathy for him because we thought he was the fellow who did it. But on the broad scale, I don't think that anybody among the professionals out there held him up to blame in the slightest, really.

Much of the discussion centered around President Roosevelt's position in this. Again, I'm speaking pretty much from hearsay, but somehow I recollect that Admiral Richardson who was commanding the fleet, somewhere around 1940, had urged that the bulk of the fleet should be drawn back to the West Coast.

Q: Yes, he had.

Merdinger: And that the President, whether it was a matter of showing the flag or what, considered it would be better placed at Pearl Harbor. And many of us really looked to that decision and, in a sense, blamed the President. I think we were even prone to believe that somehow he had not played completely fair with us, that somehow he or somebody knew that something was afoot in greater depth than it was. Again, this was an immediate reaction. Obviously commonsense tells you that it can't have been so.

Q: There's always been that school of thought, though.

Merdinger: Yes, it exists. I find it hard honestly to believe, myself. But at the time, after all, when they're looking around for a scapegoat and you're way down in the pecking order of things, it's pretty hard to get any kind of perspective. But I never felt, and I never ran into any-

Merdinger #1 - 50

body who thought that Admiral Kimmel was really to blame for this, or General Short, for that matter.

Q: As an aftermath, obviously there were the bodies to dispose of. Did the personnel surviving get involved in mourning services?

Merdinger: Yes, they did, but it's all kind of vague in my mind now. I don't remember how this was carried out. I ended up being a kind of permanent officer of the deck, and my job in the daytime was to preside over the comings and goings of people on the ship. There probably were other people who had other details and they were perhaps permitted or even sent over to some of these memorial services. I just don't remember.

Q: Could you very quickly make an estimate of the future usefulness of the NEVADA?

Merdinger: Yes, it was determined that she would be refloated and brought back to the States, which she was. I've forgotten now exactly how long it took to de-water the ship. It must have been a couple of months. My recollection is that we finally sailed her back under her own power, and got back to Bremerton around the 1st of May. So it was almost a year there that was lost in getting this thing organized.

Now, a goodly number of people were transferred off the ship very early in the game. Obviously we didn't need the full complement there. So a number of - again, I'm vague about the number, but let's say we had about 100 officers or thereabouts; we probably cut down to 25 or thereabouts in the permanent officer group.

Merdinger #1 - 51

Q: Sort of a skeleton staff.

Merdinger: Yes. My recollection is that our captain, who at that time now had become Captain Scanlon, was transferred and became captain of a cruiser. The executive officer, Commander Thompson, then became the acting commanding officer.

There's one part - in de-watering the ship, prior to its being brought into drydock, we ran into a succession of tragedies. This was due to some accumulated gasses down in some of the compartments. One man went down, and although he had a certain amount of proper breathing apparatus, he was overcome, and a man went after him - in all, I seem to recall that about six people died, one going in right after the other, after the others who had gone in.

Of course, it was very disheartening, that these fellows had survived the tough day of December 7th, and in a relatively peaceful atmosphere had suffered this kind of tragic after-effect.

Q: Did you have the benefit of professional salvage people around?

Merdinger: Yes, there was. It was a combination of professional salvage people, shipyard people who were you might say, on the fringes of the salvage business, and, of course, our own ship's company, so it was a combined effort. As the ship was pumped out, our own crew went down to clean up this place. Of course, it was a horrible mess.

Q: Decomposed bodies would be a great problem.

Merdinger: Yes, there were bodies. There was the problem of accumulation of oil all over everything, if you can visualize that; as you went down in the ship it was a complete mess. And the business of the bodies was a bit of a problem for some time. I recall one of our junior officers, Daniel Elmore by name, was thought to have been killed. He was a short fellow, and they found a body about his size up in a place that he probably would have been, during the battle. So shortly thereafter, a rather big article as I recall was in the Seattle paper, "Local Boy Dies Hero's Death at Pearl Harbor." It turned out that he hadn't been on the ship at all, that when it started he'd been over on the beach. As he was trying to get back, he ended up in a motor launch that was commandeered by a more senior officer and ended up on a ship that immediately put to sea, and we didn't see him for several days. So as I say he was presumed dead when he'd never been aboard the ship at all - kind of mistaken identity, I'm afraid, happened in a lot of cases.

I suppose it points up the kind of confusion that we had there, in terms of identifying these people. I gather that the dentists were pretty busy later on identifying people through their tooth work.

Q: Since you mention confusion, how long did it seem to take for order to be established again within the naval precincts there?

Merdinger: Well, my recollection is that things were pretty orderly by that night, as a matter of fact, the night of December 7th. Now, it is true that in scattered instances people were going around firing guns at friends but I think some semblance of organization had taken place. There was the business of setting up food ashore. For instance, we had no way of cooking any of our food aboard ship at all, so motor launch systems were devised to take members of the crews over to eat at the local barracks. Within a day or so, we were able to bunk ashore in barracks. Ultimately a number of families moved out of the housing at Pearl Harbor, and some of us moved into sets of family quarters ashore. The families apparently were taken back to the States. There were a lot of stories about families that were hastily evacuated with a roast in the oven and all that sort of thing being left. I didn't really run into any of that the first day. But I would say that in essence we had order by that night.

As a matter of fact, during the battle itself, while there was a certain amount of confusion, there was definitely order within that confusion, as suggested by the incident of hanging up the phones in the plotting room that I mentioned before. Discipline was good, and I think by and large the people performed magnificently. There were some who didn't. There were some cowards who crawled off in a corner and cried, but very few. Most of the people faced up to this thing well, just the way you would hope they would in such a circumstance.

Q: How did Admiral Pye function as the interim C in C?

Merdinger: I don't know. I had no contact really outside the ship. My world was the ship, apart from the business I mentioned of going out to talk to some of the wives. So I had no feeling for the larger relationship at that time.

Q: Did some of the VIP's come on board for inspection?

Merdinger: Yes, I recall people coming and going all the time. Subsequently, of course, they got around to giving out medals, and I recall Admiral Nimitz coming aboard to present some medals. You may know that in those days we didn't have all these intermediate medals we have now. We only had the Navy Cross. We didn't even have the Purple Heart. And I think that a number of people were given the Navy Cross simply because they had been wounded. It was felt that somehow, something was owed them. They had to be given some token of appreciation, and I think there were a number of Navy Crosses given out under those conditions. Had we had a series of other awards, they might not have been. I don't mean to demean the Navy Cross and people who got it, but I am suggesting that this did, I think, bring us up short on the whole business of medals and the varying weights that they should be given. Clearly this Navy Cross, which is a rather high decoration, should not have been given for people who simply were wounded. But this happened in a few cases. And conversely there were some people who really deserved recognition and they in turn never got anything. But this always happens.

Q: Since you mention those who had been wounded, were the hospital facilities adequate for this situation?

Merdinger: I don't really know. I know that a number of them were taken over to the local hospital and treated there. Later on I went to visit some of my friends who were over there. They seemed to be getting taken care of. Well, most of them suffered primarily from burns. This was one of the major causes, I would suspect, of the seriously wounded and perhaps even of many of the deaths.

Q: It was largely the paint?

Merdinger: No, this would be a burn from an explosion some place, as opposed to just a paint burn. As I say, it was mostly explosions. So my view of the hospital situation was very restricted, a parochial one, and all I can say is, these friends of mine seemed to be taken care of adequately and subsequently recovered.

Q: Was there any fear and apprehension of a subsequent attack of Japs?

Merdinger: Oh, yes, I think there was, and this, of course, was perhaps one of the reasons that we didn't abandon the NEVADA all together. It was nothing more than a gun platform by this time. It wasn't going to sea, obviously, for a long time. There was no other particular reason, except to man guns that might be useful in case of another attack. Yes, I think that for some time we thought that this might happen.

I think that had they had the forces there, the Japanese easily could have taken Oahu. Now, whether they could have gotten in with that many forces without being detected, is another matter, but assuming the same element of surprise and so on, if they'd had the infantrymen I don't think it would have been any great problem to have taken the island.

Q: How long did you stay with the NEVADA?

Merdinger: I stayed with her through the period of de-watering her, getting into drydock in Pearl, refitting her there, bringing her back to Bremerton, Washington. We got in there around the 1st of May and I was orderd transferred from it sometime shortly thereafter.

Q: Was that a hairy trip back to Bremerton?

Merdinger: Well, we were concerned, of course. We were a pretty defenseless hulk out there. But we didn't have any incidents with any enemy submarines or anything. So apart from the anticipation of something that never came about, it was really a calm trip. We didn't even have steering gear on the bridge. We had to communicate all the information back down to steering quarters in the lower part of the ship aft. So it was an uneventful trip, I'd say, but with some anticipation.

Then somewhere in May I guess, along with a great many other officers, I was ordered from the ship to new construction, ordered to the ALABAMA which was then building in Norfolk, and set out to go across country and joined this new ship.

One of the first things I did there was to trace out all the possible escape routes from the bottom of the ship.

Q: Nothing like experience.

Merdinger: No, I figured if I was going to get trapped another time, I might not be so lucky, and I'd better know a little more about the ship than I'd known about the previous one. But it turned out, I didn't spend much of my time below decks there. I started out in the plotting room, but very shortly thereafter was made first division officer and turret officer, turret one; so I ended up supervising three 16-inch guns. We had about 150 men in battle in the turret, which surprises a lot of people -- to know it takes that much amount of service for such guns.

Merdinger #1 - 57

These were 16 inch, and we probably were stacked in about a five story structure, if you counted everything.

Q: How far along toward commissioning was she when you joined her?

Merdinger: Well, I joined her somewhere in June or July, and she was commissioned, as I recall, in August, and we put to sea the first time in the fall, November I think.

Q: During this period before she was commissioned, what were your duties?

Merdinger: Simply organizing the ship. Well, from my standpoint in fire control, we had a lot of jobs to do, just getting the control equipment lined up with the turrets and this kind of thing so that all the fire control machinery would function properly once we got to sea.

Q: Were there any special new installations in terms of fire control?

Merdinger: Yes, we were getting systems where we'd get an automatic follow-through. For instance, by just a twist of the wrist down in the plotting room, through a series of mechanisms the guns would actually elevate and train. In other words, it wasn't the matching system we'd had before where we would transmit indicators to a turret and then men in the turret itself would change gun elevation and train by hand. But now, as I say, we were going into the automatic phase.

I must confess a lot of us were a little leery of this. We were afraid, if that went out in the middle of battle, where are we - if the whole hydraulic system is out or something? But as it turned out -

Merdinger #1 - 58

Q: - no normal operation -

Merdinger: - yes - it was a significant step forward, and, of course, made the batteries far more effective in terms of rapidity of fire and accuracy and everything else.

Q: In this interim period you had to train men?

Merdinger: Yes. Men were coming aboard. We were getting them slowly organized in the divisional structure.

Q: These were draftees now, were they?

Merdinger: We were getting a new kind of fellow on board. We had some of the older petty officers, but we had a lot of people who were new to the Navy. If I could give a general observation, I'd say they were a cut below the people - most of the ones we'd known before - in terms of their education and motivation and a lot of other things. Ultimately they made good sailors. We had a fine outstanding group.

Q: Most of your officers I suppose were reservists coming in?

Merdinger: Well, not initially. It's rather interesting. Every division officer on the ship, almost without exception, not quite but almost every one, had been on one of the ships at Pearl Harbor. So we had quite a bit of battle experience, even though the war was only a few months old, in those terms.

Q: Was that good or was it bad?

Merdinger: Well, let me say this, that the captain and the executive officer of the ALABAMA had recently served in the Bureau of Personnel, and I think they pretty much hand-picked their officers. If I were to make any remark, I would say that they had an over-abundance of qualified officers. I'm not saying that they were stepping on each other's toes, but I'm saying that there was certainly a tremendous amount of good talent there. I think they'd personally picked a good many of these people and that perhaps they short-changed some of the other ships by getting all these good people on the one ship. Now, this again is a bird's eye view and maybe a lot of other people felt the same about other ships, I don't know. I just was very enthusiastic about the quality of the officers that we had aboard that ship.

Q: They actually represented a composite of Pearl Harbor experience, not any one ship.

Merdinger: That's correct.

Q: Did you have any voice in some of the installations, since you were there before she was commissioned when things were in process? Was your wisdom or that of other officers incorporated in the installations in the ALABAMA? Was any opportunity given for this?

Merdinger: I would say that the opportunity was more in procedures and how we were going to operate things, rather than the installations themselves. In other words, the ship was designed, it was ready to go. There wasn't much that we were going to change. But as far as ways to use equipment, means of approach and so on, I think perhaps we

Merdinger #1 - 60

did contribute along those lines, but not in the design of the ship per se.

Q: Who was your skipper on this?

Merdinger: Captain Wilson was our first skipper and his executive officer was Commander Neil K. Dietrich. Later on he fleeted up to become the skipper.

Q: What was Wilson's first name?

Merdinger: I don't recall. Of course, Admiral Dietrich, would recall that one. They were a fine pair. As a matter of fact, as I say, I had nothing but admiration for the complement on that ship. They were really superb.

Q: Did segments of the personnel go off to special schools during this period to learn how to operate new equipment that might have been installed?

Merdinger: Yes, I'm sure they did. I recall going off myself to Damneck, Virginia for some instruction in fire control. Small weapons, that sort of thing. Yes, there was a good deal of this going off to school for one reason or another. I suspect, although I don't know this for a fact, that a number of the engineering personnel probably did the same thing.

Q: Was she equipped with rudimentary radar?

Merdinger: Yes.

Q: This was very hush hush, as you indicated in Hawaii.

Merdinger: Somehow it didn't seem hush hush any more. I don't know what had happened in the intervening months, but it seemed to be just a fact of life now. Of course, these radar screens were a new thing on the ship. They looked like a bedsprings, or -

Q: - they were immense in size -

Merdinger: Yes. So obviously this was something that ships hadn't had before. It was the first question that one would naturally ask, that is, one who knew anything about ships at all. So all of a sudden radar wasn't really much of a secret.

Concerning radar, I remember an incident after we were really going and part of the fleet. It was in the middle of winter, early '43, and we were operating off Newfoundland in a taskforce. We had carriers, cruisers, battleships, destroyers, the whole lot. It was 8 o'clock at night, very stormy. I was officer of the deck. This was an exposed position for an officer of the deck on an ALABAMA-type ship. The helmsman and most of the other people were inside the conning tower, but the OOD was out on a bit of platform out in front. There was a waist-high ledge that kind of protected him from the wind, but he was out in the open.

Well, we received a signal to change course and speed at this time. The seas were running very high. As a matter of fact, we had passed word for all hands to stay off the weather decks.

Just as we got the signal to execute this rather complicated maneuver, I got the word that a man had been swept overboard. Apparently he was a fellow who had been mess cooking and had decided to comeup and throw some potatoes over the side and got swept over along with them.

At the same time, with the cry "Man overboard," we get the execute, and the fellow who was plotting me into the new position was taking all of his information from the radar. What he didn't know was that the radar was swept around to try to pick up this man, who'd been washed overboard.

Because of complicating factors that I'll never really understand, we almost had the most magnificent collision in the history of the U.S. Navy, because we went across the bow of a cruiser and under the stern of a carrier and missed them by just the slimmest of margins, maybe a few hundred yards which is nothing when you're in that situation. And practically nobody even saw this. All of a sudden I recognized that we were coming up hard onto this carrier, and I swung the helm over, and as I said we scooted in between these two ships. I called the captain to let him know, but when he got out, he couldn't see because it was pitch black out there and he'd been in the light. The radar was not really focusing on the main target, and so this was just one of those occasions when your heart is in your mouth, and just by the grace of God we missed this fantastic collision. And how we got into that position, I don't know, but it's in part accounted for by the fact that the fellow who was plotting was plotting the wrong thing. And there wasn't much that I could do to see out there very far. It was hard to see much beyond the focsle of our own ship.

I think I'll recall that to my dying day -- one of those rare instances at sea when everything seems to go wrong, and yet you luck out at the last minute.

I might add that we immediately signaled the destroyers about the man overboard, and they searched for him, but the water was so cold, it's doubtful if he would have lasted 10 or 15 minutes in the water, even if he had been a magnificent swimmer. So that was certainly the tragic part of that one.

Q: When the ALABAMA was finally commissioned, where did she have her shakedown? The waters were infested with submarines, weren't they?

Merdinger: We had a shakedown cruise in Chesapeake Bay.

Q: Was that adequate for a battleship?

Merdinger: Just barely. As a matter of fact, I recall our getting stuck on a sandbar somewhere, and we actually sallied ship to break ourselves loose. That is, we mustered all hands and put them on the port side of the ship, and then when the bugler blew a signal, we all rushed over to the other side, then wait for the signal, then as we -- as I say, we sallied ship, and finally got off.

Q: That's a real ancient technique, isn't it?

Merdinger: It's an ancient technique, and I'm not sure whether that did it or not, but I recall going through this drill, and I recall our getting off somehow, and I think this maybe had something to do with it.

Q: Is that the sort of thing you would have learned in textbooks at the Academy?

Merdinger: I don't know. I don't remember reading about it, come to think about it. It certainly wouldn't have occurred to me. I always assumed it was the executive officer Commander Dietrich who thought that one up, and I don't even know why. But at any rate whatever it was, we did get off.

I remember one incident on that that falls under a form of humor, I suppose. By this time I was a lieutenant (jg), and there were a number of us who were up on deck observing the conning of the ship. Some of the very senior officers were doing this, and some of us who were more junior but who would be senior watch standers in the ordinary course of events were simply up there observing how the ship handled. As I recall, we were coming in to anchor, and it was the first time in many days that we were going to have liberty. So to help the officer of the deck out, I had a number of the liberty boats called away, I'd seen them getting into position and I knew that they were being taken care of.

Well, when the ship finally came to anchor, those of us who were extra numbers were simply secured from our jobs, and the officer of the deck continued on as the ship was anchored.

Well, I went back to my room, and about a half an hour later for some reason or other I just happened to go out on the main deck aft. There must have been a few hundred men all standing in line with one poor ensign back there trying to inspect them all to get them into the liberty boats. JO came out about the same time, so both of us decided to pitch in to help this fellow inspect these people and get them over the side.

So here we were, loading these boats - after a short period, the executive officer came back and said, "Don't you think it's about time that we shoved these men off?"

I said, "Yes, Commander, I guess it probably is - "

But we looked over, and here were all these boats bobbing out there, full of bluejackets, no crews in the boats.

I hadn't a clue as to why there were no crews. I just didn't know. And with that, Commander Dietrich gave me a lacing up and down- and also my JO. "With $50,000 worth of government education, and you two can't get a boat away from the ship!"

I was thereupon disqualified as a senior watch stander, which was rather embarrassing, to say the least.

It turned out, by the way, that these crews were up with the officer of the deck in the forward part of the ship. He was giving them some kind of instruction. But, of course, I hadn't known anything about that.

Well, I tried to plead with the exec that I was just back here trying to do somebody a good turn. It really wasn't my watch or anything else. He said, "It doesn't make any difference. You're the senior man back here, and you're responsible."

So thereupon, as I say, I was disqualified. Well, I stayed in this state of disgrace about a month, and stood junior watch under some people I had taught, and was properly humiliated.

Merdinger #1 - 66

Q: It doesn't pay to be a good Samaritan sometimes.

Merdinger: Well, it certainly bore out the old adage, "don't be a volunteer."

I must confess, I never did hold it against the exec for doing this to me. As a matter of fact, I admired him and respected him very much. But this I thought was a rather cruel blow at the time.

Q: Did you have all your trials in Chesapeake?

Merdinger: Well, no, we went out later, and went up and down the Atlantic Coast. We went to Casco Bay, Maine, and I think that we were in pretty good shape as we got up there.

I remember one other incident up there that I think is, well, kind of reminiscent of the old Navy. It seems that a new seaman was accused of stealing something from one of his shipmate's lockers. This happened about 2 o'clock in the afternoon, and the division officer was called in, and the police petty officer and a few others to check on this, and sure enough the stolen gear was in this man's locker and he confessed.

The court martial, of which I was a member, sat at 3 o'clock in the afternoon, and at 4 o'clock he was ordered confined to the brig and dismissed from the Navy under dishonorable conditions, the following day. This certainly was immediate, though not drumhead justice. We had a very impressive sobering ceremony the next day, where they cut off his buttons and drummed him over the side. Now, this is shades of the

British Navy in the 18th century. But I think it had a very salutory effect on everybody, because it was the first known incident of somebody coming in and stealing. And you know the Navy prior to this time was such that people certainly had a lot of confidence and trust in everybody. The business of having to worry about your personal belongings was certainly not the uppermost thought in people's minds. But now here we were getting evidence that this might break out, and I think it was the command's way of showing that we weren't going to put up with this sort of thing aboard ship. So I'm sure it had a lasting effect on everybody who participated in that ceremony.

Interview No. 2 with Captain Charles J. Merdinger

Place: U. S. Naval Institute

Date: 17 January 1972

Subject: Biography

By: John T. Mason, Jr.

Q: Well, it's awfully nice to see you this afternoon, Sir. Last time you told me off tape of an incident that occurred in connection with the bombing and sinking of the battleship NEVADA, and I'd like to add that to the manuscript at this point.

Captain Merdinger: Of course, my memory's a little hazy on this, but the main points that seem to stick with me are these. It took us some weeks to raise the ship in preparation to take it into drydock in Pearl, and during the course of that period I had a number of times stood the officer of the deck watch. As a matter of fact, I was more or less the permanent OOD during the day and sometimes during the night on this hulk of ours. The night before we were to go into drydock we were already floating, and suddenly a stiff wind came up. It looked as if we were possibly going to blow back onto the shore. I called the commanding officer to let him know the situation, and at the same time arranged for a tug that was standing off to help us out.

Ultimately the tug did help. We were not blown on the beach, and I more or less forget about the incident, until we got the ship into drydock. Shortly after we had been in drydock, the skipper called me to his office and told me that by and large he thought that my performance had been pretty good but that I'd made two mistakes since I had been on the NEVADA - one, the night before I had almost let her run aground which would thereby delay her return to the fleet by possibly several months, and the other, that I'd been responsible for sinking the ship on the day of December the 7th.

Well, I told him that as far as the -

Q: This was a totally unexpected charge, wasn't it?

Merdinger: It certainly was. I was so surprised, as a matter of fact, and I told him so. I said as far as the first incident was concerned, we hadn't gone on the beach. I thought that was evident by the fact that we were in drydock. But as to the second charge, being responsible for sinking the ship on December 7th, I felt this had been the work of the Japanese and didn't realize that anybody considered me as contributing to this.

Well, this subject got bandied about the ship, and one of the senior officers suggested that perhaps I should ask for a court martial so that the true facts could come out, rather than simply being accused of something that was kind of vague. It was true that in the course of the battle I had ordered a few magazines flooded because of the danger of fire. I think that the flooding of these magazine probably did contribute to the ship's going down, but as far as being a proximate cause, of course, I could certainly dispute this.

Q: And was this the nature of the captain's charge?

Merdinger: Well, this was never brought out. It was just the mere fact that I had been responsible for some of these flooding orders. As I say, I don't believe that that kind of flooding contributed materially to the ship's sinking. I think the one torpedo, of course, and some of the bombs really —

Q: Did he ever spell out his reasons for assuming an attitude like this?

Merdinger: No, he really didn't, and I just had a feeling that he was in a rather distraught state and perhaps this was an off hand remark; but I can assure you that it was taken seriously by me.

Q: Did you follow the suggestion of this senior officer on board and ask for some sort of formal — ?

Merdinger: No, but I did ask him why he thought that this would be of any use. He said that he had noticed some of the more senior officers who had come aboard later in the day who, in turn, had ordered other flooding to take place, other than the flooding I had ordered. And it's quite possible that their actions might have contributed to this. Therefore, this was one of these things that it was very difficult to assess any kind of blame to anybody.

Q: There's really not much sense in finding a scapegoat.

Merdinger: No, I don't think so. I think the Japanese had really done the job, and quite honestly I thought that most of us on board ship had performed very well, and to bring up something like this under such vague conditions, and so hard to retrace any steps, wouldn't really have been worth it.

Q: So nothing ever came of it.

Merdinger: No, nothing came of it.

Q: It's an interesting little footnote to the Pearl Harbor story.

Merdinger: As far as I know, I'm the only ensign who was actually accused of sinking any of the battleships.

Q: Well, that's quite a distinction. Shall we jump ahead to the ALABAMA again. Last time you dealt with her commissioning, and her exercises and so forth, and I think you were almost ready to assume a battle station.

Merdinger: Yes. In early '43 we then left Newfoundland, and went to Scapa Flow in England, and there we joined the British Home Fleet. My recollection is that we were even given the code calls of "Black Prince" so that we were more that just another American ship.

Q: At that point I guess the BLACK PRINCE in the Royal Navy wasn't commissioned?

Merdinger: I don't think so. I don't know if it ever was. At any rate, we were told that our basic responsibility was to stand off some of the convoys to Murmansk with the thought that some of the German raiders would come out and that we in turn would engage them — some heavier ships.

Q: Like the TIRPITZ?

Merdinger: The TIRPITZ was the one most prominently mentioned, and we spent a lot of time shuttling from Scapa Flow to Iceland to some point off Murmansk. We never went into Murmansk. I never saw it, but we made that trip many times, and we never saw the TIRPITZ. We had a lot of German submarine contact, and, of course, we ran into very foul weather up there. We would go for days steaming a thousand yards behind the ship ahead of us and never see it.

On the other hand, there was light until midnight as the year went on, so the nights were not very long, and I do recall writing my log on the bridge at about 12 midnight by natural light.

Q: But that light exposed you to the FW's too, didn't it?

Merdinger: Well, I suppose so, except for the fact of the general fogginess of the area, which again made it hard to see even with the light. I do recall that there were times when the weather was so rough and the sea so high that we had to slow down to about six knots, just to enable the destroyers to keep going, keep them from getting battered.

Q: Did you escort any one convoy that was heavily attacked? Some of them lost vast numbers of ships.

Merdinger: No, I don't recall any particular problem along those lines. We were off some miles from the convoys themselves, the idea being to keep out of sight so the TIRPITZ and others could possibly be drawn into the trap, which never happened during my tour out there.

We also were subject to bombing attacks out of Trondheim (Norway); at least we were alerted to the fact that the bombing command there was after us, but I honestly don't ever remember undergoing any bombardment from the air. But the business of the attack by submarines was very real. Many torpedo wakes were sighted and this sort of thing.

Many nights it was difficult to go to sleep, simply because of all the noise going on, of the destroyers dropping dept charges, warding off these attacks.

I do recall one time when we made a fake invasion of Norway, and this was an incident where –

Q: Was this organized from Scapa Flow?

Merdinger: Well, we had originally been in Scapa Flow, and I don't recall now whether we'd been to Iceland first or what; but at any rate, we were apparently giving the impression of an invasion off Norway. I suspect that this was a diversionary measure to draw attention from some of the things that were going on down in the underbelly of Europe.

Q: Maybe it was to gratify Hitler, because he had an intuition that we were going to invade Norway.

Merdinger: I don't know. We were never given much information about this sort of thing. As a matter of fact, during the course of this particular exercise, which lasted in the neighborhood of two weeks, as I recollect, we had a correspondent from one of the British papers come aboard, and he was my roommate for this period. He went away a very frustrated man, because he really wasn't able to find out anything about the operation. He knew we steamed around for a couple of weeks and that we were near Norway, and that was about all he knew. Nobody ever really explained the operation to him or to anybody else, to my knowledge.

Now, I was one of the few officers of the deck under way, so this meant that I was up on the bridge and knew course and speed and disposition of the force and so on. But, quite honestly, I never knew the grand plan either. I just knew the day to day cruising information, so I wasn't much help in passing any information on to him.

When he left, it was pretty much in a huff, because it was a high degree of secrecy, at least on our ship. I suspect it prevailed on all the American ships.

Q: How large a force was this?

Merdinger: Well, it's so vague in my mind now, I don't remember the numbers. Of course, we were a battleship. We had British carriers, cruisers, destroyers and everything else.

Q: How long did the ALABAMA remain on this duty?

Merdinger: Oh, we weren't there very many months. My recollection

Merdinger #2 - 75

again is that in the middle of '43 we came back to the States. We were back there just a short time and then we set out for the South Pacific, through the Panama Canal.

Q: As a matter of fact, I think the convoys were discontinued during the middle part of '43 because the losses were - had been so great that they weren't resumed again until September.

Merdinger: I wasn't aware of that, but I seem to recall that we got home in perhaps July or August of that summer. Up to that time of course, the TIRPITZ had not shown. Just as soon as we got through the Panama Canal, we got the word that the TIRPITZ was now out, following the sea lanes again.

Q: You were there simultaneously with the WASHINGTON?

Merdinger: There were some other ships. We were with the SOUTH DAKOTA, as I recall. The WASHINGTON had preceded us, I think.

Q: How did the ALABAMA perform during this time? Did she meet the expectations of the crew?

Merdinger: I think so. I think it was an excellent ship, fine crew, fine body of officers, fine morale. I think that everything one would want in a battleship, we had. In other words, it was new and we had people with a lot of competence, a lot of enthusiasm. One thing, our enthusiasm and competence couldn't overcome, though, I recall now, and that was the business of streaming paravanes. The business of paravanes was something that the British had developed a great skill in, and there was always a great competition to see who could get his paravanes over first and be ready to steam on. Inevitably the British would beat us. Of course, I had a direct interest in this because as first division officer, my division had the responsibility for streaming the paravanes.

I don't know whether these things ever did much good, but it became standard practice to go from Scapa Flow to Iceland with paravanes streamed.

Q: Did it impede progress?

Merdinger: Yes, I'm sure it did. But apparently the feeling was such that the mines were such great threat that it was important that we have these. But even after we got these streamed, we were always breaking them. It turned out that our material apparently wasn't as good as the British. We ended up using British paravanes.

Q: We first had our own?

Merdinger: Yes, we had our own, and again I'm a little vague on this whole thing. But it seems to me that we had something made of cast iron, whereas they had wrought iron. At any rate, there was a difference in quality of material and ours kept breaking, and finally we had to go the British way. I'm not sure how long the streaming of paravanes remained the standard operating procedure. I don't recall our ever doing it much in the Pacific. But up in the North Atlantic, this was standard operating procedure. The British were great ones to "Stand by to execute" and they'd be all ready, and we'd be ten, fifteen minutes later before we'd be ready. Of course, they all got a great laugh out of that.

I might add that we used to have the same kind of competition in the sending of signals. They had some signal men on the blink lights, who were hard to follow. The idea was to send it so fast the other fellow would have to ask you to slow down.

Q: A certain amount of pride involved in all this, I would think.

Merdinger. Yes. There were other things too. The British used to love to come over and eat in our ships. Particularly when we were at Scapa Flow people liked to be in the lighter alongside, because they could come over and eat in our galley. On the other hand, a number of our people rather liked to go on the British ships where they had the rum ration, so there was a certain amount of exchange there, mutually acceptable.

Q: And morale was high. The crew must have been generally aware of the vast danger of this duty in the North Atlantic, the Murmansk run, which was perhaps the most dangerous of all the routes.

Merdinger: Yes, and I think perhaps the knowledge of that was responsible for this morale. In other words, when people share a common danger, there's something that knits them together even more than the normal course of events would do. I sensed this later on, for instance, when I was up at Adak, with the weather. People seemed to knit together better simply because they were facing such horrible weather, and I think certainly part of that was true up in the North Atlantic.

Q: Well, tell me about the next assignment of the ALABAMA.

Merdinger #2 - 78

Merdinger: We went down to the South Pacific, and really the first engagement we had of significance was the bombardment of Nauru in connection with the assault on Tarawa, which as you recall was the bloodiest in Marine Corps history. This was probably the first real battleship offensive of World War II. I think you'll have to check with the historians on that one, but again I recall somebody remarking that this was the greatest assemblage of power and battleships that had been put together yet, and now we were beginning to go back. I don't recall how many battleships were in this overall effort.

Q: Was it the expectation of meeting the battle line of the Japanese fleet, or was it rather the fire power and the use of it on the beaches?

Merdinger: The primary reason for the battleships was to soften up the beaches. The secondary role probably was anti-aircraft. Of course, we had carriers in the task force too, and I think the combination there was such that we expected to dominate the area without significant threat from ships.

Q: What are your recollections of those operations? Nauru, there wasn't much opposition, was there?

Merdinger: No. I recall looking through my periscope - I was Turret One officer at this time - and watching the shots go off, almost like a battle practice. In other words, we had practiced so many times - we had really gone through this in such a similar fashion that there wasn't anything particularly new about it. Although we did have one tense occasion, I recall, where we were using sensitive fuses. The fuses capped the 16 inch shells which were six feet long. These shells were brought up from the lower deck in a vertical position, and the fuse on this one shell had somehow got mangled in the process. These fuses were very sensitive and could go off with slight penetration of oh, say a quarter of inch of wood.

So there was a certain amount of consternation when the gun captain asked me what to do with this shell that was sitting there with the obviously mangled fuse. What should we do about it?

Well, I recalled that for the thing to go off, finally, the shell had to rotate through the air so many times, so I said, "Ram it home," and we did and we fired it without any particular incident. I don't know if the shell got to its destination or not. But it was one of those things that some of the people were concerned it might explode right there in the chamber. That's the only tense moment that I recall during this whole episode, because we were not being bombarded from the other direction.

Now, in the overall course of the operation, of course, we had problems concerning ourselves with enemy submarines, and we did have enemy planes flying overhead and so on, and we had to take evasive action and many times we were shooting at the planes. But we received no direct hits on our ship at all.

Q: I think you mentioned shells. Were the 16 inch shells at that point generally functioning properly? I recall the skipper of the MASSACHUSETTS telling me about his great consternation in North Africa when he was firing at the JEAN BART and the shells didn't explode.

Merdinger: My observation is that they did. As a matter of fact, I watched many explode through the sights. It was a question, of course, were we ever going to knock that tower down. We seemed to be hitting all around it and somehow it never would go down. But that place certainly must have sustained an awful bombardment. After all, these shells were 2000 pounds apiece, and we were capable of firing two shots a minute from each gun. So figure we had nine guns, that was three to a turret - that's quite a lot of ammunition we could lay on the beach. Now, we didn't do it quite that fast. It seemed to me, every 30 seconds or so we would lob shells out of one gun in each turret.

Q: This was at Nauru.

Merdinger: That's right.

Q: Was there much resistance on the part of the Japanese fortifications?

Merdinger: Not much that we could see. I think that there was something further inshore because I recall one of the destroyers getting hit, and they transferred some of their wounded to us. I learned later that a classmate of mine was killed on one of those destroyers. It's just they were a little closer to shore than we were. I'm a little vague now as to whether this happened at Nauru or Tarawa.

Q: The Tarawa operation was a little more - you got some flak from that.

Merdinger: Yes. Well, that, of course, that was my last engagement out there. That was the end of the war for me.

Q: Since you have been in the Atlantic, around the UK, then immediately catapaulted to the Pacific and battle there, would you say something about the contrasting situation?

Merdinger: Well, I can talk particularly in terms of an officer of the deck, because the kind of facilities we had for him on the ALABAMA were such that he was out exposed, to the direct blast of the wind or the sun or whatever it was, all the time. His protection was a parapet that came about waist high; he stood outside and everybody else was inside. This was particularly rough up in the North Atlantic - very cold. If you stand a four hour watch up there in the driving rain and sleet and snow, and those howling winds and pitching deck and everything else, you've had a good physical workout, whereas down in the South Pacific it was the other way around. It was wonderful to be out there and see the sun, and in the evening the moon and stars - almost like a pleasure cruise in so many ways. So while I suppose ultimately our Navy saw more of the enemy in the South Pacific, I think it was more pleasant to be there. The enemy was the weather, in a sense, up in the North Atlantic, even though there were hostile planes and ships up there too.

So that would be the prime difference from my point of view, being outside so much of the time, subjected to so much adverse weather up there. I'll never forget that.

Q: Were there psychological factors? I can think of the situation being somewhat different in the UK, part of another fleet, another navy - it was mainly their battle. In the Pacific, we were the dominant naval factor.

Merdinger: I don't recall anything in particular, apart from this, that when we were operating with the British Navy, of course, there were certain signals that we had to change, and we had to learn, and so there was this complicated communications bit. So this was one more thing that the officer of the deck and other people had to worry about, that we'd get the right signals and that we understood each other.

In the Pacific, for the most part, we were operating with American forces, and there wasn't that kind of a problem. But as far as who was in charge or not in charge and so on, I don't recall any difference in that. In other words, up on the Murmansk run it would be a British admiral that was calling the signals. He was on some other ship. Down in the South Pacific it was an American admiral, but he was on some other ship, so there wasn't all that much difference.

Q: With these two operations, your tour of duty in the South Pacific came to an end. Did you realize that you were going to be transferred?

Merdinger: No. Very shortly after graduation, I had requested transfer to the Civil Engineer Corps at such time as would be convenient to all parties, and -

Q: What made you do that?

Merdinger: I had studied civil engineering before I'd gone to the Naval Academy. I knew we had a small Civil Engineer Corps in the Navy that was doing interesting things, and I had the feeling that that's what I wanted to do ultimately in the Navy. But on the other hand, once the war had started I felt I'd been trained to be a line officer. Certainly this was where my responsibility lay.

Q: You were needed immediately.

Merdinger: Right. I didn't want to miss the chance of getting into the CEC, but on the other hand I didn't want to simply go and leave what I was doing in an irresponsible manner.

Well, it turned out that this matter was all settled for me, because throughout the war, people were called back to go to postgraduate school and become Civil Engineer Corps officers on a class basis, and when your class came up you went and that was it. It turned out that my class had two whacks at it. I didn't go the first time so when I was finally ordered, this was my last chance to go into the Civil Engineer Corps. As a matter of fact, before I completed the course at RPI, I'd been selected as a lieutenant commander in the line, so I was one of the few rare individuals who was transferred as lieutenant commander into the CEC. I was already kind of late as far as grade was concerned, although with accelerated promotions I was still relatively young. But anyway, the operation at Tarawa was the last one. Shortly thereafter, when we were down in Efati in the New Hebrides, I got orders to go back to the States and report to Rensselaer Polytechnic Institute in January of '44. In Troy, New York, yes.

Now, the program there was a three year engineering course compressed into slightly more than two, because we were all going full blast. We went to graduation with the mechanical, electrical and civil engineers, got our bachelor's degree and master's degree in civil engineer-

Merdinger #2 - 84

ing simply because we were going into the Civil Engineer Corps, I think.

Q: Were you married at that time?

Merdinger: Not when I went there, but after I'd been there almost a year.

Q: Tell me a little about the speedup course.

Merdinger: RPI had been in business a long time, of course, as an engineering school. As a matter of fact, it's long been held to be the oldest civilian engineering college in the country, dating from 1824. And they had also had a long history of taking in Civil Engineer Corps candidates who were graduate of the Naval Academy. This went back to the early 1900s, and I think RPI was selected simply because the then chief of the bureau had been an RPI graduate himself. Through the years normally about three Academy graduate were sent back each year to take this course, which in peacetime covered three years. In the speed-up course we covered the same ground in a little over two years.

So when the three of us in our class came along, there were no choices for us. We didn't have any options. This was the course -- structures, water-supply, airports, etc. I recall, there were some periods when we were in class for as many as 39 hours a week. Now, this is pretty tough classroom schedule.

Q: There would be some background for this too?

Merdinger: Yes, many times you were supposed to have about two hours preparation for every hour in class, so it adds up to a pretty long week.

So we were pushed –

Q: You had to be good students to be selected for this kind of course.

Merdinger: Well, yes. When I was making inquiries, I was told that Naval Academy graduates ought to stand in about the first 15 percent of the class. Now, this wasn't always the case, but it is true. I think, that Naval Academy graduates who were selected for this course, were pretty good students and as a consequence I think we fared reasonably well. In some cases, we were in classes with just the three of us. In other cases, we were thrown into undergraduate classes. But for the most part we were very fortunate in having department chairmen as our instructors, and we had a very first class engineering course. I think I mentioned before that there was a difference between this course and the Naval Academy approach to engineering. I really came away feeling I had a strong background in design, and a strong fundamental grounding in all areas of engineering that I did not get at the Naval Academy.

Q: Still you felt that your preparation at the Academy was adequate for this?

Merdinger: Oh yes. The Naval Academy was fine to produce a naval officer, someone with a good technological background, but it was not oriented to produce a design engineer. You'd have to go somewhere else to get that kind of training.

Q: You just said, in some of the courses the three men from the Naval Academy comprised the class. Does this imply that there were special courses directed toward the Naval Academy men?

Merdinger: Yes in a few cases there were. For instance, one course we had was in architecture for engineers. We had the head of the architectural department, and I think that he gave us some very special programs and projects. As a matter of fact, he used to challenge us a great deal, telling us that we weren't really members of a respected profession, that people in architecture for instance had a sense of the history of their profession. One of the hallmarks of the profession was that people had this sense in their background, whereas in engineering we didn't know what happened 10 years ago, let along 100. And I think that this challenge he threw down was one of the things that ultimately sparked my interest in the history of engineering. I said, "Well, where does one find out about it?" There didn't seem to be much in writing on the history of engineering. I said to myself, "Somebody ought to write a book on the history of civil engineering."

This ultimately came to be one of the things that I immersed myself in.

I do think that this challenge in part was responsible for my going into it.

That was a typical example. We had other courses, but they had to do with contracting procedures, for instance, particularly naval contracting procedures. There was a Civil Engineer Corps captain up there who was assigned as our mentor, and he gave us a few courses along these lines. It seemed to be very practically oriented to the kind of thing that we would ultimately do as CEC's.

But for the most part, we got the undergraduate and the graduate courses that everybody else took. If anything, these special courses were above and beyond, they were not in lieu of, in any respect.

Q: It's rather marvelous that they would accommodate these special courses.

Merdinger: Yes, and I might add that we were treated both as graduate students and special people, and we were also treated as undergraduates. By that I mean, we were allowed to participate in the undergraduate life if we so chose. Among other things, I played on the varsity football and lacrosse teams there, and belonged to some of the clubs. I also acted as scoutmaster out in the town and got a little bit into the community that way. So we were not completely tied to the grindstone of studying.

Q: It being wartime, were you obligated to wear uniforms?

Merdinger: Yes, we were in uniform all the time. It was a little awkward at times because practically everybody else on campus was in uniform too. They had a variety of these naval programs, V-12, V-7 and so on, so here we were -- most of the time we were there as senior grade lieutenants -- and all of our compatriots in the class were apprentice seamen, or whatever their grade was. This was particularly noticeable when we would go on an athletic trip. The home team would assume perhaps I was one of the coaches coming in an officer's uniform, and then I'd strip down and just join the rest of the team. It always caused a little

Merdinger #2 - 88

flurry. But we were in uniform all the time.

Q: I should think this would have meant that the rest of them sort of gravitated toward you for leadership.

Merdinger: No, if anything it might have made them gravitate the other way.

Q: Did you experience any particular difficulty, coming from a battlefield to the classroom, any particular difficulty in studying, applying yourself in that way?

Merdinger: No. I didn't find any particular difficulty, nor do I recall that my contemporaries did. Now, I had some difficulty getting back in the groove with calculus and thermodynamics and a few other subjects. In other words, here were things that we had studied some years ago and I'd never had any real use for them in a practical way. Now all of a sudden we're given an advanced course when we got back in the same subject. So there was a little period there of a few weeks in getting adjusted to that. But the idea of studying per se wasn't particularly difficult

I think perhaps our minds were more or less prepared for this, because we had a chance before the term began to speak to some of the fellows in the CEC program ahead of us, and they gave us the idea that you simply studied all the time. That was about the size of it. So I think we were more or less psychologically prepared to do this. Then too, the whole campus was under forced draft, so to speak. Everybody was going through faster and earlier. So I think it was natural to be caught up in this overall environment of intensive study.

Merdinger #2 - 89

Q: How did this afford time for romance?

Merdinger: Well, I don't know, somehow - we seemed to have time to get in a few extracurricular activities. My wife to be at the time -

Q: - was she a Troy girl?

Merdinger: No. She lived in Boston. But I had met her back when I was a first classman and had seen her a few times. As a matter of fact, when the ship had been at Casco Bay, I'd seen her in Boston some. But there was nothing particularly serious when I first came back. But interestingly enough, my roommate and I had both, after several months, came to the conclusion that we'd found the right gals and were going to get married. We ultimately ended up by marrying on the same day - not at the same place but on the same day, so we broke up our apartment very neatly and went our separate ways.

Q: So your course of study extended until April of '46, I believe?

Merdinger: Yes. Yes and no - in the sense that our academic studies were over, oh, very early in the year. Then we were given two extra courses. One was a welding course with General Electric over in Schenectady, so we went over there for a number of weeks, and as I recall, actually qualified in certain areas of welding. And then we had a six weeks tour with Consolidated Edison Co. in New York City, and this was a very interesting time. We went around to a number of plants, talked to a number of people in key management positions, and in general got the feel of how one runs a public utility.

So that wasn't really part of the RPI course as such, but it was part of our instructional period.

Q: That so-called Cook's Tour is something that MIT graduates engaged in also.

Merdinger: Yes, I think it's something that has become common with certain engineering schools. I suspect that our program perhaps went a little deeper, and broader, than many of the others.

Q: It's really the implementation of some of the theory.

Merdinger: Yes, particularly some of the things we'd been studying about management and how one manages a technical enterprise. To go out and see them on the firing line, so to speak, I think is very important. One of the things that struck me, both at General Electric and Consolidated Edison, was the fact that size in itself ultimately creates a certain amount of bureaucratic procedure. Where in the Navy we might have six copies of something, I found that in these other places they might have seven or eight copies. So it wasn't the Navy that was to blame for being a great bureaucracy because it was Navy, but rather because of its size.

Q: It gets to be ponderous.

Merdinger: That's right. This is one of the things I think that I saw a little more clearly perhaps for the first time. Big business does run an awful lot along the same lines that the Navy does. I don't know whether this is good or bad, but the point was, the similarity was definitely there in terms of business procedures.

Q: Did you get a degree as a result of this?

Merdinger: Oh yes, at RPI we got a bachelor of civil engineering and a master of civil engineering degree. After the first compressed two years we got the bachelor's degree, and at that time we were then transferred into the Civil Engineer Corps. So the last two terms while we were doing the master's degree work we were actually in CEC officially. Prior to that time we'd simply been designated for it. And we also were inducted into a number of honorary societies like Sigma Zi and Tau Beta Pi and the rest. I assumed they went with the course, but I found out later that no, there was only a certain percentage of people who got these. Apparently most of us in the Navy did well enough so that we were usually inducted into these honorary societies.

Q: That must have been a very very pleasant interlude, although a hectic one.

Merdinger: Yes, I look back on the days at RPI with a great deal of fondness. I think that for many years I was fonder of RPI than I was of the Naval Academy, and I think it had to do with personalities. I got to know the professors at RPI, a good many of them, whereas at the Naval Academy I hardly ever got to know anybody. We were in a situation in my midshipman years whereby one would have an instructor for four weeks or so and might never see him again, so it was very difficult to latch onto anybody in the instruction course. RPI, of course, was completely different. So I think there was this very personal touch that I carried with me for a long time.

Q: Isn't that more typical anyway of a private college or university?

Merdinger #2 - 92

Merdinger: Well, I hesitate to generalize because you hear so many complaints today in the private universities that the students never get to know any professors, and again that's a question of size, to a degree. But there wasn't all that great difference. It wasn't a question of difference in size between RPI and the Naval Academy. I think it was the Naval Academy's approach to instruction at that time. By the way, it's changed. We don't have that today. Normally one gets a professor for at least a term.

Q: Having graduated you were then ready for what?

Merdinger: Well, fit to become a Civil Engineer Corps officer - however, not quite. We had to go to Davisville for a number of weeks to get a little rounding out on some of the practical problems in the Civil Engineer Corps.

Q: This was to draw you back into the service again?

Merdinger: Yes, in a way, but it was really more specifically to get us acquainted with problems we'd face as Civil Engineering officers, going into public works assignments, contract assignments and so on.

Q: Tell be about the school at Davisville.

Merdinger: Well, it doesn't exist anymore in Davisville.

Q: Davisville where?

Merdinger: Davisville, Rhode Island. This was also the home of the Atlantic Seabees. The school subsequently shifted out to Port Hueneme where it is now, known as "CECOS," the Civil Engineer Corps Officers' School. It ran just a few short weeks, maybe two months at the outside – and we simply had a series of short courses in areas that one would not get normally in college. In other words, these were not academic sources. They were essentially pragmatic in terms of the kind of problem one would encounter administratively in carrying out his duties as a CEC officer.

Q: This was conducted entirely by the service?

Merdinger: Oh yes, it was conducted by a Civil Engineer Corps captain, who was the officer in charge of the school, and he had a number of CEC assistants. I guess they had a couple of civilian professors too.

Q: How big was the student body? What kind of people?

Merdinger: Oh, it varied, but in our class we had people ranging in rank all the way from JG through full commander. Some of these people had spent all the war in the Seabees and they knew nothing about public works or anything else, and they were in turn coming in to get indoctrinated along these lines, along with people like ourselves who'd been line officers and knew nothing about the CBC. So it was quite a melange.

Q: And a melting pot.

Merdinger: That's right, of student as well as faculty.

Q: It must have meant good cross-fertilization, must have been interesting.

Merdinger: Well, it was interesting, but, of course, we were there such a short time that I'm not sure how much we got from each other.

Q: Then you went down to Panama.

Merdinger: Yes. This was to the 15th Naval District Headquarters.

Q: Was this something that you looked forward to?

Merdinger: Well, I was very surprised. I must confess that while in RPI I had been looking forward to going out into the Pacific with the Seabees, and —

Q: — because the war was still going on.

Merdinger: Because the war was still one, and I think that there was a sort of feeling of being let down a bit when the war stopped. I know this sounds rather horrible, but the point was that we felt we had some kind of obligation to get out there with those fellows, even thought we had been out with the fleet, but now there was another kind of job to be done.

Well, it turned out, of course, that the Seabees — this was now '46 were coming home. They were being disbanded very rapidly. I never had even thought about Panama one way or the other, but I was delighted with the assignment. It turned out to be first class professional assignment as far as I was concerned, because I really got two jobs. One, I went into headquarters as the base maintenance officer, which meant that I had a public works department of about 350 civilians under my charge, and was responsible for all the utilities and maintenance of the base in general.

Merdinger #2 - 95

Q: And the base was where?

Merdinger: This was naval district headquarters, which was at Balboa. Right next to Fort Amador. And then my other job was a resident officer in charge of construction of what may have been about the only cost-plus-fixed-fee contract we had in the Navy at the time. This was a job that called for a variety of things to be done -- in one part we knocked down the jungle and built roads and houses. As a matter of fact, it was a great thrill to me to participate in designing these houses, and then to act as resident engineer seeing them go up. And I even named the steets and did a lot of things of that nature, and just a couple of years ago, I went back to Panama after, what was it, 20 years or more, and by golly the houses were there and the people were enjoying them just as much as they had the day they moved in. They were built well. And the names of the steets were still there.

Q: This is on the base itself?

Merdinger: This was over at a place called Farfan. This was not at 15th Naval District Headquarters. I should point out that as resident officer in charge of construction I was responsible for a lot of construction throughout the Isthmus.- Navy construction in a number of different places.

Q: On Canal property?

Merdinger: On US property, yes. There were a number of things that we had to do, such as to fix the floor of a machine shop that had sunk. You see, this was a multi-use area at Farfan. Among other things we had a submarine base, which had been built on filled ground. Some of the structures were sinking, and now we were faced with the problem of shoring them up. I recall one incident, in connection with the machine shop, on the design of the piles that were in there. I'd just been studying piling at RPI, and took issue with the design that our engineers had come up with on this job. I changed it and just as a result of the savings on that alone, saved the whole cost of my education at RPI. This to me was of great satisfaction, to be able to contribute something technically to this kind of operation.

So in the course of being there less than a year, I figured that I had saved the government my salary many times over in terms of technical, not errors, but changes.

Q: Too bad the record of the General Accounting Office couldn't show that.

Merdinger: Well, I'll tell you this, it was a lot of fun building those houses. While they may not have represented the major percentage of total construction costs – because we were doing a lot of things, big water tank, this machine shop, a fire house, a tunnel, etc. – to me the houses perhaps were the most satisfying because people were going to live in them and we could put a little more personality into them. These were four bedroom places with garages which we built for $10,000. I was told later that nobody, even when the GAO came in, nobody would believe that we could build houses for this low a cost.

Q: How was it accomplished?

Merdinger: There were a number of factors. One of them - of course, this gets me into semantics about whether an item costs you something or not - but there was a lot of surplus material that the Army had, and I succeeded, in my relationship with a number of different people down there, in getting some of this stuff for nothing. So we were able to put that into the project. Then the people we had in direct charge of it, Pan-Pacific Construction Co., were very good at organizing people into little units and then giving them subcontracts. For instance, we had to dig a 300-foot tunnel through a hill. They simply offered this contract to Jose or Pedro, whoever it was, showed him how to do it, and gave him all the materials and said, "This is what we'll give you for it." "X" dollars per foot, so he had his cousins and uncles and everybody else, people coming in on Saturday and Sunday working on the thing.

Similarly when we were putting the houses together. One man might get a contract to put in all the window frames, and again he would get a lot of his family or friends to help him out. So we were able to get very reasonable prices, and pretty speedy work, and we simply saw to it that the quality was up to standard. So we put them up rather fast and relatively inexpensively.

Q: Did the Panamanian require closer/supervision perhaps than US personnel would?

Merdinger: I suppose you could generalize and say this is true, but you can always find the exceptions to that. You find certain US in overseas places who aren't particularly good. They've bounced around from one place to another. And you find some native workmen who are tremendously good. But again I suppose you could generalize that Panamanians had to be a little more closely supervised, simply because they might not have had the depth of training that the Americans had had.

Q: Did you have them bid on contracts?

Merdinger: Well, these weren't really bids, these were negotiations with individuals who were already on the job. In other words, you'd find that some carpenter was a very good man and he was doing a great job. You'd say, "Look, how would you like to be responsible for doing this particular job, and we'll pay you so much to get it done. You can get whatever people you want on this job."

Now, I don't know that you could even do that in today's climate with labor union rules and everything else.

Q: You didn't have that sort of thing to contend with.

Merdinger: We didn't have that down there at that time. As a matter of fact, that was the time when you still had very great racial discrimination between Americans and Panamanians. They even had drinking fountains, gold and silver, and this went back to the old days of the Canal's construction, when the white workers, the Americans, were paid in gold, and basically all other, the coloreds for the most part, though not necessarily all colored, were paid in silver. So when we were in Panama, you still had toilets marked Gold and Silver, even drinking fountains, and there was a differential in the amount of pay. There was not equal pay for equal work. The Panamanian who might be just as competent as his American counterpart and doing the same job - I'm speaking now perhaps more of clerical jobs - would not be paid the same, even under our civil service operation.

Q: At that time they didn't terribly resent this?

Merdinger: Oh, I think there was agitation going on. It was something that we simply didn't feel because as an employer we weren't very big. It was the Panama Canal Organization that was the big employer, and the Army was much bigger than we were, so I would say we were the minor, almost the most minor of the US government agencies down there that had any kind of native work force at all.

Q: Did you have any dealing directly with the Panamanian government?

Merdinger: I'm trying to recall. I didn't. My dealings were more with the Panama Canal Government, and, of course, the Panama Canal Government was basically Army Engineers. The governor for instance was a major general in the Corps of Engineers, but he'd taken off his stars and he walked around in a civilian suit, but he was still an Army Engineer.

Q: How did you find the climate there, functioning in that tropical - ?

Merdinger: Well, I found personally that I enjoyed it. I flourished in it. I don't know, this is strange, a boy coming from Wisconsin -

We had a house that was up on a hill, no air conditioning. As a matter of fact, we didn't have air conditioning in the offices. But our house was up on a hill overlooking the Pacific terminal of the Canal, and I don't ever recall a night that we couldn't sleep because of the weather. There was always a bit of a breeze coming through. It was always cool enough to be comfortable enough to sleep.

Q: Were you free also from the Panamanian mosquitoes?

Merdinger: Yes. Curiously, there weren't many insects in the Canal Zone. They'd been pretty well stamped out. In was very seldom you saw a fly, for instance.

Now, You've got all kinds of tropical lizards and things that run all around and so on. You get those, and termites are an ever present problem. But the normal kind of insects that bother us in this country, mosquitoes and flies, were not particularly evident in the Canal Zone, at least the part of the Canal Zone where we were.

Q: Well, you earned your spurs as an engineer there on this assignment.

Merdinger: Yes, it was a very gratifying kind of a job. I was out in the field a good part of the time, in the office some of the time, and working on contract negotiations and design changes, things of that nature. And, of course, there was the business of the maintenance of the base too, which took a certain amount of time. So I learned both the public works and construction business rather in a hurry.

I might add that it wasn't took difficult to learn because the course we'd had at RPI was such that I really felt that I was on top of all these things. Obviously when you go from an academic to a practical situation, there's a certain amount of difficulty there, but I thought that we'd been prepared at RPI very well for this.

Q: At the naval base, what sort of maintenance of naval units was maintained before? How much work was done?

Merdinger: Well, it was really mostly of a housekeeping nature. We had a good many families living there so we were taking care of everybody's quarters. We had the streets. We had to supply hot water. Refrigeration was obviously a problem. We had a small enlisted force there and of course, there was a BOQ, so we had the barracks and that sort of thing. As far as boats were concerned, we didn't have them at that particular base. That sort of thing was taken care of over at the sub base. There was also a naval air station down there. So we had all kinds of naval activity down in the Canal Zone, but not right at headquarters itself.

I might add that any kind of major ship repair that might have to be taken care of would be done by the Panama Canal people in their shops. So we weren't a shipyard. We had no shipyard responsibilities. Ours was really an operational headquarters, worked mainly ashore.

Q: Were efforts very widespread to prevent sabotage and that sort of thing in the Canal area? Were you conscious of this?

Merdinger: I'm not conscious of it at this great distance. This was just after the war. I think there was a general relaxation all over, and I suspect that there was pretty much of a letting down of the bars

Merdinger #2 - 102

on that. This is not to say that we weren't conscious that something might break out in the Republic of Panama, but there was not the same kind of hostility to the American presence that apparently there has been in recent years.

Q: Was there any discussion at that time about the need of a supplementary canal? We've heard so much about this.

Merdinger: Yes. Yes, very much so. The Canal of course, was undergoing a lot of study just before the war began. As a matter of fact, they started on what they called the Third Locks Project, and some excavation had actually been accomplished.

Then after the war there was a great deal of controversy in the technical area as to just what approach should be taken. Do we want to go ahead and build a third set of locks? Or should we make this a sea level canal? There's another school of thought that said, no, you don't want to go to a sea level canal, you want some kind of a terminal lake plan.

These studies were very much in evidence when I was down there. In fact, the Army Engineers had a beautiful big model of the present Canal, and you could see how the water moved from terminal to terminal. There's a differential in the tides at either end. As I recall it - the Pacific has a fantastic tidal range, 22, 24 feet perhaps, and it's just a few feet over on the Atlantic side. And, of course, the question was, what will this differential do to us in terms of rushing water from one side to the other? And so on. Well, I don't know that this was ever successfully resolved, although the sea level advocates seemed to have a pretty good story there. And as you know, there have been a number of studies since. They've come up with all sorts of alternate routes. But interestingly enough, practically every alternate route that anybody's ever come up with was already discussed as a possibility back in the 16th century.

Q: Columbia? Tehuantepec?

Merdinger: Right. You may or may not know that back in the 19th century, Captain James Eades came up with an idea of going across a section of Mexico - Tehuantepec - not with a canal, but with reailroads. In other words, they'd put all the ships on giant railway cars, and track them across.

Q: That would be hard to do with a carrier, wouldn't it?

Merdinger: That would be pretty tough today, but it was a practical solution with ships the size they were at the particular time.

I might add, he's the same engineer who ultimately built the St. Louis bridge, which is very famous in American landmarks. He ultimately died mad. An interesting footnote to history.

Q: Now, is there something else that's significant about your tour of duty down there?

Merdinger: Our first daughter was born down there, so that's significant from the family standpoint. And while down there, I won the Rhodes Scholarship, which certainly ultimately affected the rest of my career.

Q: Tell me how that came about, how you happened to apply for this scholarship and be considered for that.

Merdinger: The Navy for many years had discouraged its officers from competing for Rhodes Scholarships. As a matter of fact, there was a regulation I believe on the books at one time that said any officer who accepted such a scholarship would automatically forfeit his commission.

Q: What's the reason for that?

Merdinger: I don't know, but there were just some people in the higher echelons who felt that this kind of an education wasn't particularly compatible with the requirements that the Navy had.

Q: It wasn't necessary for a seagoing man to be a Rhodes Scholar.

Merdinger: Nor even desirable in the minds of some. However, the Navy embarked on the experiment once -- the group that went to Oxford in 1930. Out of 32 in the country six were Naval Academy graduates. This was the first year that Naval Academy grads were encouraged to compete. And subsequently one more went over about 1932-33. The Navy shut it off again; said, sorry, we're just not going to permit anybody to take advantage of this.

So in the postward period - this was then in 1946 - the Navy decided to allow its officers to compete. This was the first time

Merdinger #2 - 105

(apart from that initial try back in the early thirties).

Q: Did that not work out successfully, the initial one of seven men?

Merdinger: There were some people who felt that it did, and some that it didn't. One of these officers was killed in an accident, and another left the service early, but the remaining officers all stayed through for the full 30 year careers and I think contributed materially to the Navy. So in terms of their staying power, I don't think you could quarrel with that.

No, I don't know all the reasons, except that the Navy was small. There was a certain feeling on the part of the hierarchy that all young officers should go to sea immediately, and they didn't like the idea of their going off to postgraduate school somewhere, and this was, in the view of many of them, just another postgraduate school.

Q: And not particularly in engineering or anything like that.

Merdinger: No. As a matter of fact, the Rhodes trust specifies that the individual may study anything in the world he wants to study when he goes over there.

So we come down to '46 and now the Navy has decided that it wants its officers to compete for this.

Q: What invoked this?

Merdinger: A number of people had something to do with this. Frank Russell, who was very active in the Rhodes Scholar Association for many years and particularly interested in the service academies, managed to interest West Point in this way back as early as 1925, I think. And he kept after the Naval Academy and people in the Navy for this, so his was a certain amount of influence.

Q: Did West Point have a continuing program of participation through the years?

Merdinger: Yes, they did. One back in the twenties —

Q: No hiatus at all?

Merdinger: There might not be a scholar selected every year, but the point was that they encouraged their people to compete, and I do know that right up to the class of '36 at least, there were Rhodes Scholars; that is, in the pre-World War II period.

So Frank Russell was one. I think one of the proximate causes was right in our own Navy. The then six-striper, Stan Turner, who's now a rear admiral in Washington, mentioned this to Secretary Forrestal. Stan Turner had gone to Amherst a couple of years before the Naval Academy, and told the Secretary he was interested in competing for the Rhodes Scholarship but that the provision in the Navy didn't exist.

Now, there were other people who were also working on this, in other words, in the Bureau of Personnel. I don't recall who they all were, but some years ago I wrote a little article about this, and did a little historical bit on this thing as to just who these people were.

I suspect, however, that it was the Turner-Forrestal connection that perhaps had as much to do with this as anything.

Q: That moved the mountain.

Merdinger: I think it moved it. And I might add that he and I came in from the same district. He came in from Illinois and I came from Wisconsin, as Rhodes Scholars. But it was this notice that came through from BuPers encouraging us to compete that really caught my eye; and while I didn't know what one studies at Oxford, didn't know much about it, it was another competition, it looked kind of interesting, and so -

Q: Where were you then?

Merdinger: I was in Panama at the time. So the next question was, how to go about competing? One had to send in a request to the Bureau of Naval Personnel to be allowed to compete. At the same time, I wrote back to the president of RPI and told him that I was interested in doing this, and wondered if RPI would support me as a candidate. The candidate has to have the support of his college before he will be carried on in the competition. And I got back a very enthusiastic note, that RPI had never had a Rhodes Scholar, that they would be very happy to support me. Then, armed with that information, I went ahead and filled out the forms. Time was going by. I hadn't heard from the Navy. In the forms I put myself down as a graduate of RPI, and while I mentioned the Naval Academy, I did not go in as a candidate from the Naval Academy because I had no permission.

Merdinger #2 - 108

Well, it was a good thing that I did, because just a couple of days after I'd put in the papers - because we were nearing the deadline - I received word from the Navy Department that they would not allow me to compete. So I showed this to my boss, who was a captain, told him I had this dilemma, that I'd been told "No, you can't compete" but that my papers were in, and we just decided to let the whole matter ride and see what happened.

Q: What was the reason for not letting you compete, based on the Naval Academy record? This was a conflict from above and below?

Merdinger: It's like all these selection boards, you never know why somebody is selected and why you are not. There are all sorts of things you can conclude - simple that they thought there were a lot of better people in the competition, or that perhaps I'd had too much postgraduate education. I'd just come out of postgraduate school. I don't know, I have no way to --

Q: It wasn't a blanket refusal for Naval Academy men -

Merdinger: Oh no, no. This was on an individual basis. In other words, I as an individual was not allowed to compete, though other people who were Naval Academy grads competed in the district I ultimately competed in. They were given permission and they didn't win it. I was not given permission but did win it. So we had this dilemma.

Well, in the course of applying I'd mentioned to the secretary of the Rhodes Trust who was up in Swarthmore - Dr. Frank Aydelotte was the American secretary — that I was down in Panama engaged in this important construction work, and that quite honestly if I were called for an interview I didn't see how I could get back to Wisconsin, which was my home state. So he wrote back and said on the basis of the record they'd seen, they thought I ought to get an interview, so they were setting up a special one down in Bogota, Colombia, for me, just for me. The board would consist of the one Rhodes Scholar they had down there who was the head of Socony-Vacuum Oil, and the American ambassador and the American cultural attache.

So I was then set up to go down there. The next question was, how to get down to Bogota. Mind you, now, this was in the immediate postwar period and aviation was not in the same stage as it is today. Well, fortunately we had a commodore on our base who was the Foreign Liquidation Commissioner for Latin America. In the course of my responsibilities as base maintenance officer I'd fixed him up with some curtains and other such things, and apparently was in his good graces, and when I explained my difficulties he offered to take me down. He was going down to Bogota anyway about that time, so I managed to get a ride on the commodore's plane. I went down, and was met by Dr. Tong who was the Socony-Vacuum man, and he and I hit it off immediately. He was a geologist. He had gone to Oxford, having been through World War I, so he'd been in kind of a GI situation. He had spent much of his time in the oil fields, and had the same sort of outlook I suppose that I did in a general way on life, in terms of our engineering interests and responsibilities and so on. So I found myself in the company of a very compatible gentleman.

We went over to the ambassador's for lunch and the cultural attache was there, and Dr. Tong, and it was a delightful affair. We must have spent three hours or more there, and we talked about everything from Medieval French literature to labor conditions in the Canal Zone, and thoroughly enjoyed the time.

After it was over and Dr. Tong was taking me back to my hotel, I asked him, when we were going to have the interview, because perhaps I should bone up on Keats or Shelley or something, and he said, "Oh, we've already had it."

The way the interview had gone, everybody was talking about "When you get to Oxford" and so on, as if this thing were in the bag, which, of course, it wasn't.

Well, that was that, and then this information was forwarded up to my state committee in Wisconsin and then on to the district committee. It just turned out that Dr. Tong had been a contemporary at Oxford with some of the people who were on the boards up in my district, and they all had a very high respect for his opinions. So with this combination of circumstances, it put me into the winning group there, without ever appearing really before my board. Later on I had a chance to see the chairman of my state district and talk to him about this. This was on my way to Oxford. He said that quite honestly, he was biased against a military man getting it, not because of his being military but merely because the military had such a great postgraduate system that if they wanted their officers to go to

Oxford, they could jolly well send them there. Whereas he felt that a lot of these other fellows would never get a chance at postgraduate education unless something like the Rhodes Scholarship came along.

But you see, basically the Rhodes system says it doesn't make any differences as to whether one can pay or not. That's not a criterion for selection. As you know, in today's scholarship game in colleges, this tends to be all-pervasive, the question of need. With the Rhodes Scholarship need is not a criterion.

So he said, despite the fact that he felt that way and some of the others did, they voted for me anyway. I thought this showed a certain openness of mind on their part that was commendable.

Q: How many men went from the nation at large?

Merdinger: That year there were 48. Now, this took into account all the people who would have been eligible from before World War II right up to that period.

Q: There was cessation during World War II?

Merdinger: Oh yes, it stopped. The last selection had been 1939. There was no 1940 selection. So you take all these people in and really it covered almost a ten year period; whereas normally the top age for Rhodes Scholar candidates would be about 23, 24, at this time it was raised to 33, to take into its fold all the people from during the war. So I think as a consequence we had certainly an older than average group that went over.

Q: Probably a more capable one.

Merdinger: Well, they'd been around longer and had a chance to gain experience and improve themselves. Certainly this group in subsequent life made its mark here and there. Among the 48, I can name the president of the University of Virginia, the president of NYU, the headmaster of Lawrenceville - people I can think of in education. We have an admiral and a couple of generals. The attorney general of the United States, Nicholas Katzenbach was one of our number, the head of the National Institutes of Health was another, the head of the Viking Press. So we've produced people in a number of fields - law, medicine, engineering, government, health and so on, and many of them have achieved some measure of competence in their fields.

Q: How did the Navy react to your appointment when they had denied you the right to do it?

Merdinger: That was a very interesting time. As soon as I received the telegram - it came on a Sunday morning - I immediately went over to my boss and told him. And I might add that previously when I came back from Bogota, I'd told him that I just had a feeling that I might win this thing, and that we should be prepared in view of the turn-down that I had before, to do something. So he had alerted a friend of his back in the Personnel Section of the Bureau of Yards and Docks. which was my parent bureau, that this might come about.

When I told him, he immediately got off a dispatch to his friend. It went into the bowels of the Bureau of Naval Personnel somewhere, and it rattled around there for about a week and we didn't hear anything.

It took about a week, and finally I did get the approval. I found out, oh months and years later, in talking to some people who'd been in BuPers at the time, that there had been quite a discussion as to whether I should be court martialed or released without pay or what, but finally commonsense prevailed. The Navy had indicated that it wanted its officers to go after this thing, and it had somebody who'd got it. So they decided to forget the protocol involved in disobeying the rules.

Q: They would have looked mighty ridiculous, wouldn't they?

Merdinger: Oh, I think that they were in kind of a strange spot. My wife was very concerned about the thing, but I never really had any great concern. I figured this was something that was good for me, was good for the Navy, and therefore somehow -

Q: She wasn't particularly anxious for you to do it?

Merdinger: No, she was anxious for me to go over, and she was very happy that I had the opportunity, but she was a little concerned about the business of going against a regulation - it wasn't a regulation but a decision that had been handed down.

But as I say, common sense did prevail and that was the end of that.

Q: What would you have done if they'd turned you down?

Merdinger: I don't know. I've never really figured that one out. I didn't waste too much time thinking about it. I think, quite honestly, had they said, "We'll let you go over without pay," that I would have done that. I don't think I'd have resigned from the Navy. But as I say, I didn't face the thought squarely. I don't know.

Q: What did the scholarship entail in a monetary sense?

Merdinger: It was over and above, of course, my pay and allowances. In other words, I was not cut off from my Navy base. This was on top of it. I think it probably amounted to a couple of thousand dollars a year. The reason I'm vague on this is because it has changed through the years, and it's much more now than it used to be, so it's not a consistent sum. But I think it was in the neighborhood of a couple thousand dollars. I do know that at one time, I figured, because of the income tax situation and this, that and the other thing, I was making about the equivalent of $14,000 a year, which was a great deal for a lieutenant commander at that time, considerably much above my real pay. So financially it was a great deal, if nothing else, but, of course, it was far more than financial in its benefits.

Q: What were the terms of the scholarships?

Merdinger: One would go to Oxford for at least two years and proceed toward a degree. It didn't make any difference what the degree was, and as a matter of fact proceeding toward it was the important thing. They didn't say you had to get one. And there were some of our class-

Merdinger #2 - 115

mates at Oxford who didn't get a degree. Some went two, three years and they simply didn't get it and probably never will. But the terms were very generous, in that there was enough money there to pay for all your college expenses and maybe a little expense money on the side.

Q: For family? Some of them were family people.

Merdinger: No. And some of them were in pretty tough straits. No, this was designed really to support one individual, and I might add that supporting this individual was more than just going to the college, because the normal academic year over there is only three eight week terms, a total of 24 weeks out of the year that you're really living at the college, and the rest of the time you're expected to go out and -- well, broaden yourself, travel, certainly read a lot, do research. A lot of the people thought that they did most of their best work in between terms. Things were so busy during term that they didn't have time to do all the studying they wanted to do or needed to do. So this out of term period was not a time to get a job, but rather one to do the studies in greater depth.

Q: Did you have your family with you over there?

Merdinger: Yes, I did. I brought my wife and our first daughter who'd been born in Panama, and then we had a second daughter born in Oxford. But this didn't keep us from traveling. We did a lot of that, and, of course, one of the most interesting bits of travel was traveling with the university basketball team. As I recall, my wife was traveling with us. I think she was eight months pregnant on the last trip, when

Merdinger #2 - 116

we went down to the Riviera and played the croupiers of Monte Carlo and worked our way back up through France. As a matter of fact, I guess she was in her early stages of pregnance when we traveled through Czechoslovakia. We spent three weeks there playing all of their leading teams. This was in early 1948, two separate trips to the continent, and we warmed up a good many of the European Olympic teams -- the basketball team which appeared later in the Olympics in London that summer.

So we had the basketball trips and then we had just plain family trips. I should say, just the two us us. We always managed to leave the girls home with the baby sitter.

Q: A nanny over there.

Merdinger: Well, I suppose one could call her that, but in the case of the first daughter, we left her with some pub keepers. It turned out that the first place we were able to get in England was in a pub, and we became so fond of these people that they became Auntie Em and Uncle Syd, and even up until this last summer we've continued to visit them everytime we've gone back. Uncle Syd is dead now, but we went back to see Auntie Em this past Summer.

Q: What was your course of study, your particular interests?

Merdinger: I mentioned before that the head of the architecture department at RPI had rather spurred my interest in writing a history of civil engineering. When I got down to Panama, I got even more deeply into the history of the Canal. So finally when I went to Oxford, I decided that I didn't really want to study any more engineering. I'd done enough of that, although Oxford has a lot to offer in engineering. A lot of people get the idea that it's solely a non-technical sort of place, but they have some very fine scientific and engineering officers there. However, I thought it would be better to take my engineering background and the vast historical resources at Oxford, and write a history of civil engineering for a doctoral dissertation. So I told the people there this is what I'd like to do and they said, "Fine, all right, old chap, we don't know anybody who did it before, but if that's what you'd like to do, have a go at it."

And so I did. I spent a couple of years really involved in research, and research involved not only plowing through a lot of books at Oxford but going down to Rome, for example looking at the old Roman ruins and aquaducts and this sort of thing. So my main intellectual effort then was devoted to the research and writing of this dissertation which ultimately came to about 180,000 words. What it did was trace from the beginning, the time of the Pyramids up to the present day, the course of civil engineering in a number of different areas. That would be roads, bridges, canals, water supply systems, waterfront structures, all these things that we've come to look upon as the field of civil engineering. That ultimately became a series of articles in THE MILITARY ENGINEER, and subsequently they were put together in the form of a book entitled CIVIL ENGINEERING THROUGH THE AGES, published by the Society of American Military Engineers in 1963.

Merdinger #2 - 118

Now, as the result of those articles and that book I've been called upon to speak in a number of parts of the country, and so what turned out to be a little exercise at Oxford has become a lifelong avocation really. It's a fascinating subject, and, of course, the whole subject of the history of science and particularly the history of technology is really a new discipline, at least on the American scene. I think before World War II it was almost non-existent, but there are a number of people now in this area.

Q: But this was actually a pioneering effort, in this area.

Merdinger: Yes. It's not the great definitive work or anything, it's not even a very scholarly work. It's full of holes in a lot of places. But my thought was to put together something like this that would give other people something to shoot at, and in turn would span the whole field. So it was a labor of love.

Q: Did you have some knowledgeable counsellors at Oxford in the area?

Merdinger: Yes. He was called a supervisor. My supervisor was Dr. F. Sherwood Taylor, who was then curator of the Museum of History of Science, and he was a fellow who was well known in the history of science field over there. Just as soon as I mentioned at my college that I would like to do this history of civil engineering, they immediately thought of F. Sherwood Taylor.

Q: What was your college?

Merdinger: I was at Brasenose College. Brasenose is one of the newer colleges. It wasn't founded until 1509. By the way, that's the same college that George Washington's great-grandfather attended.

Q: Really? Talk a little about the differential, if there is one, between the Oxford standard and the American university standard.

Merdinger: Well, first of all, I think that the average undergraduate one gets at Oxford is liable to be much better academically prepared than his counterpart over here. Now, I suggest that this comes about from the sheer competition for space. I recall looking at some statistics some years ago that placed one American in 20 - and I don't know what the grouping was, but anyway, 1 in 20 of this particular group of Americans was in college. The comparable group, 1 in 900 in Britain. I think right off the bat that says something about the competition that got these people into the university.

My impression was that it was very difficult to get into Oxford, but that once one got there, he was pretty well assured of getting his degree if he did any kind of reasonable work at all. In other words, I think that the admission standards were so high that you were almost guaranteed that you'd get somebody who was not only capable of doing the work but who would do the work.

Q: Would this explain the custom that I've seen implemented by somebody who's attended an English University, working for a master's say, "MA (failed)" after the MA in parens -

Merdinger: I'm not sure that I understand.

The British system for the undergraduate degree at Oxford works this way. For the most part, most B.S. degrees take three years to accomplish. The student goes through, and he may take a few exams, but basically there's only one exam and this is at the end of the three years.

Q: It's certainly a comprehensive.

Merdinger: Yes, this is really a comprehensive. He'll sit for several papers during the course of a week and write reams of paper. After these papers have been corrected by the examiners - who, by the way, are not his original teachers. This is some external group, not his tutor, conducting these examinations - then he may be called for what's known as a viva, and he comes in and will then be expected to defend his paper.

Now, I don't really know the facts of the case. I've heard it said that you can't raise your grade, you can only lower it, but at the time I was there, one could get a first, and these were the ones who were in the genius class and became prime ministers - or a second, that's good solid perhaps A student, and a third is somebody who didn't set a second, and a fourth is a gentlemanly grade. Then, of course, one could fail.

Now, it took as I say three years to get the BA. Four years later, or seven years from matriculation, having gained the BA, then the candidate was allowed to go up for his MA. With the payment of a fee and certification that he hadn't been in jail, the MA would be automatically awarded. This has made some people in this country feel that it's kind of a watered down MA. Well, I suggest that it was an MA that was being studied for in the first place. But you see, the normal student I was familiar with over there, who came in as a freshman at Oxford, was probably academically equivalent at that time to our college junior. He was doing, if you will, the last two years of our college course plus a third year. I might add further that the BA there is much more concentrated in one area. In other words, you don't get the smorgasbord of courses that we get particularly in our liberal arts colleges. One is expected to have gone all through that before getting to the university. So I think that this business of MA failed, could mean that he went through the course, took his examinations and didn't pass them; perhaps that's what he's trying to tell us.

Q: Did the Navy expect you to report to them during the priod you were there, on your progress? Were you required to make periodic reports?

Merdinger: On occasion and sporadically. We were officially attached to the office of the naval attache in London, and every now and then we would show up in person down there, write a little note as to what we were doing - but by and large we were on our own.

Q: Who was NA when you were there?

Merdinger: Commodore Tully Shully.

To go back to the other business that you were mentioning, about the academic environment, I could expand on that a little more..

One of the very distinct impressions I came away from Oxford with was the fact they they put the individual much more on his own than we do here. There's not the spoon-feeding. And in particular, at that time, I think that much of our U.S. education was a one book kind of thing. That is, you read the book and you more or less disgorged it back to the instructor. Now, we've changed. We've come a long way since that time. But even then at Oxford, one was given five or six books to read and told to write an essay on the subject they covered. What made it difficult, of course, was that the authors all had different points of view, so it was important then that the student think through the whole thing, and come up with his essay that would reflect something original on his part.

Now, I'm distinguishing, you see, between the B.A. and the doctoral program which I was in and which very few people were in, by the way. Of our group there were only four of us who did the doctoral work in the two years. For the most part they "read" for the BA even though they were BA's (in the U.S.) and in many cases MA's already. But the BA-MA program has always been considered very fine at Oxford, and a lot of our people felt that this was where they would get the most out of Oxford.

The undergraduate had this responsibility, then, for digging in and thinking on their own. They also had to do a lot of writing, and I think that kind of discipline can be a big help to a person in later life. I think perhaps that some skill in writing might be a mark of most Oxford graduates. Now, maybe they were pretty good writers to begin with, because they'd been through public schools, but the point is, at Oxford they were still expected to do a lot of it.

The undergraduate reading for the BA, will see his tutor probably once a week in each subject. So he may go to one, to maybe three tutorials, a maximum of two hours for one, something like that. There he's expected to read his essay - possibly 2000 words - and then his instructor will not only go over the content with him but he may well mark his technical errors as well.

Q: This is a private affair, not in conjunction with anyone else.

Merdinger: Yes. Oh, there may be one or two other students in there, but essentially private. For the most part, the tutorial is an individual thing.

Now, I'm not sure whether this is still the case today or not. I should add further that there were many, many lectures given in the university, but many tutors would say, "Well, I think you can read that better for yourself than to go hear him read some of his own book."

So the response then to lectures was sporadic. It all depended on the individual. Obviously there was no compulsion to go. Supplementing the lectures, of course, were innumerable clubs - for example, the Cosmos Society, which would concern itself with world affairs. Then there was the Jan Masaryk Society which was concerned with Central European affairs. One could go over the whole political, scientific, social spectrum, and could find something almost every night.

Q: Stimulating.

Merdinger: That's right, and not only was it stimulating because of the individuals who were giving the lectures, but also stimulating because of the people in the audience there who could take the lecturer apart in many cases. I remember for instance, there was a lot of talk about the Arab-Israeli problem at that time. Well, it was easy to get somebody who was a rather high official from either side, out of London, but there would always be a number of people in the audience who were on the other side. This fellow would have a good stimulating time, let's put it that way. I don't mean that the people were disruptive, as they tended to be here in the last few years.

Q: This was an intellectual disagreement.

Merdinger: An intellectual interchange. It was very stimulating. So as I say, it wasn't only the lecturers, but even the audience was stimulating from that standpoint, and, of course, you had people from all over the world. London was only 60 miles away from Oxford, so it wasn't too difficult to get people really from all parts of the world and all walks of life to Oxford to lecture.

Q: Then Cecil Rhodes did well by you.

Merdinger: I think most of the fellows who went over there as Rhodes Scholars felt that it was a wonderful experience, stimulating, something that they never would have experienced any other way. I always felt that way. It certainly opened my view of the world. Whether it has any direct effect on one's career is open to argument, of course, but certainly in terms of personal stimulation – no question about it. It was a wonderful experience.

Now, not everybody who went there felt this way. There were some who were there just a short time and they said, "This isn't for me. I don't like it. I'm not getting anything out of it."

I recall one fellow who'd apparently been a very brilliant scientist from MIT, and he didn't feel that the laboratories at Oxford were on a par with MIT. I guess maybe they weren't. But he didn't see that there were other things he could get over there. He decided that wasn't for him. I understand that he's done some very good work in Bell Labs in subsequent years and so on. There were cases like that.

Q: He chose to be a very special specialist.

Merdinger: That's right. In other words, he was a scientist who didn't quite find his niche there. On the other hand, there was a fellow who was a poet who decided he wasn't finding his niche in Oxford either. He decided to go to Florence to write poetry. So it's across the whole spectrum. It isn't necessarily one class of interest that gets shunted aside there. I think it depends on the individual. But I would say that most of them certainly got a lot out of it and it was well worth the experience.

Q: How did your wife like it?

Merdinger: Oh, she lapped it up. She enjoyed being over there. She enjoyed the traveling that we did. She attended a good many of the lectures in the evening in particular. So all in all, I think that she almost got as much out of it as I did. Of course, she had to stay home and take care of the babies which inhibited her a bit, but she has always looked very fondly on Oxford, as I do. So every time we have had an opportunity to go back to England – and it's been frequent – we've always managed to go back to Oxford, to make that little pilgrimage.

Q: What did the Navy have in mind for you when you came back from Oxford?

Merdinger: Well, they weren't quite sure. As a matter of fact, when I got back the Chief of Civil Engineers called me into his office and said, "You're so educated now, we don't know what to do with you."

But I ended up in Washington in headquarters, Bureau of Yards and Docks, and I was given a job as program coordinator. This meant that I was involved with a lot of architectural engineering programs, getting their work translated into some of the work that we had to turn out from the Bureau, designs of one sort and another. I had a lot of odd jobs.

Q: Would you give me some illustrations of that?

Merdinger: For instance, we were concerned with turning out standard designs for low cost structures that would have a five year life. If we were ever to get into another war, what kind of structures should we build to build up a base rapidly? We ought to have designs all ready on the shelf, rather than just coming along and starting from scratch. Improvement, for instance, of the quonset would be a typical example.

So we negotiated with a number of architectural/engineering firms and finally chose one to prepare a series of designs for our "Mobilization Structures." I stayed with the project from inception until the designs were completed and placed in readiness for some future emergency. That would be a good example of our long range planning responsibilities.

Now, we had other work which was current - where, let's say, we were going to build a hospital some place, and we were doing the design at headquarters. Or the design might be done somewhere out in the field but there was a certain amount of headquarters coordination that had to be done. So I would get involved in that. I had a series of different areas that were within my responsibility, housing, hospitals, radio facilities and a number of others of that nature.

Then I had a lot of odd jobs. Every time a British admiral would come to call on the Chief, I was called on to be the admiral's aide. Or any time any kind of educational group came through, I was tapped for that.

The Chief used to get a kick out of showing me in uniform and introducing me as "Doctor," to these educational groups.

Q: Is this such a novelty for the Navy?

Merdinger: Yes. It was. We didn't have very many people with the doctorate.

But that was a relatively short tour, and then I went to the Public Works Department in Bremerton -

Q: You said earlier that as a result of your articles and so on, you were called on to speak various places. This happened simultaneously with your Washington assignment?

Merdinger: Well, no, not simultaneously, because the articles didn't start coming out until 1952. This was the 100th anniversary of the founding of the American Society of Civil Engineers. They had a big program in Chicago to celebrate the centennial, and at that time I was called on to present a paper which was, in effect, my first chapter on CIVIL ENGINEERING THROUGH THE AGES - in other words, a very quick recap from the Pyramids to the present day. So I gave the paper there, and it was basically the same as the first of the articles that appeared in MILITARY ENGINEER. Just as soon as that first one appeared, there seemed to be a demand for this sort of thing, so for the next ten years these articles appeared every now and then in MILITARY ENGINEER.

After the articles appeared, then I began getting letters from people, phone calls and so on. So I would say '52 really started the real lecture tour, in terms of this particular subject.

Q: When you went out to deliver a lecture, it was always under the aegis of the Navy, was it?

Merdinger: For the most part, yes. I found myself at a number of national meetings. One time I was invited to go back down to Panama. I was stationed in California, and they invited me to Panama to give the major address for Engineers' Week. The governor issued the invitation, so I was feted for a few days down there through this. Then another time when I was in Japan, I was asked to go back to Alaska to do the same thing.

I felt I was in pretty good company - Werner von Braun had been asked the year before. So that was kind of nice.

When I was in California, I was invited to go to Mississippi and to Louisville and Chicago, a number of places. I really got around the country. And this occurred over a period of years.

Texas was one of the truly hospitable places; they asked me to come twice. They got me to come the first time to talk about old surveying instruments. This was a Texas Surveyors Association. I'd done some interesting work on the development of instruments at Oxford, and I think I had a bit of a story to tell. They liked it so much they asked me to come back again and talk about Polaris and the Meridian. I didn't know much about that subject so I did a little research on it and simply added another chapter to my book. That was one that was not written at Oxford but just got thrown in, since I had to do it for this particular speech.

Q: Being called upon to speak on various subjects, did this stimulate you to write things, continue with it?

Merdinger: Well, in the case of the Polaris and the Meridian, of course, this is a very typical example where I'd answer, yes. In terms of writing in this particular field, no, although I was from time to time producing other little articles of one sort or another. I don't know if the two are really related.

Q: Do you still write?

Merdinger: Every now and then. The most recent thing I wrote was the aquaduct section of the ENCYCLOPEDIA BRITANNICA, which has not yet appeared. They've given me my check so I assume it's acceptable.

Q: It'll come out in the next edition.

Merdinger: I suppose so, and prior to that, the most recent thing was in NAVAL REVIEW, 1970. This was the article on the Seabees and Civil Engineers in Vietnam. That's about a 10,000 word article so that took some time to put together. I did that after I returned from Vietnam, I might add. I didn't really have much time on the site.

Q: You went out to Washington, Puget Sound, April '51?

Merdinger: Yes, I went out as the number two man in the Public Works Department, about 1500 people. Of course, it was essentially a civilian organization. I might add that practically all these positions I've been in, in the Civil Engineer Corps, have been primarily civilian, civil service in character. And here was the normal public works reponsibility for maintenance, utilities, transportation. I learned a great deal about how shipyards work and particularly labor unions. I had certain problems with outside labor unions.

Q: Tell me something about that.

Merdinger: Well, one of the big projects that was going on up there was the building of the Jim Creek Radio Station. Our district civil engineer had let out the contract over in Seattle, but there were certain parts of it that simply didn't lend themselves to putting in a contract document. They were a little too vague, or there was something special about them.

So, as the nearest source of skilled labor in government, we in the Public Works Department at the Bremerton Shipyard were asked to do some of the supplementary work.

This brought down some of the unions on the outside on our heads. My boss had been sick for some time, so I was the acting head of the Public Works Department. Now the whole thing fell on me, the furor raised because we were going in and competing with this union labor out there.

I had a number of the labor union leaders come in to see me. They wanted me to come down to Olympia but I told them that we were doing our work up here, so they finally came up. They were really very concerned that we were competing, and they said we were doing them - their people - out of jobs. I might add, however, that our people were also union, only they were union within the shipyards, as opposed to people out in the civilian trades.

Q: What trade unions were they?

Merdinger: They were plumbers, carpenters, electricians - the building trades. In the end, I told the union leaders that we would continue on the job and that we would certainly cooperate with them to every extent but there was simply no way of our pulling off the job. Finally, it turned out that they didn't pull their people off the job either, and our people swapped tools back and forth with them. So it ended up rather amicably, but it was just one of those things - typical needling that you get in this kind of a situation. It sounds very simple here, but it was much more complicated in the negotiations.

Merdinger #2 - 132

Q: It can get really passionate.

Merdinger: Yes. Yes.

Q: Was this the first time you'd had this kind of experience with labor unions?

Merdinger: In Panama we had it to some extent, but this was the first time I'd really run into, you might say, the sophisticated American labor unions with strength on a broad national scale. As a matter of fact, one of these labor union leaders wrote into headquarters and pointed out that I wasn't being very cooperative with them, and they wanted the national headquarters to do something through the Department of the Navy and so on. So I was given some sort of a verbal slap, why don't you cooperate with those people more? and so on, but nobody ever wrote a letter, and, as I say, we ultimately finished the job.

But this was really the first occasion I had to deal face to face with these people. Of course, I might add that the shipyard unions - or the masters, various echelons out there - were pretty tough to deal with too, very hardnosed about what it says in the book and what their rights are and what they want and so on. So there were a lot of lessons to be learned in that environment in dealing with blue collar labor movement.

Q: It's becoming increasingly a problem for the government, dealing with unions.

Merdinger: Yes. You've got a new dimension that's just been added in these last few years, and that is the business of collective bargaining within the government. For years we had the government unions, but I'm speaking now more of the white collar types -- really they weren't militant, in the sense that it's possible for them to be now. I'm not suggesting that they are militant now. But the business of the collective bargaining --

Q: The strike method?

Merdinger: Well, you see, that was illegal. In theory, the people on the job _were_ the people, and they couldn't strike against themselves. That's now gone out the window, and they do have the right to strike.

I have not been involved with any of the new collective bargaining type unions in government. It was just coming into my area when I left the Navy, so I don't know just how that one's working out.

Q: You were active in athletics while you were in that job. You might tell me about it.

Merdinger: Yes, I was the basketball coach for the base team -- a team of amateurs. This was a group of sailors who did their day's work and then came down to the gym when the day was over and we'd put together a basketball team. Well, we were fortunate enough to win the district championship, and then we went on to an all-armed forces tournament where Army and Air Force teams were involved. There we ran into the real professionals. I found one Army team, for instance, where they were 100 percent black; and if they weren't a farm team for the Globetrotters, at least they had some fellows who either had been on a farm team for the Globetrotters or were headed there. I found out that their responsibilities for the most part consisted of sweeping out the gym in the morning and practicing basketball in the afternoon. We weren't really in the same league with this class of ball player. So while we did go to the All-armed forces tournament, we didn't turn out very well there.

But, in the course of our competition at Bremerton, we were selected on two occasions to play the Harlem Globetrotters, which I guess is some sort of an honor, in itself. We had a lot of fun playing them. Obviously we didn't beat them, but it gave a thrill to all the local citizens.

So that was a great bit of extracurricular duty. I enjoyed it.

Q: Was this entirely voluntary on your part, or was this part of morale building effort within the naval establishment?

Merdinger: No, it was completely voluntary on my part. As a matter of fact, in our organization, Public Works, since we were essentially civilian, except for a few officers, we didn't even have any enlisted men. The enlisted men came from other units on the base. So I had nothing directly to do with them at all. No, this was completely voluntary on my part. Some of the people knew that I had done a little coaching at basketball, and this was the result.

Q: Your prowess as an athlete followed you all the way through, didn't it? When you were at Oxford you were an athlete.

Merdinger: Well, yes. I played on the varsity lacrosse and basketball teams at Oxford and also played on a couple of our college teams. These were not the varsity, but were more like scrub teams. I played field hockey, played rugger once, got into a game of cricket once, but really I concentrated basically on lacrosse and basketball. But it is true that when the Navy biographies showed athletics at the previous station, one almost automatically got involved in the new station.

Q: What about your intellectual activities at Bremerton, the duties in the Navy yard —

Merdinger: I don't recall getting involved in much outside. No, that all came later in California, when I became a Great Books moderator and adult education leader.

Q: You went on from Bremerton to Alaska.

Merdinger: Well, more precisely, the Aleutian Islands, Adak. I was ordered to command the 124th Seabees up there and become public works officer.

Q: Was this to your liking, something you had sought, or?

Merdinger: I was delighted with the prospect of getting a Seabee battalion, but it came very suddenly. I got a call one day from Washington. I was not scheduled for transfer. I was still some six months away from a routine transfer. But it appeared there'd been a lot of difficulties up there. A boiler had blown up, personalities had flared and so on, and it was thought that a new Seabee commander was needed right away. So in the space of less than a month, I was up there with my whole family, with our four children now, all of them six years of age or under. We flew up to Adak and lived in a quonset for a while and finally got into more permanent quarters. But I found a situation that was somewhat chaotic in many ways. Of course, Adak I think has always been somewhat chaotic anyway. You can go there about any time and find something that's wrong with the place. But we had a lot of technical and personnel problems and everything else.

Q: What was the situation when you got there? What did you find?

Merdinger: I think basically a philosophy had developed that with the war long gone, Seabees would be withdrawn from public works duties. This was a maintenance battalion, the last naval construction battalion in the Navy. It was not a mobile battalion that we're so used to today, but it was a stationary one. It was simply a Seabee public works department, but it was augmented by a number of civilians. And as I say, the philosophy had been developed that, now that we're in this peacetime situation, let's phase out these Seabees and replace them with a civilian public works department.

This, of course, had happened throughout the shore establishment in the continental U.S. I think perhaps theoretically, on paper, it probably made some sense, but as a practical matter up at Adak it didn't make much sense. And the reason for that came I think from primarily the kind of a place Adak is. The climate is just horrible. The wind scarcely ever drops below 15 or 20 knots. While it doesn't get so cold on the thermometer, maybe 14 above zero is almost as cold as it gets —

Q: — but with a 40 mile an hour wind —

Merdinger: That's right. With the winds whipping around, it was very cold, and this happens most of the year. I think if you added up all the suntime you receive from one day to the next, maybe you'd have two weeks of sunshine all told during the year. Most of the time, it's overcast, it's gloomy. Housing was not too good really, pay was relatively good for that period. You could get some really first class civilians, get some really good people up there, but they were few and far between. Most of them were people who had bounced from one —

Q: Adventurers?

Merdinger: Well — bums. Yes. Not in all cases, of course, but some of them were pretty low on the totem pole. They'd been bounced from one place to another and they ended up on Adak. Some of their personal files were very thick, crammed with contentious personnel actions. So to get a gang like this to work and pull together was a real problem. We had mixed Seabee and civilians when I was there. Numbers I'm a little vague on now, but I'd say perhaps we had three Seabeas to one civilian, something like that, and maybe an overall force of 350 to 400. I think it was ultimately 500 by the time I left. But this was the only technical force on the island, and we were taking care of everybody. There were about 4000 people on the island, but they were living in an area as big as Washington, D.C. In order to make the round of our major power plants, I had to travel something close to 60 miles, just to go from one major power plant to another. So with everything spread out this way, the problems of utilities was a very tough one, and particularly with the kind of weather we had. It was always adverse.

So we had the problem of a place that was inhospitable to begin with, and we had a number of people who simply weren't competent, and a lot of drinking and gambling and everything else. There wasn't much else to do. There is no town there. It's military establishment only. No natives, no self-respecting Aleut would live there - just the people who got sent there were at Adak. There was even a paucity of animal and bird life. I think when we were there, there were just rats and buzzards, and some wild dogs.

Q: What kind of a base were we maintaining there?

Merdinger: Well, we had a naval station, and I'm sure some people would say they weren't quite sure what the objective was, because it was the period when we were taking in each other's laundry. That is, we had the runway to bring the planes in to bring in the mail, and, of course, we had piers to bring the ships in, and they brought food and people and that sort of thing. But when you really added it all up, it was kind of hard to figure what the base was there for.

Now, that's being a bit facetious, because we had some patrol runs, and these patrols would land at Adak, aviation -

Q: Siberia?

Merdinger: Some kind of surveillance, that's right. And we also had a radio station on the island and it, of course, had a function. There were some Air Force people there, Coast Guard, I guess there were a few Army communications people there too. So you had practically all the armed forces represented, but no real great product coming out of the place.

Perhaps I could put it another way. We could have accomplished the basic mission of the radio station and keeping the airfield open with far fewer people. We had a lot of people up there supporting the other people. The more people you get to support, the more other things - you've got to have - clubs and this, that, and the other thing. Ultimately houses were built. We had families up there, so we had to have more medical people to take care of the families, and the thing sort of snowballed.

Q: Maybe this is a policy of wisdom nevertheless in such an outlying place.

Merdinger: Well, many people sold the addition of housing on this basis. I think it would be equally easy to argue that, suppose you didn't send them up there for a year - at this time, there was a year's tour, subsequently 18 months. Suppose you rotated people in on a three months basis or six months, something like that, and kept it to a minimum. I think that would have been possible too.

But here it was, this big place, as I say, of about 4000 people. So the basic problem was to weed out a number of these incompetents and replace them with competents, and this we ultimately accomplished by replacing a good many of the civilian supervisors with Seabee chiefs and Seabee petty officers. And the place began to straighten up as we did that.

Q: Authority had somewhat broken down?

Merdinger: It's kind of hard to put your finger on it, but there were a lot of civilians in this outfit who were pretty much at loose ends, and running kind of a loose ship in some ways. But as I say, as we tightened up and got rid of some of those people and replaced them with the Seabees, the whole place really moved ahead.

As I recall, during the first couple of months we had a violent death on the island about once a week. A couple of children wandered out from their house and only relatively few yards away, drowned in a creek. Somebody stepped into a propeller blade of a plane that was starting up. Somebody drove a jeep off the side of a mountain. One thing after another. A series of tragedies. Most of it, it seemed, was taking place in bad weather, caused by poor visibility or made under conditions where people didn't have all their faculties, or weren't able to use them. So it was just one thing after another that seemed to be bad.

But ultimately I think we got it organized.

Q: How did you go about organizing in a situation like that?

Merdinger: Along with bringing more competent people into key positions we moved to consolidate the population. Many of our civilians were scattered in quonsets that were out in the hills and some were practically cave dwellers. Nobody even knew where they were. I might add that at one time there were perhaps 100,000 people on Adak, and there were quonsets all over the place and all kinds of other buildings. One of the major projects that we embarked on while I was there was to move a number of buildings. We had a site about 20 miles away which had some beautiful buildings. The area was abandoned- nobody was there any more - and we moved these structures, got them down into the central village. Then we moved people into them, and thus we contracted the community, if you will, got them together where they could be a little more accountable and comfortable.

I think that one of the most satisfying things we did was to move a 350 seat chapel all in one piece, moved it two miles. It was in an area that again had been abandoned. And two miles, by the way, is a long distance on Adak. A hundred yards can be a long distance up there.

Q: You mean, in the winter snow.

Merdinger: That's right, because at times you just can't see 2 feet in front of your face.

We didn't have a chapel, for instance. One was in the new construction program ultimately, but we went ahead and moved this thing, as I say, in one piece; moved it with seven caterpillar tractors on a big skid, moved it across the airfield, and that excited a lot of comment. As a matter of fact, I found out later that there were some persons willing to bet $500 that we'd never move it a foot. Well, this was the great challenge, to see if we could do that, so we moved several buildings. We got a post office out of this, we got a lot of places for people to live, we got a chapel and so on. Thus we consolidated the community, and this in turn shortened communication lines. We didn't need as much transportation, we didn't need to keep up the roads, we didn't need to put the tractors out there and so on.

So every time we moved one building and got one more function in the cen ter of town, so to speak, we eased ourproblems. So I would say that that perhaps was at least a major portion of the answer to this problem.

Q: Then you had programs I suppose of interest going on too. Once you had a community established.

Merdinger: Oh yes. And as I mentioned earlier, I think the mere fact that we were all on this storm-wrecked island together gave us a feeling of closeness. Oh, one of the things that was very interesting that we did was to move the officers' club. Only in this case we didn't move the building, we simply moved the bar out of the old building. The original club was way down at the far end of the base. Again we put it in an empty building that was right in the center of things. This drew a lot of attention. We got a lot of people interested in working on the project in kind of a self help basis, but after a while this interest petered out. So I had to call the Seabees in to finish up the job and get that club operating right "down town." Among other things, this new site kept people from falling off the edge of their jeeps coming back from the club on a dark and stormy night as had been the case with the previous club.

Q: What about the social life, which is terribly important in a place like that.

Merdinger: Yes. There was a lot of business in the club, toastmasters, dancing on the weekends, dinners, that sort of thing. Many people entertained at home, having dinners back and forth, and, of course, we were getting inspected a lot of the time. There were some groups coming in every few weeks it seemed. So those were occasions to have dinner for a number of people.

Q: What percentage of the personnel were family people? Some drifters were without families.

Merdinger: Oh yes, there were civilian drifters without families, and, of course, we had a large number of our enlisted population and a few officers there who were unmarried. The statistics escape me now, but it's conceivable that married men and their dependents made up nearly half the population.

Q: What about your athletic program? How did you develop competition? You had no one to play on a team.

Merdinger: Well, we had various units. In other words, the Marines had a team, Seabees had a team, communications and so on, so there were plenty of opportunities to generate intramural teams. Now, we had a varsity basketball team there, and I became the base basketball coach. I took them over to the mainland, to Fairbanks and Anchorage, saw a little bit of the mainland of Alaska -- which, by the way, was entirely different. To say the Aleutians are like the rest of Alaska is just wrong. It's not the same breed of cat at all. I thought things were much nicer over on the mainland.

Q: Did you have any relationship with the Russians who were near neighbors?

Merdinger: No, although every now and then we would have an island exercise, about defending the island or evacuating it, so I suppose the Russians were in our minds when we were doing that kind of drill.

Q: Were our friends the CIA people up in that area?

Merdinger: I'm not aware that they were. No, we didn't really have much contact with anybody except ourselves.

Q: Was there any commercial shipping of any kind that touched the island?

Merdinger: No. There was a commercial airline that came in -- little planes brought in by bush pilots. I think it was called the Reeves Airline. I don't recall commercial ships coming in. This, of course, was a possibility. But for the most part they were military, MSTS ships. Sometimes they'd have to stand out two or three days. It was so rough that they simply couldn't come in and come up alongside.

Q: What is the weather pattern? What is the season there?

Merdinger: Well, in a sense, you've got winter all year round. But as you get into the summer season, of course, it does get a bit milder. And, as a matter of fact, there may be a day or two, if you get into a crevice some place where the sun is beating down, and you put out a thermometer, you might register 70 degrees. If you get out of the wind, get in the sun, get completely protected, you might get that. But that would be very rare. In other words, I'd say that you'd scarcely find the temperature much above 50 at the warmest. Generally we had either drizzle or fog or rain or snow or sleet. That we just seemed to get all year around. But the summer season is better than the winter season, I can say that. For instance, when we wanted to do some kind of construction work like the repaving of the runway, that obviously couldn't be done in the wintertime; but it was possible to get the asphalt down in the sumer.

Q: How did your family adapt to a situation so different from Washington and Oxford?

Merdinger: Well, the girls were so small. All they remember of it now is what they see on the movies that we took at the time. Of course, we only took movies when there was some sunlight, and we took them out on their sleds or something else in the snow. So they think they had a wonderful time. I think everybody adapted to it well, quite honestly. I just wouldn't want to make a life of it up there. But for the 14 months we were there, it was a great experience. Professionally I found it exhilarating, and the family certainly didn't find it inhibiting.

Merdinger #2 - 146

Q: You say you found it exhiliarating professionally. It called for a lot of adaptation, I imagine, flexible approach to everything.

Merdinger: Things weren't in the book. Obviously, in any kind of engineering situation, you start out from certain fundamentals, but then you have to adapt them to the problem you have at hand. We had all sorts of problems with the water supply, keeping the roads open, keeping the steam lines going. Just one thing after another was either breaking down or about to break down and the question was to keep ahead of it, and as I mentioned, to anticipate with some kind of planning to cut down the necessity for additional facilities. In other words, if we cut out a district by bringing all the people in from it, we wouldn't have to keep the utilities going. So there was this continual business then of trying to make this consolidation.

Q: What imperative was there for constant inspection of the whole island? Why wasn't it possible from the beginning to be in one community?

Merdinger: I suspect that it had to do largely with the big separate groups with different missions that were there originally. As they contracted, certain elements were still left out there — yes, in little islands, if you will. That was certainly a part of it.

Q: Did you have anything to do with the other islands in the chain?

Merdinger: No, not really. We had a responsibility for facilities at Attu, but this was minor.

Merdinger #2 - 147

Q: Kodiak?

Merdinger: No, Kodiak was the headquarters, but this was further up. I just don't remember many details, but we had a little airstrip there.

Q: Is this installation maintained at the present time?

Merdinger: There is a naval installation at Adak today. I suspect that it's decreased in size from the kind of a place we had. I don't know. I haven't been there since we left in 1954.

Q: It isn't the sort of thing you go back to visit. What were your recommendations when you wound up your tour of duty?

Merdinger: I had recommended that we seriously consider shutting down the island. The amount of money that we were spending to keep people up there was substantial. For instance, it cost us three times as much to build a house there as it would to build that same house in Seattle.

Q: Why is this?

Merdinger: Well, the cost of labor up there is astronomical. The cost of getting the materials out there, of course, is very great. So everything is exorbitant.

Q: If it was in the naval confines why was labor so expensive?

Merdinger: If we were to operate efficiently we really couldn't operate a construction force locally, because we weren't in the business of constructing all the time. We'd just construct every now and then, so we'd bring in an outside force. Now, sometimes this could be a Seabee battalion to come in for a special project, and this happened for a good many years. But sometimes when the Seabee units were not or didn't have the requisite expertise we would call on a civilian contractor. For instance, this big tower, which may have run 900 feet in the air, something like that; well, that wasn't a Seabee job. That called for a special kind of construction force to come in and build.

Q: A communications tower.

Merdinger: Yes. So when you get special facilities like that, you very definitely go to civilian contracts. And there are many other times when, as I say, the Seabees aren't available so you go to the civilian contractor anyway.

Q: Would this be an Alaskan contractor, or somebody from Washington?

Merdinger: Generally speaking, contractors would tend to come out of Seattle, but you might find them some other places. But it's mostly the mainland based companies - at least, at that time they were the only ones - capable of mounting the logistics to accomplish something like that. But as I say, the whole place was tremendously expensive to keep up once you got there, and the question was, was it all really worth it? I think in many quarters this was probably seriously considered, but somehow an advocate always jumps up for a place, "We've got to keep it," and I'm not sure now how valuable it is strategically at this point. At any rate, the main recommendation I had was that we shut it down or at

Merdinger #2 - 149

least put it on very reduced status, but nobody ever seemed to buy that one.

Q: What was your budget when you were up there? What sort of base budget was there?

Merdinger: I'm so vague on that, I just don't know. I seem to recall we had about 500 in the department at one time, so that would give you some clue.

Q: As you departed, did you feel you had accomplished your mission? Did you feel you had really achieved the unification of this post?

Merdinger: Yes, I did. Of course, my responsibilities pertained only to the public works department, and after all there were other units on the island, but I will say this, that ours in a sense was the unit that really affected everybody because we were concerned with such common items as utilities and roads and transportation and that sort of thing. The answer is, yes, I came away with a great feeling of satisfaction that I'd had a very successful tour in every way.

Q: The overall commanding officer was the naval officer?

Merdinger: That's right. He was a naval aviator. At various times, this had been known as a naval air station, and sometimes as a naval station. I don't know what category it's in today, but it was usual to have an aviator as the commanding officer during those years.

Q: I recall during World War II when Admiral Kinkaid was there, it was sort of a dual command with an Army general as well.

Merdinger: This could well be. I'm not familiar with it, except for the fact, as I mentioned, that probably 100,000 people were on that island at one time. Of course, this was evident to us because of all these quonsets all over the place, many of them just rotting and flapping in the wind. I suppose some day if somebody's looking for a project, he could go up and dismantle all those decaying buildings.

Q: Don't they decay rapidly in a climate like that?

Merdinger: Well, yes, they decay but not as rapidly as you'd think, because after all, these were put up somewhere around '44. This was now ten years later, and many of them were in excellent shape. Some were not. So I don't know how long it would take for the island to reclaim this kind of thing.

Q: Certainly the jungle wouldn't overtake it.

Merdinger: No, not the jungle, but the williwaw. Which, of course, is the big wind up there.

Q: Well, even though you enjoyed that, I imagine you were just as happy to get an assignment in California, were you not?

Merdinger: Yes, I was overjoyed. When I was asked what I would like to do next, not that I would necessarily be able to do it, but at least I was asked, I said I'd like to go to a naval air station in Southern California. And I was told, "Fine, you're going to the naval air station at Miramar."

Q: I would think that you'd earned some credits and had a right to more or less ask.

Merdinger: I think anybody who's put in a tour at Adak certainly deserves some consideration on his next request. Well, there was only one thing bothered me about Miramar: I'd never heard of it. And when I asked about it they said, "Oh well, you're going down and you're going to build it." To some degree this was literally true, because Miramar had existed in various forms from World War II, as a Marine base for helicopters, I guess, light planes and so on.

Q: Where is it located?

Merdinger: It's just outside of San Diego. This was the first master jet air station in the Navy. It had just emerged from the status of a naval auxiliary air station, was just commissioned as a naval air station about the time I got there. So I had two and a half years where I was not only the public works officer, but I was resident officer in charge of construction for a vast amount of new construction on the base.

Q: Did you have a budget?

Merdinger: Oh yes. My recollection is that at any given time we had about 17 million dollars worth of new construction under way. Now, this is when a million dollars was worth a lot more than it is today. So we were in the process of building barracks and BOQs, hangars, extending the runways, coming in with new refueling systems - just a wide variety of things. I was in on the planning part of it, on the construction phase, then on the maintenance phase when it was turned over,

Merdinger #2 - 152

so I had the whole range then of the technical responsibilities for this place.

Q: With a conglomerate operation of that sort, didn't this strain your training and experience? Weren't there some aspects of it which were totally new to you?

Merdinger: That's kind of hard to say, because you've got some fundamentals in laying down pavement, for instance. Now, I'd never really been involved in laying down a major runway for an air station, yet the principles I'd known. Certainly a hangar was new in my experience, although I'd been concerned with maintaining a hangar, let's say at Adak; but building a new one and incorporating a lot of new features in it and so on was a new experience. Well, it would be presumptuous of me to say that I really understood everything that we were doing, but on the other hand I had a number of people who were expert in their areas to whom I could turn for this kind of information.

So I didn't feel overwhelmed by the technical responsibilities. I enjoyed them, as a matter of fact. Some of the things I was learning for the first time, but perhaps contributing a little at the same time.

One of the things we did was plant a lot of trees while I was there. Miramar's pretty much a desert place, even though it's just outside of San Diego, and I think along with all the technical innovations we brought a little bit of habitability to the place too in some of these things. Very very interesting and exciting.

Of course, the master jet station was a new concept in the Navy.

Some of the things we were doing were being done for the first time anywhere. So a lot of people were coming to look at our station, to see just how we were doing.

Q: That was very close work with the aeronautics people, wasn't it?

Merdinger: Well, let's put it, the Navy air people. Now, the Air Force people didn't come into our picture.

Q: I meant naval air.

Merdinger: Yes. Well, this was a naval air station. We were also involved in a certain amount of work with some of the city fathers because, of course, we were involved in getting real estate right around the base so that we could protect it from too much growth. You know what the history of these aviation stations generally has been; they will be put in a remote area, then because of the installations there people will move out around it, and then the next thing you know you've got little industries and little communities springing up in support of these people, and then you've got complaints because of the airport noise.

Q: It's a boomerang.

Merdinger: Yes. So we hoped, among other things, to build quite a buffer zone around the air station so that we could ward off this sort of thing. We were never completely successful on that, because there's a problem of convincing Congress that you really need the money to buy this property. There's the problem of convincing the people they ought to sell to you, even if you have the money and the authorization and so on. We weren't very far from La Jolla, and we used to get complaints from the citizens over there that our sonic booms were destroying their peace, and, of course, we always get the problem of some farmer coming in saying his chickens weren't laying eggs because of the noise of the planes and so on, so this created a lot of action with the community. And I found myself on occasions, along with a lot of others, giving lectures to the community as to what the jet air station was all about and what we hoped to accomplish, trying to get the citizens on our side, and I think that by and large we were successful in that.

Q: A public relations job was required.

Merdinger: Yes. Of course, San Diego, the whole San Diego area at that time at least was pretty much of a Navy-oriented town. I think we were starting out for the most part with sympathetic audiences. Not completely, but for the most part. So this job then was technical and was public relations; it was a number of things. And because we were building up, of course, the public works department was building up, so this involved hiring new people, and we got a lot of fine civilian workmen. This was completely opposite to the problem we had at Adak. Here we were getting very competent civilians and they were really great. We built up I think a very fine public works department there, and I was very pleased to have been in on the ground floor when we got so many of these people.

Q: What were some of the problems that had not been anticipated in building a new base of this sort?

Merdinger: It's kind of hard to say. I know, one of the problem areas that we had was with the rapid refueling of planes. Now, this was really a mechanical problem, but after all, we were the ones that installed them. It was part of the overall construction effort. I think that initially nobody knew how to really work these units in conjunction with the planes, and this took a lot of hard work down at the chief and first class petty officer level, just wanting to make this thing work. Now, the same installations had gone in at a couple of other fields, and the impression I had was that they'd practically abandoned them, said, "No, it won't work, can't work," - but people at our station said, "By golly, we will make these work," and they went out and they just worked with them until they got the whole system going, so we were again leaders in this area.

This then was an area that couldn't be anticipated. It was a brand new development, I suppose, in aircraft refueling, and just one of those things where the bugs ultimately had to be worked out.

A lot of things that looked good on paper somehow didn't work out when the fellows were there trying to do the job.

We were continually faced, as you always are when you're in the building business, with trying to bring these things within cost, so although we had a very interesting hangar, good hangar in many ways, and the first hangar that was built at Miramar, the second one was not a mirror image of it at all. We had a lot of developments in terms of where certain items should be, how certain spaces should be laid out - even in the material of the thing, because of costs. Costs had gone up so much we couldn't build in the same "permanent" fashion that we had with the first hangar.

And, of course, there was the experimentation with training, how you get your flight patterns so that you get the maximum number of people who are taking off and coming in, and bounce drill - the simulated carrier landing. You're trying to work with that while you have a lot of other traffic coming into the station. So this posed problems of runway layout, and the taxi ways, how to get the planes off rapidly and so on, because after all this was in the early jet age, and we were still learning about how to operate jets efficiently. So we had a lot of problems of that sort in there, more on the master planning.

Q: There was no friendly foreign experience you could draw from?

Merdinger: No. If anything, we were leading in this area. So in a sense you might say that Miramar was a prototype for a lot of things. I know of no jet air stations that preceded it in size or sophistication. Now, some have surpassed it. LeMoore I think is the biggest jet air station. But at the time, Miramar was the first.

Q: Did this mean you had to go back to Washington for consultation while the job was going on?

Merdinger: Yes. Frequently. And much of the time was spent in trying to convince people who were holding the purse strings back there that we were growing, we needed more people to operate this plant. Here was a new station. We'd just put on another row of buildings and this, that and the other thing, and we had to have people to maintain them. If we were going to operate the next bank of buildings, we'd have to have

Merdinger #2 - 157

additional utilities. This sort of thing. So the answer is, yes, we found ourselves going back. Normally the commanding officer of the station, the supply officer and I were the three, the major figures in this kind of sortie on Washington

Interview No. 3 with Captain Charles Merdinger

Place: U. S. Naval Institute

Date: 1 February 1972

Subject: Biography

By: John T. Mason, Jr.

Q: Well, it's good to see you again, Sir. I hope that little accident yesterday is not going to prevent you from your usual facility of expression. As we concluded last time, you were talking about setting up the new jet air base at Miramar in California. Do you have anything additional to add to that story?

Captain Merdinger: No, not really, except as I mentioned there's an anecdote about building the dog house.

Q: Do tell me that.

Captain Merdinger: Well, the skipper of the station, as I may have mentioned, was Captain "Gloom" Mills out of the class of '27. Gloom was a great dog lover, and on the station we had a number of guard dogs who'd been placed there to stand watch over some material that was valued at about 5 million dollars. Originally the station was more or less on a path that was used by the wetbacks coming over from Mexico. They'd cross the plain and they'd see a lot of this loose material and they would pick it up, so I think in the course of time, the guard dogs came into existence to take care of this material. But by the time I got there, there was a fence around the station. There in turn was a fence around the material, and there were Marines on the station in addition to the guard dogs, so I would say as a sort of bureaucratic organization they'd lingered on while events had preceded to pass them.

But this didn't make any difference to Gloom. He felt that we really needed these dogs, but he didn't like the place they were housed in. They were housed in an old World War II theatre, and he said, "We've got to get them into something that's better than that."

Q: How many were there?

Merdinger: Oh, there may have been 10 to 15 dogs, something like that. And as I recall, four or five handlers and all sorts of other paraphernalia that went with this group. But he put the burden on me to get a project for a doghouse started. I might add that at this time we had under construction in the order of 17 million dollars - runways, barracks and so on, but the most important thing in my life for a while became this dog house.

The first thing I did was to write back to our parent bureau of Yards and Docks to inquire about criteria and designs for dog houses, and they didn't have this, so it was then necessary for me to send our chief architect out around the San Diego area to take a look at typical dog houses.

Q: This was entirely a new problem for Yards and Docks?

Merdinger: This was a new problem. I was rather disappointed that this fount of all engineering knowledge didn't have this kind of criteria. But at any rate, we sent the architect out and he came back with some sketches. Ultimately he sketched a very nice 20 dog kennel with the appropriate appurtenances, and the estimated cost of this thing came out to $15,000. This didn't seem unreasonable because it was less than a thousand dollars a dog. I then presented this to the skipper and he said, "Well, I'm sorry. This would never get through. $15,000 is too much, let's make it $9500."

So we go in with a project for $9500. This is how you make engineering estimates in some of these cases. We then presented the package through channels to Washington. I had to write the letter and I recall giving all sorts of reasons for going ahead with this project, ending up with the fact that the present place they were living was "not fit for a dog." And this, of course, drew a few chuckles.

But nobody took the thing very seriously even when it got to Washington. Elliott Roosevelt's dog was still the subject of some public discussion, and so dogs were regarded as sort of a "hands off" item, per se.

Well, we went back to Washington, our group, and I went in to see my counterpart, the civil engineer down in the lower echelons of the Bureau of Aeronautics, but Gloom went to see his old classmate, the chief of the Bureau of Aeronautics. Whereas my civil engineer friend was more or less laughing me out of the place, Gloom in the meantime was getting the money, so we did get $9000.

We were so pressed with our own engineering force that we had to let out an architect/engineering contract for $500 just to design this thing, which now left us $8500.

Well, it was put on the street for a bid, and you've guessed it, the low bid was pretty close to $15,000, which is what we'd originally estimated, for which we didn't have the money.

Well, Gloom was beside himself on this one. He vowed that this was the one thing he wanted, and he was going to make sure that I got it, and I told him, "Well, there's one way to get around this and that is, we can build it with our own station forces and we will use reclaimed materials." This is the old dodge where you pretend that the materials don't cost you anything because you paid for them some time before under some other category.

So this seemed to satisfy him, and we were all ready to start work but the trouble was, it was now the end of the fiscal year and the funds had expired.

Q: You had to start all over again.

Merdinger: Fortunately the new fiscal year's funds were forthcoming again. As a matter of fact, we were back to the $9500. But a couple of days after the money arrived, the Inspector General arrived on the station, and one of the things he wanted to check on was this guard dog project, why did we need such a project?

In the course of things I was called upon to testify, and I might point out that we had all these handlers. We were also using somehing like $25,000 worth of meat a year for the dogs, and a number of other items, which added up to make it questionable whether this was really an economic proposition or not, but in the course of defending it I managed to confuse the issue such that the Inspector General and his party were not able to make a decision on the spot. So they called for an ad hoc committee to be formed to consist of the Chief of the Bureau of Aeronautics, the commandant of the 11th Naval District, and the Commanding officer of Miramar to look into this problem of guard dogs, and to make the recommendation later.

Well, Gloom thereupon convened the board of these three, and, of course, the Chief was in Washington and sent his proxy out, and the commandant rode our station plane so he sent his proxy over, so Gloom convened this board consisting of himself and two proxies, and came to the conclusion that no only was the guard dog project desirable, it was mandatory for the future security of Miramar.

So then once more I had to write a letter, this time pointing out that if we didn't hear from them by April 1st or whenever the date was that we would assume that there was no objection to the project and we would go ahead. We sent it through varying channels, much like the British - if they don't know what to do with a sticky problem, they send to the Commander-in-Chief Australia for comment, and by the time it comes back, nobody's quite sure what the problem was to begin with.

I think this is what happened with the guard dog project. We didn't get any negative reply so we did begin the project, and it was really a very handsome structure - concrete block, trees at the proper spaces; there was a first aid station for the dogs, a place for transient dogs as well as the permanent group, and all in all, a very really handsome first class facility.

Well, on the day we completed the project, we put a hard hat on the Skipper and a number of us in the construction force went out to the site, took the leading dog and had him bite the ribbon that opened the facility.

I might add that the buildings on one side of the road were all numbered K for Kearney Mesa, and in checking over the building numbers we found that we had a building K-8 and then for some reason skipped to K-11 so obviously this building had to be K-9.

This is a true story. Then, as a climax, we forwarded the drawings and with a final letter to the Bureau of Yards and Docks pointing out that we did have what might be considered a prototype for guard dog houses, that while it was really based on Southern California living, I felt that the Bureau's Architects could in some way change it around to make it useful in any climate. We simply requested that if they gave out this information, that they would indicate that it was a "Miramar-type dog house."

I'm happy to say that the Skipper was pleased and the dogs were pleased.

Q: May I ask a question in the nature of a second footnote - when you were in Danang, did you build a doghouse similar?

Merdinger: Oh, there were some doghouses there but I never had anything to do with them. They were just a little bit of wire and posts that were put up by the Marines. Well, really, these were field dog houses if you will, as opposed to the home base dog house we had at Miramar.

Q: You'd come a distance from the wetbacks.

Merdinger: That's correct.

Q: Well, having accomplished that, which was a very impressive accomplishment, I would say, you went on to another California station, Point Hueneme.

Merdinger: Yes. I went up to the Naval Construction Battalion Center at Point Hueneme, and there I was commanding officer and director of what originally was called the Naval Civil Engineering Research and Evaluation Laboratory. Later on that was changed simply to Naval Civil Engineering Laboratory. This I felt was one of my great accomplishments, in shortening the name of this establishment.

Q: Did that have any bearing on the duties? Were they changed?

Merdinger: No, the duties weren't really changed. It was a laboratory of about 300 people. There were only two other people in uniform on the staff besides myself. These both were Civil Engineer Corps officers who were atomic energy experts. And the rest of the organization were civil service. We had a wide variety of engineers and scientists, physicists, chemists, biologists, every brand of engineer you can think of, geologists, across the board, plus a number of supporting personnel. These people were engaged in a variety of research and development activities.

Q: Would you illustrate that?

Merdinger: Yes. One of the major problems we concentrated on was the toredo. This is the worm that eats the piles. You've seen wooden piles that are riddled with all sorts of holes. These result from attacks by various forms of the termites of the sea. Now, they don't eat only Navy piles, they eat civilian piles too, so I like to think that much of the work we were doing had direct bearing on advances in civilian life. It wasn't only our fight against the toredo. We were working in a variety of areas, again all over the world. We had people at the North Pole, the South Pole, out in the Pacific Ocean. One of the projects we worked on was the formation of ice airfields, compacting snow so that we could land planes in the polar regions in better fashion. In other words, actually take the material, the snow and the ice and compact it with combinations of sawdust and other such things to make it a good hard base.

This had its practical application in the winter Olympics of 1960, up in Squaw Valley. I might add that we had a research unit that used to go up to Squaw Valley area, around the Truckee area in winter to work in all kinds of arctic problems, and this business of the snow compaction came to the attention of the Olympic authorities. They were faced

Merdinger #3 - 166

with a tremendous problem of parking a lot of cars up there, so they came to us, and with our techniques and the help of some Seabees, the laboratory was able to help out in the parking situation up there in the Squaw Valley area in 1960.

Well, that, of course, was not a prime responsibility of the laboratory, but it gives you some idea of the fallout, of the kinds of things we were doing.

Q: Did this take you down to the South Pole?

Merdinger: I never went down there but some of our people did. We were working on all kinds of equipment, construction equipment that would work at very low level temperatures, and we had a giant ice box at the laboratory where we did work out a lot of this equipment at extremely cold termperatures.

One of the other activities we were involved in at the time was the designing of shelters against atomic blast. You may recall, in the fifties there was a great deal of concern over the effects of the atom bomb tests.

Q: They were building shelters all over the country.

Merdinger: Yes. And we were in that picture very heavily. We built at the laboratory during the time I was there, under contract, the first atomic blast simulator. This enabled our engineers to analyze the effect of an atomic blast on various structural members, full size. In other words, you wouldn't have to go out to Nevada and have a bomb test to analyze the effect of an atom bomb on various kinds of structures.

With the moratorium on the atom bomb coming up, of course, this was a very great tool in terms of design engineering, and we were very pleased. I think we were if not the first laboratory, certainly one of the first laboratories anywhere to have this kind of a device.

Q: Did you work with Civil Defense on this?

Merdinger: Yes, and I recall one time being invited to the atomic tests in Nevada. The skippers of a number of the major research laboratories engaged in affiliated work were invited out there, and I actually saw an atomic blast. I must say it's certainly some sight.

Well, those are a few examples.

Q: How closely did you work with Scripps - La Jolla -

Merdinger: I don't recall working together very closely with them. This business of worrying about the toredos was something that we worked with scientists in two different places, but I don't recall Scripps being in the picture at that time.

Q: There must have been other things too in the area of atomic energy.

Merdinger: Generally speaking, we were only concerned with civil engineering type problems incident to it. In other words, how do you build a shelter that's going to withstand this kind of a blast? And these would be all kinds of shelters. They might be homes, might be military command type structures and so on.

There's another area that we worked very strenuously on too, and this was on all phases of amphibious landings. In other words, the business of getting cargo off of landing ships and getting the floating decks in to bridge the distance between the ship and the shore, also the business of getting fuel from offshore to the land. This involved much experimentation with couplings of various sorts, materials of different kinds, so we found ourselves cooperating with the Marines and with the Army in this kind of effort. All sorts of, you might say, civil engineering gear related to amphibious landings.

Q: Where were these projects generated or spawned?

Merdinger: All over the Navy. In other words, somebody would come in with a request. In might come into Naval Research, might come into Bureau of Yards and Docks, any number of places. Of course, we would get our projects from headquarters in Washington which would say, "These are the things we want you to work on," so they would act, you might say, as a central collection house for all this. But the Marines might come o over and say, "We've got a problem with helicopter pads, and we want this kind of a thing. It doesn't exist and we would like you to work on it."

As I say, this would come from a number of parts of the armed forces, but for the most part we were more oriented to Navy than anything else, Navy shore problems. I think the title "Naval Civil Engineering Laboratory" is a fair one to describe the range of our responsibilities.

Q: It occurs to me that a group of scientists who are working with a variety of projects are necessarily stimulated in the act and probably generate ideas of their own. Were you at liberty to develop such ideas?

Merdinger: Yes, we had a certain range there. Now, you get to the point, however, where there's the fellow who's sitting around and just wants to Seek Truth and he's not sure what it is that he's after. And while you want to encourage a certain amount of this, there's the other pragmatic side. That is, you've got a limited budget, there are people at the other end who are in a sense funding you so that you give them a product they're looking for. So we didn't have too much leeway for people just to sit down and think about new things. But there was after all a certain amount of that. We were not on a production line, so to speak, in turning out ideas. They just don't come out that way.

Q: No, I realize that, but one idea will lead to another.

Merdinger: Yes. That's a real problem, I think, in running a research laboratory of this or any other kind, and that is almost the necessity in a sense of making a profit. Somebody is footing the bill, he wants something in return from it. Generally speaking his interests are relatively narrow. There aren't too many places that exist just for the sake of pure research or pure science. So you might say that you've got a kind of a practical orientation in an environment like this, that you've got some problems that have to solved and most of your energies should be devoted to those specific problems.

Q: Did you, as a person and as the commanding officer, learn any valuable lessons in presiding over this stable of scientists?

Merdinger: I think I learned one thing, and that is, the group - and I hesitate to generalize, but let me give you a first impression, and that is that a number of them simply hated to be organized by anybody. They wanted to be free spirits. They wanted to go off on their own. They didn't want to be checked on. And I would say that a lot of them would have been happier if they weren't in any kind of a structured environment whatsoever. Now, they wanted all the materials and they wanted the money and the equipment to go ahead and do the work, but they didn't really want to be herded, if you will, down some channel. So it's a great problem, I think, to get creative people in an environment like this and then somehow channel their energies so they're all pulling generally in the same direction.

Q: This kind of aura of public-spirited cooperation of scientists with the federal government and the military which was so significant in World War II, this aura had been dissipated by this time. Were they as willing to work on military projects as they might have been to work on projects outside?

Merdinger: Well, I couldn't distinguish any difference. I was going to say, you've got to realize that these people were civil servants who'd come to work in a Navy laboratory. They were on a Navy base. There was a certain environment there that shouted Navy, and I would say that if they didn't really like the idea of working in a defense-oriented place, then they obviously ought to go somewhere else. This isn't to say that there weren't a few of them who would have liked to have done this and who, quite honestly, probably would have liked to have done nothing but completely civilian research. On the other hand, to go back to my original point, that most of the things we did, while they were to benefit certain military aims, were in themselves readily translatable into civilian operations. For instance, we were concerned with the desalinization of water. We were concerned with various kinds of portable sewerage systems and this kind of thing, all of these all obviously adaptable to any civilian end. So I would say that we were in the ecology business before the word became popular.

Q: Take something like desalinization of water, this was an idea which was worked on extensively in places like Israel where there was very great need. Were you in touch with people elsewhere in the world who were working on particular subjects like this?

Merdinger: Yes, we were to some degree. There's always this problem, I think, of keeping up with the literature in given fields. One of the greatest problems perhaps that we have today in scientific research is really keeping up with what's going on all over - to have the librarians and translators and general facilities, even the funds to get the works that are generated in other places is quite a problem. I suspect that maybe in the next several years, the computer somehow is going to play a big part in this information retrieval world-wide.

Q: At that point in time, in order to advance your own efforts, what steps did you take to be in touch with some of these?

Merdinger: I'd say that the majority of our people were in touch through this medium, that is the writings people had published. We were really not sending people all over the world to go talk with somebody in Sweden or down in South American or something like that. It's just that in general perhaps we were aware of what was going on. There wasn't all that amount of travel that would bring our people face to face with their counterparts. Of course, we did encourage our people to go to a number of professional meetings and in the course of going to those, they came together, - a number of people from all over the United States and in some cases all over the world.

Q: There was no scientific clearing house in the Department of Defense or in the federal government? - that might have been useful in these areas?

Merdinger: Well, not really. There's always under way some sort of scheme to corral all this information and knowledge. I'd probably be speaking out of turn if I said "there wasn't a clearing house somewhere," but as a practical matter I'm not aware of anything that really would have suited our needs.

Q: What efforts did you make personally to keep abreast of things and keep on top of things?

Merdinger: I think that, again, the media that I've already talked about, namely, the tremendous volume of literature that just gets poured out from every source, and the other, going to scientific meetings, knowing people here and there. I found it particularly useful at times to confer with some of the directors of the Army Civil Engineering - oriented laboratories. Perhaps I had more in common with them that I might have had with the skippers of other Navy laboratories that might have been dealing in some fields that were really more related to the ships themselves, or may be the electronics area, something like that, that we didn't have too much interest in. So we tended to, you might say, seek out fellow civil engineering organizations. By that I don't mean to imply that everything we did was civil engineering, because I've already pointed out that we had a lot more, chemistry, biology and other fields that were of interest to us throughout.

Q: What a fascinating job. What percentage of your effort was under wraps, so to speak?

Merdinger: Not very much of it. The atomic tests tended to be in this category. Every now and then there may have been something, but by and large, in most of the things we were doing were not really top secret.

Q: Your specialized field of education, higher learning, must have found some application in a job like this.

Merdinger: Well, from this standpoint – at least I was able to be somewhat sympathetic with some of the aims and procedures of some of the scientists and engineers working in this environment. I think that my practical experience in public works, in the construction field and so on, was helpful from the standpoint of knowing what was really needed out there. In other words, I think the combination of this practical aspect of my background, plus the theoretical, which could appreciate at least in a small way the scientific viewpoint, was probably helpful in the overall management of the laboratory. It's kind of hard when you had a position like that to know what you really have contributed, because you're not really one of the people down there in the lab working on experiments and so on, and after all that's where the work is done. That's where the real payoff is.

One of the things I tried to concentrate on was a logical flow of work through the place, so that we could convince those who were supporting us that they indeed had something worth supporting at our end; in getting some kind of planning and estimating system set up so that there would be a businesslike way of handling these things, so that we would not have a whole group of projects come in and not really have any idea as to how we would handle them, how long it would take or anything else.

So I think I was more involved with personnel, scheduling, generally seeing that the environment for these people was right for them to work in. Much, I suppose, the same as my present position as college president. I'm not doing any teaching. I'm trying to provide an environment so that teachers and students can work best together.

Q: I can see where you had a ready acceptance of it. With your scholastic background you had a ready acceptance of scientists even though you were not in their field.

Merdinger: Well, I would like to say that's true, and it probably was true in general. But there were a few people who really resented this. As a matter of fact, there were some who resented the idea of anybody in uniform coming in as head of the laboratory. Kind of an anti-military bias, if you will, on the part of some of these people, even though they were in this kind of a laboratory. And don't ask me to explain it, I can't. I don't know, but it was there, and we had our problems with a few of those people. Fortunately some of them chose to move on, and I think we managed to get a lot more production and I think the place was a lot happier when we replaced them with some other people.

Q: Possibly a few of them who felt that way were there because they liked to eat and bread was probably plentiful with a civil service salary at that time.

Merdinger: Probably. Of course, a number of these people are pretty thin-skinned anyway, and getting into a research climate like that probably accentuates some of these feelings.

Q: Was it a happy experience for you, all in all, to do that?

Merdinger: Oh yes. There were times when we found the going pretty rough, but on balance I felt it was a productive and very interesting tour. Again, I'm not sure that I really contributed much to the whole thing, but I certainly did get a lot out of it in terms of the experience with all these different projects and getting a feel for the whole research and development area that I hadn't had before.

Q: When you say the going was rough at times, was this in terms of frustration because some of these projects wouldn't work out?

Merdinger: Well, no, in terms of a few personnel who simply felt that they didn't have time to devote to their projects, that they had to devote it all to their own personal aggrandizement or something else - you find a few like that in every organization, I suppose.

Q: How large a segment of the total R and D program in the Navy was

Merdinger #3 - 176

accomplished in this particular locale?

Merdinger: It was a major laboratory, by definition - I guess anything in those days was called major if you had more than 100 people in it and carried more than a million dollars in business a year; after all, it's a relative term - yes, we were a major activity. But in terms of the overall R and D effort in the Navy, I would say very very minor, just a few percentiles.

Q: How many laboratories were there extant at that time?

Merdinger: I'd hesitate to guess. Maybe ten or so in the Navy. Maybe more than that.

Q: Was there pretty good exchange between all these laboratories?

Merdinger: Not necessarily, because as I mentioned there weren't any others who were really doing much of the kind of work we were doing. We were very specialized in our plant. I don't know, maybe I'm wrong when I say ten. Perhaps there were more than that. I just have no way of recalling now, if I ever knew.

Q: At this time, was there any effort to curtail appropriations for R and D in the Navy, or was this a time when you could count on this?

Merdinger: Well, my recollection is that we were always scraping for funds. In other words, we didn't have unlimited amounts. We were always having to take a hard look at the budget, a hard look at the number of people that we had on board and so on. We were not in the cutting down phase.

Merdinger #3 - 177

I would say it was simply a level phase.

Q: Shall we go on to the next period, the next assignment? You were there for what, two years?

Merdinger: No, I was there for three years. That was from '56 to '59.

Q: Did you have pleasant living quarters?

Merdinger: Yes, we lived on the base at the construction battalion center there at Point Hueneme, and had no complaints at all. The quarters were small but they were adequate, and the children were close to school. We were just a few steps away from the base swimming pool in the summer, so it was very nice, very nice accommodations.

Then we went to Japan. I was ordered out as public works officer at Yokosuka, and this I think perhaps was one of the most pleasant tours in our whole Navy experience. We spent three years there. I had a Japanese force of some 2200 people. Almost everybody in the organization was Japanese. We had a few Civil Engineer Corps officers and a few American Seabees, but everyone else, as I say, was Japanese. Among other things I had five former admirals of the Imperial Navy working for me; one who was called the general manager, and in fact he was a sort of senior staff advisor to me, was Vice Admiral Baron Nabeshima.

Q: He was a baron?

Merdinger: Yes. His wife, I understand, had come from the royal family and his family went back many many years. He showed me a family scroll that went back as I remember 500 years, and a samurai sword that had been in the family for some 300 years. We went over to his house a number of times. I understand this is quite an honor, to be invited to a Japanese house. I might add that I've been back to Japan a few times since our tour there, and every time I've managed to get over to see him and reminisce about it. He was a great admirer of the United States Naval Academy graduates. He always felt somehow they had a little something special. I'm not sure if he was particularly right, but this was his bias anyway. We had I think an awful lot in common in, if you will, a common love for the Navy and you might say a certain set of standards in relation to working with people and so on. I never had a happier working relationship with people than I did with the Japanese in general. Now, I've worked all over the world and had all kinds of different native laborers, here, there and everywhere, and this I think was certainly as pleasant a group as I ever had the opportunity to work with.

Q: What characteristics made it more pleasant than some others?

Merdinger: Well, there's a certain group discipline about the Japanese. They will take care of things among themselves with a kind of a group consensus. Just an aptitude I guess for working in groups, not quarreling among themselves. Now, I'm sure they're human, like any other group they quarrel among themselves, but it didn't seem as evident to me. They were very eager to get to work. They didn't wait until the whistle. They would get there the first thing in the morning and they would start to work and when the whistle blew at night they were still working, and particularly in the offices, you'd find many of them staying one or two hours late. They wouldn't be getting any overtime pay, but this was just in their nature to work hard, to study, really to throw everything they had into the job.

Now, it may be that some of them had some rather bleak places to go back home to at night, so it wasn't as particularly attractive as the place in the suburbs that one might have over here. That may have accounted for part of it. I don't know. The point I'm making is that these people were hard workers, and they did make a real attempt to improve themselves, in terms of studying, -- whether they'd be in school or studying on the job. I find it hard to express it except to say that there was this great feeling of a beehive of activity all the time with these people.

Q: Then there's tangible evidence in the fact that out of that came this remarkable resurgence of the Japanese economy.

Merdinger: That is quite understandable, seeing how they work, and really, having gone a few other places and seen how other people work in other parts of the world, these Japanese are just dynamic as a people as a group.

Q: Did all of the ex-Imperial officers have recognizable jobs, or were some of them in small spots?

Merdinger: Well, they all had some relatively important jobs, but the next most important one, I would say, was Vice Admiral Nagazawa, who was the head of our maintenance shop. Now, I understand that at the end of the war he had been put in prison as a war criminal because he had been the chief of personnel of the Imperial Navy, and when he was released from prison I understand that he came back to work on the base as a janitor. I find it a very hard thing to understand. But nevertheless, when I got there he was now head of our maintenance shop in public works with about 800 people. I don't know what he knew about plumbers and carpenters and electricians, but he sure knew how to run 800 people and he ran a great shop down there, very fine.

I didn't really say too much about Admiral Nabeshima. I ought to go back to that a moment, because we had some interesting conversations about the war. At the time I was there, he was perhaps over 70 years of age. I don't think he had anything really to gain to try to fool me, to lead me off base some place, so I suspect that the remarks he made to me were probably part of his genuine feeling and philosophy about the whole thing.

He remarked that really in the long run it was a good thing for Japan that the United States had won the war, and that MacArthur had come in with the kind of occupation that he had. Admiral Nabeshima pointed out that in the years prior to the war, the Japanese Army, of course, had gained the political ascendancy in the country, that most of these Army officers had had really a limited knowledge of the world. They'd gone over and knocked over a few villages in Manchuria. They thought - perhaps I should say that their view of the rest of the world was limited. The naval officers, on the other hand, according to Nabeshima, had been over the world in much greater fashion, knew the sophistication, the power of the West, and therefore, were not eager to extend these military ventures to the point where they'd come in conflict with the West. So there was this real difference of opinion, if you will, generalizing it, of course, between the Army and Navy.

So the Army was pushing on for more conquest in Southeast Asia regardless of running into the United States and the other Western powers. And I gathered that their aim really was simply to get a stalemate in the Far East so that they could go ahead and extend this Japanese Co-Prosperity Sphere all over Southeast Asia.

Well, once the Navy got into it, of course, or I should say once Japan was committed to the war, the Navy did all they could to do their part. But he pointed out that a real dictatorship existed in Japan, and had Japan been successful in its aims, even stalemate, that in some form or other this dictatorship probably would have persisted. But the fact that the Americans came in, and under MacArthur got what we conceived to be a democratic system going, that this completely turned Japanese life around. And it was Nabeshima's thesis that it was the MacArthur occupation primarily that brought this about, and that Japan did have a good sense of being a democratic nation in the sense that we think of democracies.

Now, he didn't think this was all good, because he pointed out that we had in some way taken away the national soul, that prior to the war there was a great devotion to the Emperor. The Shinto religion was tied up in this. And that when we came in and destroyed the Emperor and the Shinto religion as a unifying spiritual force, that nothing took its place. Then, of course, this great materialism cropped up in these young people, and they simply weren't like their elders. They'd lost a lot of the grace, the courtesy and those other things – the same kind of thing that we complain about over here, and we didn't lose the Shinto religion and the Emperor. So I'm not sure it wasn't more of a world-wide phenomenon than simply Japanese. But this was the way it looked to an old Japanese admiral.

Q: Now, what was the principal function of this outfit?

Merdinger: We were the public works department, and we had jobs in three main areas. One was to maintain the base at Yokosuka, all the physical facilities – this is to say, all the buildings and the roads and the drydocks. We ran all utilities. In other words, we were the telephone company and the power company and the heating company and all these other things. We supplied all the utilities to the base.

Q: This had been a Japanese naval base?

Merdinger: It had been a Japanese naval base. I'm not sure to what degree they were organized along the same lines, but down in the utilities department, for instance, we had old Mr. Sato, who'd been the utilities man there for years, and he was still in the same seat; and he was responsible, of course, for running all the boiler plants and getting the water supply in from the hills and a number of other areas of that nature.

So you've got maintenance, utilities, and then finally transportation. We were the taxi company and the bus company and the general garage. At one time we had something like 500 chauffeurs in this organization, just to give you an idea.

Q: Why so many? Why were they required?

Merdinger: Well, we just had all kinds of transportation running all over the place - sedans taking people from one place to another, running bus systems, running school buses.

Q: American naval personnel?

Merdinger: Yes. A large number of our children went to school in Yokohama, which was about an hour's ride away.

Q: They were bused there.

Merdinger: They were bused there, so we were in this busing of school children long before it became popular or unpopular depending on your point of view.

Q: The purpose of that busing, however, was not integration, was it?

Merdinger: No, it was simply that that's where the school was. At Yokosuka we had the lower grades, and for junior high and high school, the students had to go over to Yokohama. Then, of course, some of the students didn't go to the public schools run by the Americans. They went to private schools run by the Japanese. I had four daughters and they all went to St. Maur's up in Yokohama. It was only a few blocks from the Navy school.

This was a Japanese school run by Irish nuns whose mother house was in Paris, and they made a great point of teaching French from the third grade on up. Now, there were a lot of Japanese children who went to this school and a number of mixtures, various kinds of Eurasians, and some Americans but the standard classrooms were conducted in English. Unfortunately our daughters didn't learn much in the way of Japanese because the Japanese language was forbidden in school so that the Japanese girls would learn English.

There were a number of children who went to that school and there were a few in other schools, so it wasn't just the school run by the Americans themselves. But schooling was a big item over there.

But to go back to transportation - we were always in the business of supplying transportation for visiting ships. A group of sailors would come in and we'd bus them out to a picnic area or entertainment spot. This was a great rest and recreation place for ships of the Seventh Fleet at this period. It was the home base for the Seventh Fleet. So we always were accommodating many, many ships - a large transient load in addition to the steady base load.

Now, on the base itself the total population with the workers and everyone else could have been 12,000 people or something on that order.

Q: How many naval ships did you have to repair in a given year?

Merdinger: This was a big shipyard really. It didn't have that title; it was called a ship repair facility. I don't recall figures on ships repaired but there must have been 4000 workers directly engaged in shipyard operations at that time.

Q: These were all Japanese?

Merdinger: Practically all Japanese. A few American supervisors. The ship repair facility was very much like the public works department, in that it had a few American officers at the top and the rest of it was completely Japanese. I might add that it had an outstanding reputation as a ship repair facility. I never ran into any skipper in the Pacific during those years who wouldn't rather have his ship overhauled at Yokosuka, because of the quality of the work the Japanese did and the relative efficiency and the amount of cost to his budget; all these factors were important. And then I think it was a very popular liberty port. Japan was, at least in those days, a very popular place for the American sailor to visit.

What I started to say -- we were talking about this base of 12,000 -- another prime responsibility of public works was family housing. I seem to recall we had about 600 families housed on the base. But of this number, over 50 were captains or admirals who were in charge of something important, operating in or out of Yokosuka, including the Commander of the Seventh Fleet.

Q: Who was that?

Merdinger: Admirals Griffin and Schoech were Seventh Fleet Commanders while we were there.

Q: They liked to have their ships repaired at Yokosuka with the Japanese workers. Was there any flak from the U.S. because of that, that some of these ships were not sent home for refits, etc.?

Merdinger: Yes. I heard about this in a kind of second hand way, since my responsibility wasn't directly with the ships. I had a public works responsibility, to keep the shipyard itself repaired; that is, all its facilities. As a matter of fact, our public works people ran all the shipyard cranes, so we were in the ship repair business to that extent in my organization, but I didn't have any direct knowledge of difficulties back in the States. But I do recall hearing in a few instances some complaints, whether they were from Congressmen or shipyard workers on the West Coast or whatever, about this competition in the Far East.

Q: What about the problem of supplies for your own particular job there? Was the flow forthcoming?

Merdinger: Well, I think when you get so many thousand miles from the United States and you're depending on U.S. type things, you invariably have some kinds of problems along these lines. My recollection is that one of our acutest problem areas was the lack of automobile spare parts.

Now, for a while there, during my time, we went to some Japanese buses and some Japanese vehicles, the thinking being that we'd at least be closer to our spare parts. This also had certain difficulties built into it because of some of the regulations under which we were operating. It was difficult though not impossible to purchase foreign equipment, vis-a-vis American. Certain regulations almost insisted that we buy a piece of equipment in the States and spend all the money to ship it over to Japan, rather than buy it directly in Japan. I'm rather vague now as to just what those regulations were, but I remember the general outcome.

But during my time we did buy some Japanese equipment and in a sense that resolved some of the spare parts problem.

I might add that in our garage, which was a major overhaul place, we not only repaired our own vehicles but we took in a number of vehicles that the Marines had at Okinawa. In those days the Seabees were already operating in Southeast Asia. and we were getting a certain amount of cargo trucks and jeeps and other such things back into Yokosuka for repair from these organizations.

Q: And from Korea too, I suppose.

Merdinger: Yes. I'm trying to recall. Probably, but I don't recall specifically.

Q: What was the general Japanese attitude toward their own self defense in that time?

Merdinger: There were a few people, of course, who were engaged directly in the self defense forces who were very concerned. A good many of these people I knew had served - these were Navy people - had served in the Japanese Navy before, and this was simply a continuation of their careers. I would say that for the majority of the population, the self defense force wasn't anything they particularly paid any attention to. In other words, it was a kind of a nonentity. The no-war provisions that had been placed by the MacArthur occupation I think had cut very deeply.

Q: They really accepted that.

Merdinger: They accepted it, yes. I know there were a number of areas where perhaps we had a building or we had a section or some warehouses or something that perhaps we would want to give the Japanese self defense force. We always had to be very careful about this, because there were commercial interests on the outside who wanted them, and it would seem that they were far more powerful in getting their way in picking up excess land or buildings than was the defense force itself.

For instance, the admiral who was essentially commandant of the base, Commander Naval Forces Japan, lived in a house out in town in Yokosuka that had been occupied by some of the top Japanese Navy people in years past. There was no particular reason for him to live out there. We did have accommodations on the base; that is, by shifting houses around we had admirals' quarters on the base. But for a long time, I know we were very concerned that if our admiral were to move out, the Japanese Navy was not powerful enough to move in. That is, it would become kind of a civilian place.

So we always had this to contend with. I suppose it says something about the relative political clout of the self defense forces at the period.

Q: It has never seemed quite compatible to my mind with the Japanese character, to permit somebody else to do the job for them.

Merdinger: You mean, in terms of defense? Well, after all, they were recovering. They were building up certainly their electronics industry, optical industries, shipbuilding industry. Everything was booming there. The Japanese economy was such that they were eager to get every worker they could, and the business of self defense simply didn't seem to be part of the public consciousness. Not only that, but you had a number of American bases there anyway. We were there taking care of the job, and that was fine with them.

Q: I should think there'd be some resentment toward our occupation of some of the bases.

Merdinger: I never sensed that in any real respect while we were there. I'm sure there were some people who felt this way, but certainly it was not evident. There were some strikes outside of the bases. They always had what seemed to us rather peculiar strikes. They'd call them from one period to another. They'd say, "From 3 o'clock today until 5 o'clock tomorrow we're going to be on strike," and a few people would walk around outside the front gate and everybody else would go home, and that would be about the size of it. We in public works, of course, were always particularly conscious of our responsibilities at this time because we had to keep enough of a force inside the gates to keep the utilities going and this sort of thing.

Usually these strikes were against reduction in force of Japanese workers on the bases themselves. As time went on and budgets got tighter, we still had to raise the pay of our workers. There was only so much money to go around and so we would have to lay some of the force off. So there was always the possibility of this sort of token strike, against not our abandoning the bases but our reducing the force on those bases.

Q: Basically against us.

Merdinger: Well, it was kind of hard to know who it was against, because you see these people theoretically worked for the Japanese government on a master labor contract, and we in turn hired them from the Japanese government. As a practical matter, obviously they worked directly for us, but on paper at least they were working for the Japanese government, so in a sense they were complaining to their government that they were being let go.

Q: Why that seemingly cumbersome system of employment?

Merdinger: I don't remember now. It existed when I got there, and certainly made for more Japanese jobs, because you had to have people to administer this kind of a program.

Q: Was there any question of language ability as a result of this whole setup? Did you have to do anything about Japanese in order to communicate?

Merdinger: Well, no. Put it this way. All of our basic work was conducted in English. For instance, when I would dictate to the Japanese secretary, I would dictate in English, and I guess whe would translate it into Japanese and then back into English again when she was putting it down on her typewriter. But all of our drawings, all of our official work was conducted in English. However, at a certain level it got translated into Japanese, because obviously all of the Japanese working for us couldn't speak English. Very few of them could, as a matter of fact. But we had a number of translators, both men and women, who were very adept at this, and they kept the communications going.

But as far as my own attempts at Japanese go, my wife and I studied a book called "Japanese in 30 Hours" and we studied it for the three years we were there.

Q: You finally mastered it?

Merdinger: Not really. We found it a very tough language, although we got to the point where we could exist - for instance, we were on a skiing trip where we didn't see another Caucasian or run into anybody who could speak English for about two or three days. Now, during the course of this time we managed to order our meals and get on trains and buy tickets and generally maneuver our way around with the little bit of Japanese that we knew.

I might say that there were many times when I addressed the Japanese workers - a number of ceremonial occasions. We'd be giving our awards or there'd be a special day, and I would always make up a simple message in English, have my secretary translate this into Japanese, and then give it to me phonetically, so that I could read my speech to them in Japanese. I suspect that if they understood about half of what I said, I was doing better than I had a right to expect.

Q: An effective technique, however.

Merdinger: I do think that they appreciated the mere fact that I tried to communicate in their language. But with the studying I did, and I must admit I was a rather poor scholar at this thing, I didn't work as hard at it as I wish I had nor did my wife. But we found -- and most of the Americans found -- it was very difficult to carry on small talk, the kind of political conversation you'd have at a party some place with the Japanese, with the amount of Japanese language skill we were able to generate.

Q: It was idiomatic.

Merdinger: Well, and there are all kinds of inflections about one's place in rank versus another. We caught these subtleties every now and then when the secretary would talk to the maid or something like that. There's a definite way of using your inflections over there that immediately places one above someone else, and we never caught onto that at all.

Q: Did you take any trips to Okinawa or places like that when you were there?

Merdinger: Oh yes. We traveled all over Japan itself, through all the islands, north to where they're having the Olympics now. We were up at Sapporo, and we toured all the major places, down south to Hiroshima, the Japanese Inland Sea - sometimes just my wife and I, sometimes our whole family. We found it a delightful country to visit. We enjoyed tremendously the business of staying in Japanese Inns. I can't say that we ever thoroughly enjoyed eating Japanese food, just certain

Japanese foods, sukiyaki, for instance, was always a popular meal with us. But some of these breakfasts that they had were pretty hard to take.

I'm reminded now that my wife taught English to the professors in the electrical engineering department at Bodai, the Japanese defense academy. The academy was located just outside of Yokosuka, and I might add at the time Dr. Maki was the president of it. This is their combined, West Point, Annapolis and Air Force Academy really. Dr. Maki had also gone to Oxford as I had, and we had a few pleasant chats. As a matter of fact, my wife used to comment that he reminded her of her father, although he was very definitely Japanese. She went to the Academy about once a week to teach English conversation to these professors. Well, she was the first female instructor I think they'd ever had. They weren't quite sure how to react. But in the long run, it was a very happy association. They invited us to many things that most Americans never get invited to. For instance, we were invited, my wife and our four daughters and I to go with the skiing club of Bodai. These were all the cadets and some of the professors. We went to one of the skiing resorts with them, and this is where I recall these Japanese breakfasts that didn't suit us too well. But we really lived Japanese style with the rest of the cadets, and this was a lot of fun. Of course, it raised a lot of comment on the slopes because we were —

Q: This slope being the American sector?

Merdinger: No, no, I'm sorry, I'm talking about the commercial ski slopes at Zao that they took us up to. But they all had banners on.

We couldn't read them, of course, because they were written in Japanese characters, but they said "Japanese Defense Academy," and to see these girls go by with "Japanese Defense Academy" on their blouses raised a lot of eyebrows, I guess, among the other Japanese who read the signs.

We were also invited to climb Mount Fuji with a group, and this again was a family venture. Two of our girls didn't quite make it to the top. They got a little altitude sickness. But my wife and I and two oldest girls managed to get all the way to the top, which was about 12,400 feet elevation. We were treated to a number of instances like that, where we were brought right into the Japanese group; we were the only Americans in the group, and they were very solicitious of our welfare.

I might add that even when we weren't with Japanese friends — and we did develop a number of them over there — even when we weren't with them, we found the Japanese so pleasant and so cordial. There were times when, perhaps up in the ski country, we were getting on a train and the conductor or the fellow taking the tickets knew that we wanted to go in one direction and we ended up on a train going in the other direction, I recall one time when the fellow crossed over about three or four tracks to help us. He couldn't speak English, and all he did was grab us by the shoulders and bring up back and put us on the right train, having noticed that we were foreigners and couldn't really read the signs.

Every time we ever stopped any place, it seems, to consult a map or look a little bewildered, somebody would come up and want to practice his English, and at the same time show us where to go.

Q: You spoke about Japanese inns. How are they different?

Merdinger: Well, the whole layout of the place. As you know, you go into a Japanese house or Japanese inn and you take your shoes off at the doorstep, and immediately you are on (straw) tatami mats. You eat in private and to some degree you bathe in public, which is an interesting switch to westerners. Now, there's been a lot said about Japanese bathing, but there's only one place we ever went to that had mixed bathing, and this was up in the Noboribetsu, up in the very northern part of Japan. Apparently mixed bathing was a very popular pastime up until recent years, but then all that changed, and there aren't very many places that you find that any more.

Q: Were you welcomed and received in the same friendly fashion in Hiroshima?

Merdinger: Yes. I don't recall ever being any place in Japan at any time where I felt unwelcome. As a matter of fact, these people have a great capability I think for making people feel welcome. Very friendly. After all, we have lived all over the world and I don't recall ever feeling more welcome anywhere than we did over there in Japan. All I can say is that the whole tour was a delight from start to finish - the people we worked with, the kind of job we had to do, the tours we took and the friendships we made. I might add that those friendships still continue. The head of these electrical engineering professors I was mentioning ultimately became the dean of the school, and as part of his job he came over to the United States with his wife to visit a number of our academic institutions. When they visited the Naval Academy they stayed with us as our guests for a few days right on the Naval Academy grounds. And then only a year ago, he was a member of some government mission that came over here to study airports in the United States and we had the opportunity to have him at our house in Chestertown. So these friendships have endured through the years. Of course, we've been delighted with —

Q: I notice that you didn't overlook our athletic prowess either when you were there. You were the basketball coach on the base.

Merdinger: Yes, that's right, I coached the Sea Hawks. Yes, we had a lot of fun with that group and I did coach them for a couple of years. I can't say that we had the same success that we had with our Bremerton team that I previously mentioned, but we did have a lot of inter-service competition, and we got to a lot of places in Japan playing, mostly Air Force teams and Army teams in some out of the way places.

Q: This is all basketball.

Merdinger: Basketball.

Q: Not baseball, which is more eagerly embraced by the Japanese.

Merdinger: Yes, I would say that baseball when we were there was far and away the most popular sport that we have in common between the two countries. They have sumo wrestling, which is a tremendously popular spectator sport, and I don't know how to find the equivalent over here to that one.

Q: That sounds like a fun period. You probably didn't want to leave, did you?

Merdinger: I must confess that we never loved a place more than we did Japan, and the only thing that made leaving Japan tolerable was that we were ordered to the Naval Academy, and that again was a wonderful period of our lives.

Q: There's such a variety of assignments you had, each radically different from the other.

Merdinger: Well, I moved from a job as public works officer - it's a kind of combination city manager and city engineer, that type of job - and then I was ordered back to the Academy to become head of the English history and government department.

Q: This assignment at the Academy, was it something you had sought?

Merdinger: In a way I did. I'd always thought it would be nice to go back to the Academy and teach, or at least be affiliated with the academic program. Traditionally Civil Engineer Corps officers have had very little opportunity along these lines. Up to that time there'd never been a Civil Engineer captain to my knowledge who had had that opportunity.

Q: You were a captain by that time.

Merdinger: Yes. I was a captain when I went to Yokosuka in '59. There were from time to time Civil Engineer Corps officers at the Academy in teaching positions, but none in department head positions. If one became a Civil Engineer captain and went to the Academy, he went as public works officer. That was generally it. So this was quite a change, I suppose, for everybody to find a Civil Engineer not only in as an academic department head, but over in humanities on top of it.

Q: It was obvious why this went to you, though —

Merdinger: Yes, it stemmed from the Rhodes Scholarship. Now, I'd had orders to go back to Washington, Bureau of Yards and Docks. Two jobs had been specified for me. One was director of engineering, the other was director of research and development, so it looked as though I were going to stick pretty much along the lines I'd been before, but then I gather there was the move to get officers to the Academy staff who'd had more extensive experience in education, and as a result I got tapped. I was one of them.

Q: Was this philosophy of the then superintendent?

Merdinger: I think it probably went even further than the superintendent. I think it went right up to Chief of Naval Personnel, maybe even Chief of Naval Operations, because Admiral Rickover in these years was particularly vocal about the quality of education at the Naval Academy. There was a great deal of hue and cry about upgrading the whole academic effort at the Academy, and I think that an effort was being made throughout the Navy to get people particularly with doctorates and those who had had some greater exposure to higher education back to the Academy to participate in this general academic upgrading.

Q: As you pointed out elsewhere, there weren't that many naval officers who had doctorates to begin with, were there?

Merdinger: No, this is true and that counted. So I don't think that the assignment was unnatural from that standpoint.

So while I was here, I taught a course in history of technology, which was, of course, one of my avocational interests, and participated in another course in historiography, and was very active on a number of committees that had to do with revising the curriculum.

Q: Who was superintendent?

Merdinger: For the most part, Admiral Kirkpatrick was the superintendent. Admiral Davison just was leaving when I came in. We probably overlapped about a day. Admiral Kirkpatrick was relieved by Admiral Minter and just as I was leaving Admiral Kaufman was coming in. So I was here for three years and had exposure at least to four superintendents, only two of whom really served during my time. But that was only in the course of three years.

I had a number of miscellaneous jobs, chairman of the Naval Academy Foreign Affairs Conference, for example, which was an exciting thing.

Q: Tell me about that. It had been in being?

Merdinger: Yes, it had been going on under the general guidance of Professor Paone for a short time before I arrived, and we simply continued it and perhaps expanded it a bit, improved on it.

Q: What was the objective of it?

Merdinger: The objective was to bring students from all over the country to sit down in the Naval Academy setting for about three days and discuss some aspect of world politics. Generally speaking, this focussed on a region. One of the years we talked about Southeast Asia. Now, we'd get students from some 130 different colleges throughout the country to confer in small groups and to attend a few plenary sessions. A number of the ambassadors of the countries under discussion would come over and talk to our little round table groups. We worked basically with round table groups of 15 students or so, and we not only got the ambassadors but we got people from business, from government, a few from education, but more people who were more or less on the firing line in that particular area under discussion -- economic, cultural, political, that sort of thing.

Q: How many of the midshipmen participated?

Merdinger: We had a foreign affairs group who were directly involved in the arrangements, 50 midshipmen or more. But in terms of some of the seminars and large assemblies, we'd get a great deal more participation. I think it was a good thing from the standpoint of the midshipmen because it brought a breath of fresh air from the outside. They were exposed to a number of other students with divergent interests.

Q: Who financed the other students coming here?

Merdinger: This was a privately financed operation. This is where I learned a little about going to foundations and companies, to get funds to operate something like this. The U.S. government didn't pay for this. That is, the transportation, meals and all that sort of thing. This was paid for by funds that were solicited from various organizations -- General Foods, for example, was a perennial booster. The Naval Academy Alumni Association gave to this, and Naval --

Q: Naval Institute too?

Merdinger: I wouldn't be surprised. I don't recall, but probably. But a number of others were simply industries who were persuaded that this would be a good thing.

Now, it wasn't only a question of bringing light to the midshipmen We also had in mind the fact that we were bringing together a number of students who ultimately would be taxpayers and perhaps leaders in their communities and so on, and we were exposing them to the Naval Academy. Lots of them who came here with some rather fixed ideas about the military mind and what a horrible place this might be, and that the midshipmen would be all automatized. I recall - it's so typical - this girl from Radcliffe came in and spoke to me the first day, commenting on how she expected a group of wooden soldiers around here and that sort of thing; and then our getting together three days later after she'd been exposed to the place, and she was completely won over. She said she was so surprised to find that the midshipmen were individuals, that they had different points of view, that they were articulate and alert and bright and informed, and this wasn't her idea of "the military mind" at all. So she was completely taken. This kind of reaction I found time and again. Of course, I went through a similar kind of operation at West Point, and I served as one of the chairmen of the groups up there and ran into the same kind of enlightenment, if you will.

Q: Cross-fertilization.

Merdinger: Yes. I think really that the students who came from outside to the Naval Academy in many ways learned more than the midshipmen learned from them. That is, they had these stereotyped opinions that were suddenly shattered once they got into some intellectual discussions with our midshipmen.

Q: They were selected by the individual colleges and universities?

Merdinger: Yes. As a matter of fact, I just signed off a letter to Admiral Calvert here the other day. Washington College was invited to send two men, and one woman, from our student body over to the NAFAC which will be held in April this year, and this is fairly typical. A college will be asked to send a man and a woman, possibly only one, but normally they try to get at least two.

Q: What about this course in historiography? What was the background of that?

Merdinger: Let me point out that I was a co-teacher in this. Historiography was simply a course in the methodology of research in history. How do you go about performing research in historical areas?

Q: A very useful technique to know.

Merdinger: Oh yes, and I think it's a fascinating subject in itself, whether you use it or not. I think it's just one of those courses that can be a lot of fun.

Now, the one that I concentrated on was the history of technology. This was the one that I generated myself, and had just a seminar, a handful of really bright students, really good.

Q: Was this an elective?

Merdinger: Yes, this was an elective course. I tried to conduct it along the lines of an Oxford seminar to the greatest degree possible, and made them do a lot of writing, and got some very fine papers out of it. As a matter of fact, some of them were published in national magazines, and there were one or two prize winners in the papers they produced on some aspect of the history of technology. So I was very delighted at the kind of response that I got from students in this course. Of course, as I say, they were the brighter ones and capable of doing more extensive work.

Q: Does that go on now?

Merdinger: It has alternately been on and off. I was talking to the professor who helped me out with it, Professor Neville Kirk, and he said it looks as though it's going to go again next term. I hope so.

Q: What about the students who majored in history, government, English?

Merdinger: It's difficult for me to say, because when I was here, they didn't major to the extent that they do now. We had a core curriculum that everybody took and that was about 70 percent. If someone majored in our area, he wasn't wholly centered in the social sciences. Today somebody majoring in the humanities doesn't get very much in the way of science and mathematics. That is, he doesn't get it to the extent that he did in the days when I was here on the faculty.

Q: Why this change in emphasis from then to now? Because of the specialization in the Navy?

Merdinger: Well, I suppose it's a difference in orientation in the attitude of the people responsible for the basic education program now. When we were worrying about the curriculum in the early '60s, we spent a long time saying, "What is it we want the modern naval officer to know and what curriculum will be best?"

Then we went back in our experience to think, who are some of the successful people we knew who came through the reserves – who didn't come through the Academy but through some other source and were very successful, very competent, first class naval officers. Did they all have engineering degrees? In other words, an engineering background? And the answer was, no. What was it that they had that brought them to this point?

Well, we came to the conclusion that it was the fact that they had studied something in depth, and it almost didn't make any difference what it was. I seem to recall one fellow who was outstanding who had majored in music, another in theology. These fellows were outstanding naval officers, but they had gone very deeply into one subject, and that seemed to tell us something, when we were zeroing in on this.

We came up with the philosophy at that time that there are certain areas that we want our officers to cover. It's a technological Navy, therefore he's got to have a certain background in mathematics and science. Certainly the art of communication demands that he have a certain capability in handling the English language. We want him to have a certain background in history and so on. This came to about 70 percent of the curriculum at that time. As for the other 30 percent, we said, we don't care what he studies. If he would like to study in an area not directly Navy oriented, it's immaterial as long as he goes into depth. Not too paradoxically, I hope, we didn't want him to get too specialized at this time. I had some students, some midshipmen ... who came to me and said they would like to get into the Civil Engineer Corps ultimately in the Navy and what would I recommend that they take in this extra 30 percent?

I suggested that they might take a little bit of Shakespeare and some of these other subjects that had nothing to do with the technical areas they were going to study, and this surprised them. My point was: "Look, if you're going to be a civil engineer, you're not going to get enough here from us anyway, we're going to have to send you to postgraduate school and there we're going to concentrate on these engineering areas which you need to perform successfully. This may be the last chance you'll get to take Shakespeare or something else. We'd like to see you give yourself that chance and broaden yourself a bit. But we also want you to do something in depth."

Well, that attitude I think over the years has changed, and we get back to your point about specialization. I could see over the years after I left that this idea was beginning to gain headway, namely, "We need so many people who are going to be in the political military area, we need other people who are going to be engineers and so on, so we'll get them to start to specizlize at the Naval Academy in those areas."

I'm sorry to see this come about. I think that the philosophy we had developed before, this 70 percent -- now, you may argue whether it should be 70, 80 or whatever -- but the idea that there is a common body of knowledge we would like our midshipmen to have, and that we would like them simply to explore any kind of area in depth regardless of its relationship to what they are going to do later -- perhaps that might have afforded us richer returns.

Q: Doing it in depth brings on a certain amount of intellectual discipline?

Merdinger: That's right. Who was it, Montaigne who said something about the educated man who knows something about everything and everything about something -- well, I guess it's somewhat along those lines.

Q: I expect the idea of the broadly educated man is sometimes neglected in a technical school.

Merdinger: Many people have argued this, although I see the other side of the coin too. I think if one can generalize, those in engineering schools, tend to be much more interested in certain non-engineering areas than non-engineers are in technical areas. In other words, engineers will go out and take a look at political science or a look at humanities, whereas you get people in the humanities schools who are not about to take a hard look at science or mathematics or anything technical. It seems to be kind of a one way street as far as understanding and broadening oneself is concerned. Humanities consider themselves very human, humanized already, and really they miss the point of the liberal arts. After all when the liberal arts were originally defined they did encompass the scientific and mathematical side of the house. But today, certainly, I run into a preponderance of liberal arts students who have no interest, have no capability, just nothing at all in this scientific side.

Q: Isn't it, beyond capability, the lack of aptitude for it?

Merdinger: That's part of it too. Or they won't even try. In other words, they don't want to stretch their minds in that direction. So I suppose I've got a bit of the bias of the engineer when I think along these lines. But I do think that the engineers make a greater effort to understand the other culture than vice versa.

Q: What was your attitude at that time in terms of faculty? What percentage should be naval officers, what percentage civilian, that kind of thing that seems to be on again, off again?

Merdinger: From its founding the Naval Academy was always 50-50, civilian and military. In certain departments the ratio varied considerably from the average. In English, history and government, we had a department of somewhere between 80 and 90 professors. About two-thirds of those were civilian, one-third were military, but a good percentage of the military were really civilians in uniform.

These were young officers who'd only been out of school a few years. They were really oriented more toward teaching than they were toward the naval profession. So I don't know that they were serving the function the naval officer originally was intended to serve on the faculty, namely, serving in part as an inspiration to the midshipman to want to make the service his career. I don't think we were achieving that with this kind of officer who was brought back.

Q: Only this past weekend I came across an example of the philosophy of the Naval Academy which was rather extreme in the other direction - this superintendent back in 1902 who believed very strongly that there should be no civilian faculty people and that if adequately prepared naval officers were lacking, then they should draw on petty officers for the balance of the teaching staff.

Merdinger: Well, I think that's a bit of an extreme case today. As you know, West Point and the Air Force Academy have all uniformed faculties. On the other hand, they have gone another route in that they have permanent heads of departments and what they call the "not-heads." These are officers who really have withdrawn from the mainstream of the Army or Air Force to become permanent professors. Now, some of those people have become very eminent in their own right. They've developed some first rate scholars, first rate intellectuals, people who are well known in the academic community, who have very great stature. We've never really developed anything like that there at the Naval Academy. Now, I think that the possibility exists in terms of our civilian faculty developing along those lines, but certainly our military faculty would only by chance develop along those lines.

Q: Because of the method of rotation.

Merdinger: Yes, because they only come in for a few years and one can hardly call them professional academicians. I'm thinking for instance now of Colonel Abe Lincoln, who was head of the social sciences department of West Point for many many years, who by the way had been Dean Rusk's boss in World War II. He was a brigadier general at the end of the war, but then he took off his stars to go back to be a colonel and full professor at West Point. He served there for many years, but there were occasions here and there when he was called in to Washington or other places that called for an expert, and he was an international relations and social sciences expert. As a matter of fact, not too long ago when he retired from the Army and resumed his general's rank, he was called in to the immediate office of the President, and he was the man who was basically responsible for running the initial phase of this price freeze. He was the director of the Office of Emergency Preparedness. He's one of the few men around the President in this particular area.

Well, the Navy's never generated anybody who would be called in to do that sort of thing. But he was there at West Point many many years and developed this national reputation.

Now, I often felt that was a great system, that at West Point the officers were very definitely hand picked to go back there to teach, and in preparation for this they were given some intensive preparation through the master's level at least before going back, and then others, like the professors I'm talking about, of course, were fellows who had been there much longer and they, many of them, had gone on for their doctorate. I often thought perhaps that was a superior system to the one we have here, from the standpoint of giving some sort of inspiration to the cadets to continue on for a career in the serivce.

I don't know how valid that argument is. Meanwhile we're having a tough time, both West Point and Annapolis, keeping our graduates these days. I understand that the attrition is in the neighborhood of 50 percent, as soon as they finish their obligated service.

Q: Why was this system not tried ever at Annapolis?

Merdinger: I don't know. I just don't know the arguments behind it, except that there is a feeling abroad, rightly or wrongly, that maybe the Naval Academy assignment is not career- enhancing. So there are many people who felt that, while, it would be pleasant here this would not help in their subsequent careers.

Q: (crosstalk) belies that argument.

Merdinger: I don't know. I've seen the evidence both ways, and one can argue either way, I think. I'm just saying that this was a feeling that was certainly shared by a lot of people here.

Merdinger #3 - 211

Q: I've interviewed so many senior officers of the topmost rank and many of them have had their tour of duty here, sometimes twice.

Merdinger: Well, I think that you'll find that there is a lot of correspondence along these lines where others feel a different way.

I don't know - I feel this, that it has not been the same kind of a prestige assignment in the Navy that West Point has been in the Army. I think that's fair to say. In other words, to go back to teach at West Point is a much more desirable thing for an Army Officer, is considered much more career-enhancing, or at least it was until recent events.

Q: Is there a different emphasis in the Army from what there is in the Navy on intellectual attainment and powers?

Merdinger: Well, put it another way - I think that the Army by and large spends a lot more time in school. After all, the Navy, whether it's in war or peace, has to operate its ships, so in a sense you're in a wartime footing to a large degree all the time or much of the time. The Army, if they're not out shooting somebody, they're not operating all those machines, and you have a good percentage of the people in school. So I think that there is a greater tendency for people to spend more time in training positions or in school, in the Army than in the Navy. Again, this is a general observation; the facts may not bear this out.

Q: During your period here, did you take in any professional gatherings that would cut across military academy lines, secular schools.

Merdinger: Yes, I went to a number of meetings of higher education administrative officials – of course, I always went to national meetings in my own discipline, American Society of Civil Engineers for example or Society for the History of Technology would be another group, that I spent a lot of time with.

So I guess the general answer to your question is, yes, I got out and mixed in a number of different groups that might be considered straight professional in terms of civil engineers, or might be something a little broader, might be administrators.

Q: As head of the department when you were here, what sort of contact did you have with the superintendent? Was he actively interested in the progress being made in your particular department? Was there any real rapport, educationally speaking?

Merdinger: Oh yes, I think so. Of course, I was a member of the academic board.

Q: Tell me about its functions. How valuable was it?

Merdinger: The academic board consisted of the superintendent and ultimately the dean, the civilian dean who came into the picture during my tour here, and a number of academic department heads. The function of the board was really to oversee the basic educational policy of the Academy, but as a practical matter, much of our efforts were devoted to determining who's going to remain a midshipman and who's going to be dismissed.

Q: Specific cases.

Merdinger: That's right, specific individuals. We always had quite a chore at the end of the term, when a number of people had failed their subjects and the question was, do we keep them or don't we? Of course, we would have all their records and grades and people to speak for them and so on. They'd come in individually, and we'd make a decision as to whether they would go or come or be turned back, and this applied also to cases that were disciplinary in action. In other words, while they would go through the whole route to the commandant and his side of the house, ultimately they had to come before our board for the final decision. So we - in that capacity, we saw more people who didn't remain midshipmen than those who did.

Q: Did your department sponsor those public speaking courses?

Merdinger: Yes. We had the after dinner speaking program with the first class. As I recall, each first classman had to make two satisfactory after dinner speeches. During the time I was here we went from a strict grading system to merely determining, did he or did he not give a satisfactory speech? - which, of course, was the whole point.

These were very nice affairs. They were always done in a special room over in Bancroft Hall with candlelight and special waiters. Various lady guests would be brought in as well as male guests, and I think that for the most part they were pleasant occasions. But I'm remembering them as a department head who wasn't really committed to making a speech. My recollection as a midshipman when I went through the same thing is that

Merdinger #3 - 214

it was much more dreadful, that I didn't really appreciate all the candlelight and so on. But I think it was a useful kind of an exercise. I think that the people got something from it.

Q: What led up to it: What basic preparation was there for these first class men doing this?

Merdinger: No particular preparation. I suppose you're thinking in terms of a course in speech in which this would be the laboratory. No, we didn't have such a thing.

Q: It was not felt there was a need for it?

Merdinger: Well, I'm sure that some people felt there was a need for it. I think that in colleges throughout the country, speech courses have tended to disappear. For instance, in liberal arts colleges we don't have courses in speech, and we did some years ago. Except for those who are going to major in the area, this doesn't seem to be in most curricula that I know of today. And, of course, we didn't have it here today.

Q: Tell me, since you are currently involved in the academic world, in a private institution, and have had this experience at the Naval Academy, could you evaluate the application of discipline in the Academy, with the lack of application of discipline in a free wheeling educational setup? What, in your opinion, is the most valuable system? Can you make any judgment?

Merdinger: I guess it's a little hard to make a judgment, because during my time on the faculty of the Academy, we began to make a lot more concessions to the general loosening up that was going on all over the academic world. For instance, up until a certain time here, all lights had to be out at 10 o'clock. Studying stopped at that time. Then we allowed the midshipmen to study as long as they wanted; we said, all right, they're big enough to arrange their own hours.

I think there were still some kind of brakes on it. I don't think you could keep the lights on all night. But this does happen in the private college. I'm not sure if the students are studying or just sitting up and having bull sessions. Great bull sessions. I'm sure that many students learn something in these, and I'm sure that a lot of them don't learn a darned thing, but this in turn makes them more tired in the morning. They get up later. Early classes tend to be a disaster, because the students are too tired or not prepared or not there.

I guess I opt for a little bit of the discipline, simply because for some reason the American students that I have known at least find it difficult to discipline themselves. Now, I specifically said American students because I'm thinking of my time at Oxford, where there was absolutely no restriction whatsoever and yet there was a high degree of scholarship going on. The students there somehow had learned to discipline themselves. As a matter of fact, the Oxford system is such that there are very few examinations before the final one where one gets one's degree, whereas we've found it necessary in a good many institutions in this country to examine quite frequently, to be sure that the students are getting in there and studying the subject.

Q: By examinations you make him do it.

Merdinger: Exactly. So I suppose that's part of this discipline. There was more of this kind of hewing to the line in the Naval Academy than one finds out in the civilian institutions. Again, I'm talking of a few years ago, and I'm not sure how far the Naval Academy has gone in this business of dispensing with frequent examinations and general recitation and so on.

Q: But you were there at a time when they were beginning to loosen up on some of the rules of discipline. And what was the philosophy back of this? Why was it necessary to do this, to depart from the practice of the past, in deference to what was happening in the whole scholastic world?

Merdinger: I think there was just a feeling on the part of a good many of us who came back that the restructions were simply unnecessary. They were perhaps restricting unduly the role of free thought with the midshipmen. I think we were perhaps bringing a bit of our own developed philosophy into this. I don't recall that much of this stemmed from demands on the part of the students themselves. I think that much of it came from the faculty. Now, I don't know how true this would be today, as I understand many of these students are demanding all sorts of things. I don't mean midshipmen necessarily but I mean students in general. So perhaps some of this sort of thing today would come up from the bottom, but ten years ago it was coming from the top.

Q: Perhaps it would have been interesting if you'd stayed on for a year or two under Kaufman because he did change things vastly.

Merdinger: Yes. Well, of course, the change didn't start with our coming in, at the time I came in. The changes had started before. I think they were accelerated in our time and continued after. As a matter of fact, they continue today. It's been almost a state of perpertual change here in the academic program, possibly for the last 15 years. Now, it isn't only the Naval Academy. It's been going on a good deal in the academic world at large too.

That, of course, brings you to the question, are we moving as fast as the rest of the academic world? That's a tough question to answer.

Q: And is it necessary too, to move that fast?

Merdinger: Yes. I sometimes wonder, are we just changing for change's sake? But one little set of statistics disturbed us back in the '62 and '65 period. The senior naval officer at MIT who was concerned with the E.D. program - the Naval Constructors - had taken a set of statistics over a long period of time, probably went back over 25 years or more, and he found that there'd been a steady decline in the average grades of the Naval Academy graduates taking his postgraduate course at MIT. Back 25 years or so before they tended to be pretty much A students at MIT, but as you went through the years they became B and finally C students. And these were Naval Academy graduates who were coming from essentially the same cut of the class. Which is to say that either the Naval Academy in terms of its preparation of these people had declined, or the people we were getting in were not as competent, or else there'd been a tremendous acceleration outside so the people going to MIT had somehow made a significant jump ahead of our people in their ability to do this work. There are all kinds of combinations here, but what it seemed to say was that somehow, relative to these other people, our Naval Academy graduates had slipped. Now, I don't know if this is very good argument about the quality of education at the Academy. It's merely a set of statistics that are interesting to observe, and perhaps a little disturbing.

Q: There certainly are some exceptions to that statistical table, too.

Merdinger: Oh yes. We still produce A students up there at MIT, no question about that. Most of my comments on this subject of postgraduate performance, by the way, are based more on hearsay than on statistics.

A number of people have commented on Naval Academy graduates going on into postgraduate work in various places, it may be that people who went on to postgraduate work were better in the old days. I have heard it cited a number of times that the fellow who didn't have a particularly outstanding record at the Naval Academy went on and did very fine postgraduate work at a number of places; whereas today, our Naval Academy graduates do not do as well across the board as they used to.

This gives rise to another theory, that perhaps we're not getting the same cut of the college population in our midshipman population today as we did years ago. One might argue that maybe we got the top X percent, whatever that was, maybe 5 percent or 10 percent or something in terms of their academic potential. That's dropped a bit now. Again, I don't know how one proves this. It's a theory that a lot of people have kicked around.

The point is that some feel that our people are not doing as well in some of these postgraduate programs as their counterparts did years ago.

Q: Do you think the picture will change, if Senator Javits sends his wave?

Merdinger: Well, I think that's an interesting newspaper article but I doubt that we're really going to move in that direction.

By the way, one question that I'm not sure that I really answered completely - this was the business of the civilian/military. We got off into the West Point system, and some of my thoughts along those lines I think that the whole argument, at least the major argument, one can have for the existence of the academies is that they produce people who become career officers, and that motivation is a big part of this. Now, you want them to have a good education in the course of this, but it is also important that they have this motivation to become service-oriented, career-oriented, in many quarters it was felt that this motivation would best come about through a uniformed professoriat. Now that you look at West Point and Annapolis these days, I'm not sure that one is doing considerably better than the other in terms of retainment figures, so maybe that argument tends to fall by the wayside.

Then the other side of the coin is, you're trying to give a good education. Obviously if you have civilians who are professionals, particularly in fields that are not directly related to Navy operations, I'm sure they can provide a better kind of instruction. That is, theoretically they ought to be able to. This all depends on the individual. There are some people who haven't had much formal training - by that I mean they may not have had their doctorates -- but they make great teachers, because they've just got a certain something about them; whereas others who have had more advanced work still may never become very good teachers.

Just given the laws of chance, I think that we're going to have a better professoriat among the civilians, in those areas that are not strictly Navy. But a similar case can be made for officer instructors in fields of their prime competence. Why should a civilian know too much about let's say ordnance and gunnery or navigation? Our answer has been a mixed military/civilian faculty.

Q: What was the criterion for selecting a civilian professor in your time?

Merdinger: We looked for a fellow who had the requisite degrees in a particular subject from, in our opinion, "good" institutions. Naturally, his experience and references were highly important. We would go country-wide really in trying to get somebody, even as an assistant professor. We would certainly look toward his having the PhD. We were also concerned with his personality and demeanor, factors which were evaluated in the personal interview.

Q: His ability to turn out books, was this any factor?

Merdinger: Not required certainly, but it would help. We'd say, "This is fine, we seem to have a scholar here." Obviously we wanted to get somebody who could also draw on that scholarship and impart it to midshipmen. We would hope that he would have some teaching experience, and we would get evaluations from his superiors. It was quite a lengthy process, searching these people out, because we would go back to as many references as we could. Sometimes you get a little fooled by the written word and you get a little suspicious of the fellow. Then you might call up the dean of that school and find out what the true matter is. "Well, I don't think you'd want this fellow because he's a drunk." is the word I got on one candidate. He looked awfully good on paper, but there was something about the write-ups that seemed to say "We're not giving you the full story."

So I would say that our search was thorough, and our criteria were scholarship, personality, leadership, teaching ability to the extent that it could be inferred. I've often wondered, will this fellow really fit into this community? I don't know how it is today, but in our day I think it was pretty hard to get a real weird kind of a professor in this place. There was a certain accepted mode of dress and behavior that, while never expressed, was certainly there, ever so subtly.

Q: What about a man's attitude or lack of attitude toward the naval service?

Merdinger: I don't know that that every really came into the picture. Of course, this was before all these anti-war feelings that have been demonsteated so forcefully here in recent years. This was '62 to '65, and I don't recall in several years preceding that period that there was much of a pro or con feeling. It wasn't an issue one way or the other.

I do think that we tended to want somebody who was a manly sort of a fellow. That almost goes without saying. There may have been some who were brilliant teachers, but were eccentrics, flamboyant and so on - that wasn't the type who usually got hired. Whereas in a civilian school you might very well pick somebody like that and say, "Yes, we need a few characters around here, and this fellow would just fit the bill."

Q: You've indicated that it was during your time here that there were various suggestions that the academic field might be a good one for you to pursue. Do you want to talk about that?

Merdinger: Yes. This was the time when suddenly a number of people began to ask me if I would like to be considered for this or that college presidency, and I must confess that it had never occurred to me before that time. I'd always had an interest in academics one way or another - maybe teaching, I think I mentioned that I used to be a moderator in Great Books and I used to be a leader in seminars in political philosophy and foreign policy. But I'd never really considered the idea of going into the academic world ultimately. However, as I say, it was during this time that not only was I approached by a few people, but I actually was offered the presidency of a couple of colleges even though I wasn't an avowed candidate.

Q: While you were still in uniform.

Merdinger: Yes. And it got me to thinking that -

Q: Who came after you?

Merdinger: Well, there were a variety. They tended to be mostly state institutions, state universities or state colleges, and as I recollect now, something on the West Coast, something in the Middle West and something in the East, so it was kind of widespread. Now, some of this really generated from some of my old RHODES Scholar classmates who by this time had become university presidents in their own right, and they are very often asked, "Who do you think might be approached along these lines. Some, knowing I was at the Naval Academy, said, "Well, it's about time he got out on the firing line with us," and so my name I think got into the hopper that way.

Q: How did you react to it being in the hopper?

Merdinger: I was, of course, first surprised, then flattered, and then I began to wonder whether I should really seriously consider something along these lines. I never quite could bring myself to taking the final step, but I began to think seriously for the first time of, what am I going to do when I leave the Navy? I'd never really thought about that before. And I began to weigh the question of staying several more years in uniform, or getting out perhaps a little earlier and getting into some kind of career that really in the long run would last longer than a naval career would. So these were the thoughts that were generated by these overtures.

Q: How did your wife feel about these overtures?

Merdinger: Mixed feelings, as I did. We loved the Navy. We'd enjoyed going to different places, getting new jobs, and, of course, I always had, it seemed to me at least such interesting and challenging jobs and such different ones that the idea of settling down to one was pretty dull. It almost sounded dull. And yet you realize that this delightful life can't go on forever, and you really ought to think of something else along these lines. Then the Vietnam War came into the picture, and I really felt that somehow I had to go there first, and then when I came back from that, that would be the point of decision.

Q: That's very interesting.

Merdinger #4 - 225

Interview No. 4 with Captain Charles Merdinger

Place: U. S. Naval Institute, Annapolis, Maryland

Date: 24 February 1972

Subject: Biography

By: John T. Mason, Jr.

Q: Captain, it's mighty nice to see you today, and I'm very grateful to you for having made the trip through the snow over here for this interview. Last time you concluded with a very interesting discourse on the Naval Academy during the time you served there as head of a department, and now I think you're ready to turn your attention to BuDocks and the department in Washington. You went there, I believe, in August of 1965.

Captain Merdinger: Yes, that's right. I went back to be what was then called the Assistant Chief for Maintenance and Operations, and shortly thereafter, when Bureau of Yards and Docks was changed to the Naval Facilities Engineering Command, a whole new set of titles evolved, and this title changed to Assistant Commander for Maintenance and Operations.

Q: This was part of the McNamara reorganization?

Captain Merdinger: I suppose you could say that, although we weren't particularly conscious it was McNamara who was really forcing this. This was an internal Navy thing that brought all the materielle commands under the command of the Chief of Naval Materiel. So this is when we moved into the systems command concept. Really we did the same thing. It just had a new name.

Q: Was it an advantageous development, would you say?

Merdinger: There were those of us who felt that it had some disadvantages. I suppose that you always look to see where your chief is, in terms of echelons of command, and he was moved down just one rung lower. I remember a statement attributed to Admiral Moreell, who, of course, had been our great chief during World War II. I might add that at that time when he was chief of Bureau of Yards and Docks and chief of Civil Engineeers, that he reported not only directly to the Secretary of the Navy, but in many cases directly to the President of the United States himself. When our chief, under the current situation, was having some difficulties, I recall somebody saying that Admiral Moreell had remarked, "Why doesn't he go see the President about it?"

Well, the situation was completely different. He was now down many many echelons. So I suppose from that standpoint we regarded it as a downward move.

Q: Moreell had given birth to the Seabees, had he not?

Merdinger: Yes, he was the chief when they were brought into being.

Q: And this was a very special contingent.

Merdinger: Yes, that's right. Returning, for a moment, to this reorganization there's another factor too; that is, many of the other commands in this organization really did have related functions, as procurement of ships and airplanes and this kind of thing - design co nstruction, procurement, the whole lot - whereas our organization really was different in many ways. It was difficult to find the same kind of niche for us as for these other material commands under this same wing.

So there was some argument that we had a unique character somewhat along the lines of BuMed, which was not brought in under the materiel command organization. But that's really neither here nor there. From the standpoint of my operations, this didn't really change anything. I had an office of about 165 engineers, systems analysts and what not, and our job basically was to monitor the whole naval shore establishment insofar as public works was concerned, that is the maintenance and operation of the shore establishment.

At this particular time, we had what was called the one manager concept of the shore activities, so BuDocks and later NAV Fac had the responsibility to fund directly all the public works departments or the majority of the public works departments world wide. We did this through our various field divisions. Our command had offices in various spots - in Seattle, San Francisco, San Diego for instance on the West Coast, and then at Pearl Harbor there was one big office that administered the whole Pacific. The chain then ran from our office to them to the stations, and in this way, our office was concerned with you might say the funding and general operations of public works departments in about 500 different naval shore establishments world wide. These might be ordnance stations, airfields, hospitals, whatever, just the whole naval complex.

The budget at that time - this was just for maintenance and operations - was about 400 million a year, and we administered that out of our office. Now, apart from that side of it, we also were responsible for the setting of standards in maintenance of shore facilities, utilities, and automotive transportation. In other words, the whole business as far as technical standards for operating public works departments was concerned. I might repeat the responsibilities of the normal public works department. They include design, planning and estimating - all the administrative and engineering area - and three main subdivisions called shops. First is the maintenance shop - plumbers, electricians, carpenters and so on - concerned with maintenance of all facilities, whether it be an airfield or port, the lighting system, roads, houses, that sort of thing. Second - utilities - water, electricity, sewage and heat. Finally, ground transportation. This is to say that we were responsible for all the wheeled vehicles, whether they be sedans, trains, trucks, cranes - the whole range of transportation equipment.

Q: Responsible for them and for their maintenance?

Merdinger: Oh yes. Maintenance and operation of all these. So you see, there's a combination in a public works department of a number of things. It is a utility company, the bus company, the taxi company, the local garage, the roofing contractor, the local architect/engineer, all these things rolled into one.

Q: Since you mention trucks and automobiles and their maintenance, were you able to use the facilities in some of the shipyards in this area?

Merdinger: No, generally speaking. Now, you may fix up a crane or parts of a crane in a shipyard for instance but if you're talking normally of trucks and automotive equipme normal rolling stock, if you are not capable of repairing it in the public works garage you'd probably go to some commercial automotive organization for that sort of thing. There was a great drive, naturally, to get us out of as many such activities as possible and lean on the commercial area.

Q: Didn't that become more expensive?

Merdinger: No, not necessarily. For instance, let's say that you've used a lot of tires. It may be a lot less expensive to go to a local tire place to fix these than attempt to fix them yourself, because it may be that your volume of work is not such that you can keep a man fully occupied doing that sort of thing. I think it all depends on how large your organization is, as to whether it's justified to have that kind of expertise in your shop. When I was at Yokosuka, we had a big shop in public works so that we did practically everything, and we felt we could compete pretty well with commercial enterprises.

Q: I remember you said that distance, of course, made this more feasible and necessary.

Merdinger: You can't generalize on these. You can only say that you keep an open mind, that you don't operate everything necessarily in-house; you take a look, if you can do it more economically outside, that's the way you go.

Q: Within your organization, did you have a section that dealt with keeping abreast of new things on the market, new materials, new metals and that kind of thing?

Merdinger: Yes, we did. There's another section of Nav Fac on the research and development side, and, of course, I'd been associated with that group in my laboratory days. They are concerned in part with this kind of thing, bringing information back to us. In the maintenance and operations office, we were subjected to all kinds of literature and visits from every kind of entrepreneur you can imagine in the country, wanting us to adopt this kind of asphalt or that kind of doorstop, or anything, you name it. Sooner or later somebody came to us trying to get our OK on it. Normally we didn't do this, in a general way, but we would note that something was of interest - we might let other people in the field know that this existed, without putting any kind of stamp of approval on it. Let them make up their own minds.

Q: When you did utilize something new in the area and it was fairly expensive, then I suppose it required some education, did it not, for your people out in the field?

Merdinger: Well, yes, of course, it would. I'm just trying to think of some examples of this and off hand nothing comes to mind.

Q: I can think of an example in shipbuilding that required a very expert effort, and that was the use of aluminum on board ships.

Merdinger: We had so many stations world wide in so many different climates with so many different problems. It became difficult to standardize let's say on materials. We could standardize more on procedures, that is, how you will attack your maintenance problems. As a matter of fact, we set up a number of guidelines in control of maintenance in that part of our bureau, much of this before I came, and we set up a number of different ways to maintain certain items. These came out in pamphlet form and these were ultimately picked up by industry. So the Navy led industry in this controlled-maintenance program by a large margin.

Q: I can see you turning out lots of manuals.

Merdinger: Yes, we did this.

Q: Who published them?

Merdinger: These were published by the government.

Q: What was your particular cognizance there?

Merdinger: I was responsible to the chief for running this huge budget, this 400 million. So we had quite an analyst's problem at central headquarters. I had the responsibility if you will, focussed in my office ultimately, of taking all these requests from the field and putting them into one big budget, and in turn justifying this up the line — in other words, going to the Department of Defense — controller organization, and defending our need for this kind of money, simply to keep the shore establishment going.

So I was both, you might say, a supplicant before the higher authorities in the Pentagon to get the money, and once we had the money I was responsible basically for parceling it out, to the various organizations world-wide. That was one side of it.

Q: Did that entail getting involved with cost analysis?

Merdinger: Oh yes, very definitely. You might say that we were right in the middle of that kind of operation. This entailed, then, a fair amount of travel. I did get around the world to a good many of these stations. I certainly got to all the field divisions that were the local agents distributing these moneys. So I did see a good bit of the naval shore establishment that I hadn't seen before, and this included Europe, South America, Asia, all around.

So you might say that I had financial responsibility as well as technical responsibility, that is in terms of acting for the chief, at headquarters organization.

Q: Going back to cost analysis, it's such a widely diversified operation. Was it a feasible approach to things. Were you able to come up with figures in this area and that area which were definitive?

Merdinger: I think we had a reasonable approach to it, yes. Prior to this single executive, as they called it, under BuDocks, each one of the various materiel bureaus had administered its own stations, giving out this public works money, and some of the stations did very well indeed. The air stations seemed to be pretty well favored. But some of the naval stations that were sponsored let's say by Bureau of Personnel -- which somehow had not been able to get as much a share of this maintenance and operating money - had deteriorated quite badly.

I think that one of the things this single executive under Bu Docks did was to level off the amount of help that was being given to the shore stations. Now, there never was enough money to go around. There never is when you get into this kind of business. So it's a question of sharing the poverty. But some of them were less poverty-stricken than others under the old system, and I suppose in this way we brought everybody down to an equal level. At least this was the view of some who got cut. Now, others thought that we were bringing them up and that they had been brought up to a level that some of the others enjoyed. It all depends on your point of view of this thing, depending on how well you were doing before this single executive concept came into being.

Q: And considering the fact that we were involved in various types of activities in various parts of the world, were there not priorities within the whole thing, as to what outfit got preference?

Merdinger: Well, there would tend to be priorities. Of course, we didn't feel that we could judge those absolutely in Washington. We'd leave those to the field divisions where these people were able to go to the scene and make a better judgment.

Q: I suppose your proclivity for traveling also put the responsibility on you, then?

Merdinger #4 - 234

Merdinger: To some degree, yes. At least it made me better, more aware of some of the problems in the field, and particularly when I was arguing upward, asking for a certain amount of money in the budget, I could by personal experience say, "I have been here and this is the situation." So I think it perhaps would lend a little more credibility to budget presentations, or to my authority at least.

Q: Did you get involved with Congressional committee hearings?

Merdinger: Not in that job particularly. Most of the people I dealt with were budget analysts in either the Navy Department or Department of Defense, of the Bureau of the Budget. Now these Bureau of the Budget people, of course, were acting for Congressional committees. Every now and then we'd be in on the tail end of some Congressional hearing, but normally most of our business in this line was with the analysts themselves.

Q: How did you find the group within the Department of Defense, whom some refer to as the Whiz Kids, not in the most complementary fashion?

Merdinger: Well, it's interesting that you should mention the Whiz Kids because prominent among them was Alain Enthoven, who's a good friend of mine. We got to know each other because we had been Rhodes Scholars - and furthermore we ended up in a little religious discussion group that used to meet frequently- every two weeks or so.

Q: A religious discussion group?

Merdinger: Yes, a religious discussion group. So we got together quite often on a social basis as a result. This went back to the days when I was in the Naval Academy. And the friendship has continued on through the years. When you speak of the Whiz Kids, of course, his name immediately comes to mind. I didn't have really very many official dealings with him, because he was dealing with the broad national issues, much more so than our relatively little problem of maintenance of naval shore establishment. I found him a very reasonable individual. I don't think he felt that the kind of thing he was doing was the last word. It was just that his people were taking a hard economic look at a number of items that came along, and he said, "From our point of view, this is the way it seems to be."

Now, this was contrasted to many field commanders or operational organizations that said, "We need it. We don't know exactly all the dimensions of this thing but we know on the basis of personal experience, we need it."

So his office at least forced a lot of people to rethink their own positions, to quantify many things that simply had not been quantified before. There are dangers in this, of course, and many people felt that Mr. McNamara, in making his final decisions, perhaps lent too much weight to the Whiz Kids and their abstract analysis of the problems, versus the experience.

Now, this is putting it in black and white and obviously there are all kinds of shades of grey in this kind of decision making. But I think it may have been true - it certainly seemed from a distance many times - that McNamara's decisions did seem heavily weighted on the side of the recommendations of systems analysis, and possibly this wasn't the best way to make a particular decision. But I think that the concept is a good idea, because it does make the operations people justify their position a lot more than by just saying, "I have the experience so give it to me."

Q: It seems to me that you as an individual could walk in both fields, so perhaps make a better judgment of the merits of the approach than others. I find that in talking with various naval officers who bristle at the mention of the Whiz Kids that the reaction is based on what they feel the Secretary's attitude was towards men in uniform. They felt he looked down on men in uniform.

Merdinger: I'm not sure. Of course, I never had any contract with the Secretary so my impressions are certainly second hand at best. I only know that Enthoven, whom I respect very much, respect his opinions, had a very high regard for Mr. McNamara, said he was not this cold precise machine that somehow seemed to come across in the public media, that he was a fine, bright, articulate individual. Of course, he worked hard and he demanded a lot from his subordinates, and he came in many times with very preconceived ideas about how something should be done, and then proceeded if you will to make this come true by his studies - by various studies. There's no question about it, the man had tremendous grasp of what was going on there. I'm not sure whether this is best for such an establishment, however, regardless of the competence of the man.

I certainly must say this - there were many times when we felt frustrated the way things went. So many levels of decision making had been placed on top of us, in many respects, that it made Washington duty a fair horror to many people. At least I never felt particularly happy there. I felt too far away from where things were happening. I also had the feeling that perhaps, no matter what you did, there was always somebody looking over your shoulder and the decision was never final. Somebody else was always in there, even though in theory you might have the final say.

Q: You'd had so many experiences where you were your own boss. I suppose it was frustrating.

Merdinger: Yes. I think you get a little spoiled, shall I say, in positions like that. To generalize - maybe this has changed now - but there was a period when naval officers in general disliked Washington duty. I think they felt it was an imposition on their time and they weren't accomplishing very much. They were used to being doers at a given station or on ship. Whereas Army people, I had the feeling, were much more receptive to the Washington idea. The good ones gravitated to staff duty and they looked forward to Washington, for this was very career-enhancing. I suspect it may have had something to do with the fact that in peacetime the Army is not as actively engaged as is the Navy. You run your ships, whether or not you're in war, but you don't run the tanks as much in the Army. So this is a generalization that probably isn't true any more, because more and more Navy people also seek these staff jobs in Washington.

Merdinger #4 - 238

Q: And more and more have fewer opportunities to get on board ship.

Merdinger: Yes. I think the scene has changed. But from my point of view, I never really considered Washington duty as really desirable.

Q: Well, what were the high points of that tour of duty, two years?

Merdinger: It wasn't even two years. It was about a year and a half. I suppose the highlight for me was learning the intricacies of the bureaucracy in Washington. I didn't come away with any feeling of great accomplishment. On most of the stations where I'd served, we had done something. I'd seen it happen. Here, we were just keeping the show going. I'm not sure that we really came up with anything new. We did improve this system that I was talking about, this single executive management of all the shore facilities, but shortly after I left we lost that single executive. It was to fragment into something along the systems that they had had before.

Q: How did that happen?

Merdinger: Well, I don't know. There were strong forces in the Navy itself that felt this single executive idea wasn't good. They felt that the Bureau of Yards and Docks, now Naval Facilities Engineering Command, was too strong, that it was the tail wagging the dog. Their argument ran that the operators, who have the final responsibility in the Navy, should have control over their logistic support, and they argued that they weren't having that control, that it was just concentrated in the public works department because of this broad system. So you might say

I had not initiated it, it had started before I got there, and it didn't terminate while I was there, but I was kind of an interim manager of a system that ultimately collapsed.

Q: While you were there and while you learned about the intricacies of the bureaucracy, did this stand you in good stead when you went out into the field again? Did it help you to cut corners and ?

Merdinger: I think, to some degree. I would think that my first tour in Washington was even more important in that regard because you see, I only had two tours of duty after I left the Bureau this time. The first time, I had many more. As a young officer I had a preconceived idea as to how things got done back in Washington, and then I found that people fumbled around back there just as we did in the field. I no longer had the same awe and ignorance of how things were working back there. So the answer is, yes, the tour in Washington is essential I think for the field man to know just how things do run back there.

Q: While you were there, '65, '67 were there increasing demands being placed on the Bureau for developments out in the Far East, in Vietnam?

Merdinger: Yes, there were, but that was really on the other side of the house. You see, there wasn't much in the way of a public works organization out in the Far East, and so my eyes were focussed more on the activities that were already in being. There were other sections of the bureau of course, that were concerned with this. You had this big RMK BRJ contract that was building up. You had the buildup of the Seabees in a number of battalions. All this kind of thing. There was a

Merdinger #4 - 240

mobilization going on. I wasn't part of that. I was aware of it because I was one of the assistant chiefs and sat in on the conferences and heard other people report on their areas, but I had no direct connection with it.

Q: Did it create in you a desire to go out and become a part of this?

Merdinger: Oh yes, I felt that as a career officer, this is where I have to go. As the months rolled on from '65 on, it became pretty clear I think that most Civil Engineer Corps officers were going to end up in Vietnam, and I think at one time perhaps one-third of the whole Corps was out there. So this was a place that our eyes were truly focussed on, as the big thing for the Civil Engineer Corps.

Q: Maybe this would be an appropriate place to begin a sketch or history of the development of that project in the Far East even before you came on the ground.

Merdinger: I can only speak with any authority at all on the public works department at Danang. The Civil Engineer Corps was engaged in three different areas. One was this huge civilian contract out there, the RMK. Raymond Morrison Knudsen and then ultimately Brown Root Jones, RMK BRJ. This contract had started in the early sixties with some very modest construction out there, but ultimately it built up to a construction force of over 50,000 people under this one contract. Somewhere in 1966 or thereabouts. In other words, it peaked at this number and then it started to go down. As more Seabee units were activated and came over to take up combat construction, the RMK combine was not as much needed. Furthermore, they had accomplished much of their mission.

Q: Was that contract something of an open end contract?

Merdinger: Oh yes, cost plus fixed fee contract. Ultimately in the latter sixties it became a modified kind of contract. There was an award fee. It was a contract that was cost plus an incentive award, as opposed to this fixed fee that it had started on. They went over and built millions and millions of dollars worth of ports and airfields, cantonments, hospitals, everything you can possibly think of, this outfit did. Now, at any given time, probably no more than 10 percent of the force was American. The rest of it they recruited out in the Far East to a large degree, mostly Vietnamese. They trained these people to become artisans of one sort or another. But they had a number of other Asians on the forces. So here was a construction effort really that was devoted to all the armed forces. Of course, first of all it was devoted to the Vietnamese government, because as I mentioned it was there in the early sixties and it wasn't until '65 that we had forces in strength over there.

So that was one side, you might say, of the Civil Engineer Corps effort, and that was directed out of Saigon. Then you had the Seabee battalions over there. They ultimately grew to a brigade, and their headquarters were at Danang, really at Red Beach. These were battalions that essentially serviced I Corps. The Army, first logistics command, had basic engineer responsibility in the other three corps areas. I might add that in terms of their kind of public works operation - they called it Repair and Utilities, R and U, - this was done largely through civilian contract with Pacific Architect/Engineers. The Army was responsbile - it let a contract to this civilian organization, which came in and staffed a number of these Army bases and cantonments and gave them Repair and Utilities support. Up in I Corps, we had a slightly different operation. That's where we had the big public works department.

Q: May I go back to the question on the RMK effort, since it ties in with your article. You say they worked largely with Vietnamese and trained them in various skills.

Merdinger: Yes.

Q: I wanted to ask how difficult this process was. Did they have a real problem in this total effort with training?

Merdinger: My information on that is sketchy. I talked with Bert Perkins, who is the general manager over there, about this, and my recollection is that he indicated it wasn't the easiest job in the world, but they were trainable. I think they had the same experience that we had, and I'm speaking now of public works in Danang, because we did exactly the same thing. We brought in a number of Vietnamese and we trained them. It was difficult at first, but after a while we got them to do a number of chores quite adequately.

Q: I suppose it was this joint experience of this contracting outfit and your own efforts at Danang which brought you to say that one of the positive results of the whole thing, the whole effort, would be, when one

Merdinger #4 - 243

looks back in retrospect, the training of the native population in various new skills.

Merdinger: That, I think, is the real legacy that our American venture in Vietnam will ultimately have left.

Q: That's a pretty tangible one, isn't it?

Merdinger: I think so. I'd like to say one thing, now that we got off on the public works venture that I know something about.

Q: I don't want to distract you from the main stream of your story.

Merdinger: I was public works officer in '67-'68 and got involved a great deal, of course, with the Vietnamese in training because we had quite a large contingent of them. But along with them, we had a large number of Korean civilians that we had hired through the Philco-Ford Corporation. Now, the parallel I'm attempting to draw here was the fact that these Koreans some 15 or more years before had been somewhat in the same situation as the Vietnamese. Our armed forces had gone to Korea. They had found these Koreans there, trained them to be artisans, and lots of people had felt that they weren't really trainable or for one reason or another this wasn't a good route to follow. But now, less than a generation later, here we were utilizing Koreans to train Vietnamese. I should like to point out that a good many of these Korean artisans were better than our Seabees—and I don't mean to take anything away from the Seabees when I say this - because they were pretty good, but these Koreans had been in it even more years and they were good plumbers, carpenters, electricians. This I think was the legacy that an earlier American force had left from the Korean War.

Q: They have the basic aptitudes if someone trains them.

Merdinger: That's right. And I do think that this will be one of the very positive effects of the American adventure, if you want to call it that, in Vietnam.

I was talking about a more or less three-pronged approach here of the Civil Engineer Corps involved in Vietnam. I mentioned the contractor. I mentioned the Seabee battalions. We also had Seabee teams over there. These were little groups of 13 that operated on an independent basis, all throughout Vietnam. They were in all of the corps area, and they ultimately came to be little military Peace Corps. Initially when they went over they had a function of helping out some of the Army advisors, who were placed in various hamlets. When they needed a bit of construction or utility help these teams went out to help them.

Ultimately, as we got more forces over there, these teams were not needed in this capacity, and they ended up being assistance teams in little villages, so as I say, they tended to become military Peace Corps operations.

Q: Was the direction of them coordinated in any way? Under whom?

Merdinger: They were loosely coordinated out of Saigon and ultimately back in Pearl Harbor. The USAID organization initially wanted them, and then USAID became Cords and I'm not sure what it became. This was a U. S. civilian organization devoted to helping the people in the countryside that called on just about any organization it could for help, and these Seabee teams seemed to be just the right thing for helping out in these little villages. So you might say that the Seabee teams were an arm of the civilian agency, even though they had their own military chain as well. See, it gets kind of complicated.

Q: Yes, very much fragmented.

Merdinger: Well, I mention those because they don't quite fit in these other categories. Then the third major category, of course, is the Public Works Department (one in Danang and one in Saigon), and this is the area that I know most about, having been in the middle of it.

Q: Would it be feasible before you deal with Public Works Department to say something about the Seabee battalion, its accomplishments and objectives, also the teams?

Merdinger: Basically the Seabee battalions were assigned as construction units. If you could generalize, you would say that the RMK contractors were building large complicated things, in relatively stable areas. The Seabee Battalions were building things that were in the more forward areas, in less secure areas, that tended to have more of a tactical dimension to them, and were much lighter. But this is a generalization that doesn't hold up very well, because you will find that the RMK people were not in secure areas in many cases.

Q: No area was secure.

Merdinger: That's right. And many times they were building relatively small things. On the other hand, the battalions might be in a rear area some place and they might be building relatively big things, and sometimes it's a little difficult to determine just where that dividing line was. As a matter of fact, there were many cases where a contractor might be working on something and a battalion came in to take it over. Or vice versa. So there was much interchangeability there, in terms of the kinds of projects they attacked.

Q: By whose order would this happen? Would it come out of Saigon, Pearl, where?

Merdinger: It tended to come out of Saigon. Along in the latter half of the sixties, a Joint Construction Agency was born in Saigon, this under a major general of Corps of Engineers, and this attempted to set construction priorities throughout Vietnam and give directives as to what should be built and where and in what order. But priorities in the early days, of course, were established pretty much in Saigon. As a matter of fact, there was a lot of red tape connected with these major construction projects over $25,000; they had to go through practically the same peacetime processes we have to build anything in the shore establishment over $25,000. This is a long complicated chain, I can assure you.

Q: Then I take it there was a fair amount of decentralization in this whole effort, contrasted with the operational where centralization became the thing, centralization right out of Washington.

Merdinger: Yes, I suppose, when you talk centralization and decentralization, you can make any point you want in connection with what happened in Vietnam.

Q: I was thinking of some of the commanders complaining about being inhibited by directives from the White House, "You shall not in this operation go beyond the ten mile limit" or something of this sort. That's real centralization.

Merdinger: Yes. We weren't in quite that situation, although many of these projects had to be approved at the Washington level before they could be built, so that this was something in the same class.

Q: What about the mortality rate among the men, the battalions and so forth, when they were exposed?

Merdinger: Well, everything considered, when you compare them to infantry troops, of course, we didn't suffer near the casualties that they did. Compared with Seabee casualty rates in World War II, it was significantly higher in Vietnam. I don't have the ratios now, but I do know that there were significantly more loss of life, percentage-wise, as well as wounded - possibly 8 to 1 or more.

Q: Did it have any impact on their morale?

Merdinger: It's hard to say, but I think if anything the sharing of this common danger probably promoted morale rather than inhibited it. I'm not sure anybody's morale is particularly raised when his buddy gets killed.

But I'm saying, there's something about this business of not only common danger but trying to protect yourself against it that brings people together. I think there is a morale-enhancing factor - if the enemy action is not too overpowering. And in general, it was not too great with our Seabee outfits. Again, if you were one of our fellows who was at Khe Sanh, I'm not sure he'd particularly agree with that observation, that is in the period when Khe Sanh was under such heavy attack - as some of my men were, by the way.

Q: You said a little earlier that Seabee teams were sent out into the hamlets, more or less tied in with the U.S. program of building up the knowledge and the skills and so forth. Could you say more about that? As a necessary factor in this kind of war.

Merdinger: Well, it was a crazy war. I don't know how to express it. A number of these teams went out into little villages, and they brought sanitation, water supply, sewage, this kind of concept for the first time to these places. Each one of these teams had a medical corpsman with them, and these corpsmen did all kinds of wonderful things for villagers, in terms of treatment of their health. From that standpoint of course, this was a real people to people operation. For the most part, they had nothing to do with fighting the Viet Cong, except indirectly in terms of their works, but it was not a combat role at all.

Q: Was it received readily by the people?

Merdinger: As far as anyone could determine, I think it was. You must remember that even the Marines did this sort of thing. The Marines were in I Corps. They took great pains to help – all kind of schools that got built, little compounds, and houses – some thing to make the lot of these people a little better.

Q: I talked with General Krulak and I know how vital he held this whole effort to be.

Merdinger: Yes. So you can't say that the whole military effort up there was devoted to fire power, by a long shot. There was this other element that was going at the same time.

Q: Is this something that one could attribute almost solely to Americans? This "altruistic" effort?

Merdinger: I don't know. I hate to wave the flag, but I will say this, that certainly there was a high degree of altruism on the part of our people over there. This is something I think that the public has missed in this country. They've got pictures of GI's on patrol, and fire fights in the middle of the night –

Q: And My Lai.

Merdinger: That's right, massacres and that sort of thing, and they don't really have any concept of this huge outpouring of good will on the part of our troops over there, in endeavoring to bring these people up to a better standard.

Q: To digress, why wasn't this visualized? Why wasn't it understood by the military element and utilized for what it was worth?

Merdinger: Oh, I think it was understood by the military element, but the point is that the word never got back to the United States.

Q: Why wasn't an effort made by the Army, Navy and so forth to do this, to replace the more adverse publicity that has been spread?

Merdinger: I'm not sure that I understand your question.

Q: Well, it was obvious that an adverse picture of our military effort in Vietnam was being put across in this country. Why was it not counteracted by the military itself in terms of its efforts in other directions?

Merdinger: Let me give you a personal example. In Danang, one of the responsibilities of my public works organization was to take care of the living accommodations for correspondents. In other words, we fixed hootches, we fixed up their dining room, provided air conditioning, painted the walls, made them comfortable. I had occasion to go over and talk to some of the correspondents every now and then, and many times I made the point that perhaps it wasn't much of a story but there was something going on here in Vietnam that I hadn't seen reported in any way. I thought they ought to come over and see for themselves. I was referring to this effort on the part of the Seabees in my outfit who were teaching these Vietnamese how to be plumbers and carpenters and what not - in other words, this great uplifting effort I've been talking about - or to come over and see the dam that we built to bring in the water, any number of things that we did. This never seemed interesting. They didn't want to come out and discuss it. There was always something that was more interesting to them. This simply wasn't a story as far as they're concerned. Now, maybe I wasn't very persuasive in telling them what we were doing. Perhaps the fault was mine. But a number of people I knew had the same experience. This simply wasn't exciting enough, with all the firing and shooting and everything going on – I guess maybe the battles tended to be a little more important in their eyes. But in the long run, as I mentioned, I feel this was the important part of our effort there.

Q: The military was cognizant of this effort. Why didn't they on their own, with their own publicity channels – ?

Merdinger: We did. I've got examples here. I can show you some of the stuff that we put out. But somehow it never made any kind of news. Usually good news doesn't travel very far.

When I was there in the '67, '68 period, I don't think the war was unpopular at that time. I think if you go back over the Gallup Polls and so on, you'll find that most of the people supported our effort there. And yet, the word was not coming back about this altruistic part of our effort there. I think that most attention focussed, as I mentioned, on the battles.

Q: This is what turned the tide in terms of public opinion, I mean, when we could see in our living rooms television scenes of battle and blood being shed and so forth. I don't recall seeing anything about the uplift effort on television.

Merdinger: No, and yet I daresay without having access to any real figures on it that we might have had more people engaged in that than in the fighting end of it.

No, I think that inadvertently, perhaps, whatever it was, we didn't get as good a press over there as perhaps we deserved for what we were trying to do, in this peaceful side of it.

Q: Well, will you focus on your own daily life in Danang and your efforts there?

Merdinger: I arrived in Danang in March of 1967 and stayed the regular tour of a year. I went over to take charge of a Public Works Department that was already very large by our Navy standards, probably 2600 people or so in it. By the time I left it had almost doubled to 4500, and we had plans which ultimately came to pass, to build a force of some 7000. Well, even in my time this was the largest Public Works Department the Navy had in the world. There was never anything quite like it. It grew like Topsy, in a way, because this kind of thing was not originally planned. I think if you go over some of the original documents, you'll see that the top people in the Navy in Washington really had no intention of committing large numbers of Navy men ashore in Vietnam. They felt this was either an Army war or a Marine war, and that their job was to get the Marines ashore and perhaps to get them some supplies, but that would be it. I think that where this whole concept changed was when the Marines became firmly committed to I Corps. I think we were normally accustomed, at least in recent years, to Marines making a quick landing ashore and taking an objective and then pulling out again.

Q: Island hopping sort of thing.

Merdinger: Yes, and now you've got Vietnam; they went in and just settled there. They were not equipped basically, with their table of organization, to furnish the huge municipal support that they ultimately came to need in all these big places, particularly in Danang, the kind of municipal support that is in fact the Navy Public Works Department.

Now, when the Navy first went in, it went in with the understanding that this was to be temporary. I mentioned this Public Works Department in Saigon that had been in existence from the early sixties and went out of business in 1965, at which time the Army logistics command took over. Now, with the Marines coming in in the North in the spring of '65, most of the correspondence of that time seems to indicate that the planners felt that the Marines would be supported by the Navy initially, but that after they were there for a while, 180 days I think the figure was, that the 1st Logistics Command would take over and help them.

Well, the Army didn't have the people. They weren't around. The Marines didn't have them. Ultimately the Navy just came in kind of piecemeal. And I think if you'll look over some of these documents, you'll find the sequence of events and even the confusion that led up to the formation of the Naval Support Activity Command. One month it was on, the next month it was off, and there was some question as to whether it was a Navy responsibility at all. I believe, one piece of correspondence between Admiral Rivero, who was Vice Chief of Naval Operations, and General Green, Commandant of the Marine Corps, came up with

Admiral Rivero stating that the Navy would give support to the Marines initially, but that they didn't foresee any long term support, and that he intended to get a decision as to whose responsibility this was. Well, the responsibility turned out to be the Navy's, so we ultimately got involved. It was a naval support activity, originally visualized as operating a part at Danang and auxiliary ports at Chu Lai and perhaps Hue-Phu Bai.

Danang, of course, was to be the center for it, and it was. Practically everything came in there directly and then it was transshipped from there in smaller craft, to the two places I mentioned, and then ultimately Qua Viet came into the picture. That was about four miles below the DMZ, and we had another supply operation going on there. But this concept of just operating a port, fell apart after a while since the Marines needed all kinds of help, including the Public Works Department which in the original planning wasn't even mentioned . When they were talking about the establishment of NSA they never even mentioned the words Public Works Department. But I think after a few months it soon became apparent that this was needed, and this was in '65 when the department was activated. We started out with a CEC lieutenant in charge. Shortly thereafter he was relieved by a commander, and shortly after that a captain came in. That will give you some idea of the rapid growth of this operation.

Initially this Public Works Department was concerned with real estate acquisition. It concentrated first on getting NSA itself established. Renting buildings and places to live and so on right in Danang while they got a toehold there.

Q: Was this a difficult job, the real estate operation?

Merdinger: Well, the real estate operations were always kind of tricky over there. I think that one thing that might be said, in terms of establishing some of our big camps. The sites weren't picked necessarily for their military desirability but simply because the real estate could be negotiated at those particular spots. We had to get in, so we took the expedient route and got whatever we could. So some of these places were not the best from a military standpoint. It wasn't the kind of terrain that you might have gone in and just taken; it had to be bargained for and haggled over. It was much more of a commercial operation than a lot of people realized.

In the early days the Public Works Department was just concerned with taking care of itself, getting itself established later on, just about the time I got there, it began to serve the Marines extensively. The first Marine Air Wing was at Danang, and we took over the responsibility for maintaining a whole airfield there. This support for the Marines was a piece meal sort of thing. First of all we sent a few Seabees over to take care of their generators, because they had a lot of fuel generators that they'd brought along with their engineer units. We'd repair them, maintain them, and then the next thing you know we were beginning to operate the electrical system. Then we were operating the water system. Shortly thereafter we were answering trouble calls to fix up structures, one of their hutches or something like that. In the meantime we were concerning ourselves with their real estate requirements, with design, planning, and future construction. So after a while we began to give them full public works type support that they would get in the stateside organization.

Q: You were filling a vacuum.

Merdinger: Yes, because their engineer groups were limited in size and they could only go so far. In addition to augmenting them, we began to replace those engineer groups as they went forward into more combat-oriented situations. Ultimately, of course, it didn't really make any different. Everything was a combat situation. But we initially, at least, talked of the secure areas, and Danang was one of them. It was relatively secure until we got hit in the summer of '67. I remember that well – a number of rockets and mortars hit the Danang air base and among other things hit the ammunition dump there. We had a couple of hundred buildings damaged, some of them completely caved in, brand new, had just been built. This included barracks and mess halls and just about every thing you can think of.

And that is the time our Public Works Department at Danang then got into the battle damage repair business in a big way. We jumped in just as soon as the place got hit. Of course, they always struck at night on these things. Anywhere from 11:30 at night to 3:30 in the morning. But we were over there immediately on the scene of the damage to make plans, so that just as soon as the dawn came up we had repair crews over there, putting back utility lines, repairing the buildings, that sort of thing. We ultimately I think got to be pretty competent at this sort of thing, because there were all kinds of attacks in the Danang area as well as further out.

Q: How frequently did they come after that initial one?

Merdinger: Well, things were relatively quiet right in Danang, until the Tet Offensive, and then we were getting something every night. We were getting hit on the periphery all over the place. I mentioned that first of all we started giving this sort of support in Danang. Then we had a public works detachment at Chu Lai. Then we went on up to Hue-Phu Bai, and the next thing you know we're at Qua Viet. Then the advisors - generally they were Army people, but there were smatterings of Marines, Air Force, even the Australian Army was connected with the operation.

Q: They were the first ones to get involved?

Merdinger: These were the advisors to the Vietnamese forces. They were in all sorts of hamlets up and down I Corps. They were not really taken care of to their satisfaction by the Army logistics command organization, so they requested that we start supporting them. So the next thing you know, we had more splinter groups out of Public Works, Danang, in all the little villages up and down I Corps. There were five main places that these advisors were located.

We assigned Seabees from Public Works to all the major advisor compounds in I Corps. These included Quang Tri, Hue, Hoi An, Tam Ky, and Quang Ngai. Included in our buildup was the augmentation of Seabees from CB MU 301. This was a specially commissioned unit, a

Seabee battalion, which came under the operational control of public works. As I mentioned before, our basic Seabee battalions were construction battalions - new construction. This outfit was really designed to do maintenance. However, there's a certain fine line of distinction here too, because the theory behind public works was that it would do no construction, it would simply maintain and operate facilities that were already built. We found that we were in the construction business too, for many reasons. Sometimes the RMK people or the Seabee battalion that built something might leave it 95 percent complete and then they were called somewhere else. Well, it might be 95 percent complete, but it couldn't be used. Some important ingredient such as the lighting had to be finished or something else, and this meant that Public Works had to go in and finish up a lot of these construction jobs. Then there were times when the construction forces were completely committed somewhere else and we needed something right away, so we went ahead and constructed it. A typical example was a water supply for Camp Tien Sha, which was a 4000 men Navy cantonment in the Danang area. There was water coming down off Monkey Mountain, but it wasn't being channeled where we could use it, so Public Works built a couple of dams up there and conducted the water down into Camp Tien Sha. This was very definitely new construction. But there was nobody else to do it, and we needed the water and we needed it immediately. I can cite any number of instances where we had to do the same sort of thing.

When we went up to the Qua Viet, there was a Seabee battalion up there that was doing some new construction, but they were fully occupied. We had to put up, what amounted to a little village up there and we had to do that with our Public Works people.

I'd like to say one thing about this Public Works Department. I mentioned that during my time it grew to some 4500 people, but a third of these were Seabees. In other words, it was one-third military and the other two-thirds civilian. The civilians were mainly Koreans hired under the Philco-Ford contract, or Vietnamese, but we did have a smattering of Nationalist Chinese, Filipinos, all sorts of people from all over Asia, but the main forces as I mentioned were Koreans and Vietnamese. The Koreans in the main were skilled workmen, the Vietnamese in the main were unskilled. Of course, one of our jobs was to try to get them trained.

I recall when I first got there, one of my warrant officers coming to me and saying, "We're never going to train these gooks. 20 percent of them never show up on a given morning. They're listless. They're not very bright." Just a whole list of negative things about these people.

I pointed out to him that basically we were training our reliefs, so let's get out there and get these people trained.

Q: That's a great incentive.

Merdinger: Well, I think that there were some people who were a bit reluctant. They felt there just was no getting these people into the artisan class. But they went out and tried anyway. I was very heartened when the same individual came back to me six months later very proudly pointing out that they had developed some cadres of artisans among these

Vietnamese, that they were now under their own Vietnamese foremen, that they were out there – this was a group of carpenters – out constructing hutches they were on occasion beating the Koreans. They were having a little competition out there. We had developed something that was very fine, indeed, I think in terms of expertise and confidence in themselves. So I think this was a successful adventure, the training of these people. Many times you would find a Seabee, Korean and a Vietnamese, all working next to each other, and the Vietnamese in a sense being trained by both of these.

Q: This would be a footnote – you mentioned the Ford contract with the Koreans several times. What is it?

Merdinger: In a sense it was a body contract. That is, we paid Philco-Ford to put one Korean on the line for us, in the skill that we were looking for. We would tell them, "By next October we will need 25 or more carpenters, 15 electricians," and so on down the line. Philco-Ford would go to Korea, recruit them and administer them. But in a sense they then turned them over to us to be incorporated into our public works operation.

Now, there were certain areas that were completely Philco-Ford people, and they would operate completely on their own. There were other cases where they were integrated through the whole organization. But there is a basic difference between our contract with Philco-Ford and the Army with PA & E that I mentioned before. In the PA &E contract the Army said, "You go out there and you run it." The Army would have a major some place who was overseeing this contract, but PA and E were really doing the public works functions. That is, they were supervising the maintenance and utilities and so on - without any direct supervision by the Army itself - whereas in our Philco-Ford contract, we incorporated these people into our military organization. It was being run by Civil Engineer Corps officers. We had a source of artisans, but we had not turned over an operation to these people that we could no longer control. In many ways the Army didn't really have significant control over its support organization, whereas we did.

Q: Why Philco-Ford? I associate that with magnetos and automobiles.

Merdinger: They got into this business of training people, foreign nationals and so on at some prior time. It happened before I got there, and all I did was take advantage of the contract already in existence. I think it would be an interesting sidelight to go back to, to find out how they did get this, and I guess somebody told me one time but I've forgotten.

Q: We were talking about the success of the effort.

Merdinger: Well, I think it was a great success. Here you had an international mixed military and civilian brigade, speaking all kinds of languages, scattered out over 200 miles of I Corps, in various positions and yet we made this thing work. And I think that it says something for our ability to organize, and somehow to see a problem that's really shifting day by day and go out and solve it. Admittedly it was in something of a piecemeal fashion, but I do think that we accomplished the mission very well.

Q: Pressing need was a real factor in this.

Merdinger: Yes. It wasn't unusual at all to work 90 hours a week, so there wasn't much else but work. I know I started office hours or field hours - normally I'd go to the office first - 7 o'clock in the morning. Basically we worked right through there till 6 o'clock at night - go back for a little dinner for an hour or so, then go back, and still be on the job till 10 or 11 at night. This, seven days a week. We knew it was Sunday because we used to go to church, but really one day moved into another and we were tremendously busy. I mention this, these office hours, because, of course, we did have main offices, and they did keep, like any other stateside office in business. But, of course, there was a lot of traveling to be done. I had an obligation, I felt, to get around to these units, up at Khe San or Hue and other remote spots.

Q: How did you travel, by helicopter.

Merdinger: Normally by helicopter, but sometimes we'd hop a ride on a Marine general's plane, one of these little things that carry four people - maybe get on one of the C-141's that was carrying a mob up to some place. We traveled in all sorts of conveyances - most of them not really suited for the greatest comfort. But there always seemed to be a reasonable amount of airlift around. Obviously, we couldn't go to most of these places on the ground. Most places were Indian country, and we would be relatively safe in the enclave, but once you got out in the open road, that simply wasn't the way to go. Armed convoys, of course, made their way periodically. Many times they were attacked, particularly at the Hai Van pass - groups going north from Danang, Hue and on up, had to go through the pass, and this was often a very precarious trip. Lots of people got killed. They were ambushed.

Q: You mentioned briefly the real estate problem. You made a point of that in your written article. I wish you'd elaborate on it.

Merdinger: I think that one of the things that continually seemed to confront us was real estate acquisition. One obstacle stemmed from the estensive number of graves in Vietnam - it seems the whole of Vietnam must be a series of cemeteries. To take a piece of property that had some people buried on it was quite an intricate process. It was more than simply buying the land. One had to go through all kinds of religious rites to move the spirits from one place to another.

Q: These were civilians in times past.

Merdinger: Yes. That's right. Over the centuries. Of course, it didn't help us any to find that we were coming along, say building a road, and we would stop one evening, and then the next morning find a number of graves out in front of us. Now, these, of course, were planted by some opportunists among the Vietnamese who wanted to hold us up. These were just fake graves. In other words, you had the bona fide ones as well as the ones that weren't so bona fide.

Q: What was the advantage to them?

Merdinger: Well, a fellow could demand an exorbitant price for his ancestors to get out of the way so we could continue our road.

Q: But a price would accomplish it?

Merdinger: Ultimately. I'm not aware of many times when we weren't able to move them. But sometimes it was just so difficult. The problems were so immense, moving all the bodies, getting together with the people involved, that sometimes we simply gave up and went some place else. So this real estate function was the culmination of a lot of things - horse trading, diplomatic, engineering, just a complicated business.

Q: You say there were so many religious rites. The Buddhists?

Merdinger: The Buddhists were there. Other religions were there, Confucianism, Taoism. There is a large Chinese culture as well as Vietnamese, and I guess you've got quite a mixture of religions, when you add it all up. I was never able really to distinguish among most of them.

Q: There was then I take it no real sense on the part of the property owner of, this is a war effort and this is our country, these people are helping us, therefore we should make some sacrifices ourselves?

Merdinger: Oh, I suppose there were some people who felt that way, but it didn't seem to us to be a factor. We always seemed to be running into tough obstacles, where a person simply wanted to be sure that he got his money's worth. Now, we leased a lot of property too. In the early days particularly in Danang, as I mentioned, there just was no place to live, so we leased a number of places. As a matter of fact, during the time I was there, I lived in a leased house in the town of Danang, as did our admiral. At one time practically everybody lived there. Then as we began to build accommodations over at Camp Tien Sha and China Beach - junior officers and enlisted men moved over there. Ultimately the whole naval operation in Danang moved to China Beach, when accommodations were available. So in essence just about everybody moved out of town. But even as late as early '68, a good many of us were still in town in rented houses.

Q: Then were did the owners go? When they leased their property?

Merdinger: I don't know. We always seemed to be dealing with some absentee landlord in Saigon. These were not at all, all the time, local people that we rented from. Of course, there was a ceiling put on rental rates, and that eased the burden somewhat financially.

Q: How useful was the South Vietnamese government in assisting you in your efforts?

Merdinger: The South Vietnamese government was definitely in the picture, and much of our work was done through them, if you will. In other words, even though we were ultimately renting from an individual, in a sense we were going through the South Vietnamese government.

You asked, how helpful? I'd say in some cases, very helpful.

Arm twisting in the right areas would be a big help to getting something that we really needed. In other places it wasn't, so I guess you'd just say that it ran the whole spectrum.

Q: The reason I asked that is because we've heard so much about graft and that sort of thing in South Vietnam.

Merdinger: Well, yes, there's a certain amount of graft. I think of it more in terms of problems of getting workers on the base. For instance, we had a number of Vietnamese workers at the Danang air base, and to get on that base they had to go through a Vietnamese security check. Now, while we had been the ones to build it and it was largely an American base, nevertheless utlimately it was considered a Vietnamese base, so Vietnamese could only get on and off it with permission of Vietnamese officials. At times, to get a pass and get on the base apparently involved a certain amount of money under the table, and we were continually wrangling with the Vietnamese about this. Here we were, trying to give their country military support, and somebody else in the Vietnamese government or the army or the establishment of some sort was holding their own people up, making them pay what amounted to bribes, in order to come to work for us so that we could support the war effort. So the whole thing was kind of crazy, and many times we complained to the local commanding general about this, and somehow the word would go down. It would let up, and then after a while the same situation would creep up again. Our people weren't getting on the base because they weren't paying enough in order to get their passes to get on the base. So this kind of graft was very annoying. I don't think they ever were able to stop it.

Q: You spoke of a government security check. How adequate was that?

Merdinger: I have no way of knowing. In theory, I suppose the South Vietnamese could tell whether this person was a VC or not, but I have my doubts about that. In one of our naval security checks, we discovered that one of the contractors public works had in Danang for hauling away garbage was a VC. Well, it took us about a month before we got rid of him, however, because he was providing us a service. We really didn't have any alternative choice just off the bat. We decided that his being a VC was of less danger to us than letting the garbage accumulate. So we kept a known VC on the payroll. And this I think was repeated many times. I was told that some of the convoys going north - in order to get through - would pay a certain amount to the VC and the VC let them get through. Perhaps they were hauling oil, gasoline, something of that nature. So this seemed to go on in a number of places - people paid off, even to the VC. Well, as I mentioned, it was a crazy war.

Q: Were you bothered in Danang by the blackmarket?

Merdinger: I'm sure there was a small black market, but we were never aware that there was anything significant there, certainly not on the scale that there was in Saigon, for instance.

Q: Had the drug problem become apparent when you were there?

Merdinger: No. The first I ever heard of it - the first at least that remains with me - was when I went to Australia. This was in late January of '68. And at that time, as we came through customs, we were subjected to a rather thorough going over by the Australian customs officials, and an official took me aside and said he wasn't going to strip me since I happened to be a senior officer on board, but that they were concerned about this problem, that at that time they'd picked up a handful of Americans with marijuana cigarettes, and apparently they'd impounded them in the country, in Australia. He asked me if I knew what marijuana smoke smelled like, and I didn't know. I was certainly not aware that any of my troops were involved in the drug traffic. I was completely naive about the thing. I'm inclined to doubt that we had any serious problem at that time in my outfit, in early '68, because I did get around, I saw the troops quite frequently in the field, and it certainly was never brought to my attention that they were high. But again, with a force the size we had and spread out the way they were, it would be again naive of me to think that there was no problem at all. I just don't know. I don't think there was a problem. Certainly none of my officers and none of my chiefs ever spoke about it. I should think that if it were a problem at that time, somehow the word would have filtered up to me.

I might add that morale was extremely high at that time.

Q: How would you analyze that?

Merdinger: Oh, just the general attitude, spirit with which they went about their work. I used to hold personnel inspections every week, with a different segment of the organization, which meant that a specific group had personnel inspection once a month. The pride they took in their uniforms and work I think was an indication. Here we were, right in the middle of the war, and they went through what was more of a peacetime maneuver, but I think it was good for all of us to get out and do this once in a while. So just looking at the way they prepared themselves for that, and comparing it with their daily routine, which was slugging in the mud; they were out in the boondocks and really involved in all sorts of tough labor - I saw them under all these conditions, and I talked to a good many of them, and in general their spirit seemed to be one of "I'm proud to be doing what I'm doing, glad I've got a job here."

Let me take one example. I recall talking to this Seabee, asking him how things were going, how he liked it, and he said he had always wanted to be a plumber and he became a plumber. Now he was in the Seabees and he was doing a plumber's work, and he was teaching Vietnamese over there how to be a plumber. He felt that we were engaged in an important enterprise, that he was part of it, and he felt proud of doing this. He felt compensated - his was an important role.

He pointed to a fellow over across the field and said, "You see that fellow over there? with the machine gun? He wasn't a machine gunner before and he won't be again. He was assigned to that role. I feel sorry for him. I feel like a very lucky man, to be doing what I want to be doing."

All I can say is that I came away feeling that this had been one of the most constructive years in my life, that I had served with some very able and dedicated people, and I came away with no sense of frustration, in the sense that we now seem to consider the whole Vietnam war. Oh yes, there were frustrating times, and I don't mean to belittle those. As you have in any kind of a situation. After all, what kind of a war ever went off very neatly? But the overall feeling I had was that we were doing something important and that our people were really dedicated to doing it.

Now, in terms of prosecuting the war as a whole, I think many times we felt that our hands were tied behind our backs, that we couldn't cross a certain line, that these people could come over and harass us and then go back across the line and be immune. There seemed to be some better way to bring the war to a conclusion more quickly, but somehow we didn't pull out all the stops. When you're getting shot at, it makes you a little annoyed with some of the decisions higher up. These were decisions coming from Washington that were part of a grand political design, and perhaps were the best course in the long run. But, when you're getting shot at, the normal reaction is to get the fellow who's doing the shooting, and get him out of your hair.

Q: That combined with all the brickbats.

Merdinger: Again, let me say that at that time we were not conscious of the war being an unpopular war. I wouldn't say that it was a popular war either. I would say that it was a kind of neutral situation at that time. To illustrate: when I went off to Vietnam, I went down to the airplane, my wife said good-bye. It was a commercial plane, no bands were playing and flags flying, no great movement off to the war zone that we'd seen in earlier wars. It was a very individual thing.

Q: It was an undeclared war and this made a difference there.

Merdinger: Yes. And coming home was the same thing. Nobody there to greet you. You just came home. As I say, it was essentially a neutral thing. But I didn't have in any way the sense that it was an unpopular war, while we were there. It simply wasn't popular. Maybe somewhere in between.

Interview No. 5 with Captain Charles Merdinger

Place: U. S. Naval Institute, Annapolis, Maryland

Date: 27 March 1972

Subject: Biography

By: John T. Mason, Jr.

Q: As usual, it's nice to see you again, Sir. Last time we talked about your year in Vietnam and the vicissitudes and triumphs of that period. I believe you wrote an article that covers some of this, did you not?

Captain Merdinger: Yes, I did. As a matter of fact, come to think of it, there are really two articles. One is a report in depth which I made to the Chief of Naval Facilities Engineering Command, and the other is the report in the NAVAL REVIEW, 1970, entitled "Seabees, Civil Engineers and Bases in Vietnam." I think that anything we may have missed here may well be covered in one of those two documents.

Q: I perused this and it's very interesting, parts of it quite technical.

Captain Merdinger: You're welcome to keep it, because I have other copies, if that would be of any used to you.

Q: Your period of duty there was for just one year, was it not?

Merdinger: Yes. That was the standard tour.

Q: What relationship did you have with the Commander Seventh Fleet, CincPac, any of these?

Merdinger: As far as naval personnel was concerned, my boss was the commander of Naval Support Activity at Danang.

Q: Who was that?

Merdinger: It was originally Admiral Lacey and then the last couple of months, Admiral Osborn. Now, they had a naval boss in Saigon, that is Commander Naval Forces Vietnam, but there was another chain, and this was back to Commander Service Force, Pearl Harbor. Admiral Hooper was very much in evidence in that role. In the naval chain, we really went more to Pearl Harbor than we did to Saigon. In a sense you might say we were detached from naval duty, and were really responsible to the Marines. The commanding general, 3rd Marine Amphibious Force (3MAF) was really the big boss up there, and we looked to him. In turn, I used to deal with the commanding general of the First Marine Air Wing, the First Marine Division, Force Logistics Command, and the Second Marine Division, but they, of course, were all reporting to Commander General, Three, MAF.

Now, the responsibilities we had that brought us directly in contact with the Marines were very simply these. We had to take care of the airfield that the Marines were running, and a number of the more settled though still advanced bases, from Chu Lai, all the way up to Keh Sanh. So you might say that in many ways, from a public works officer's standpoint, he had a number of bosses. The prime boss obviously was the Admiral in Danang, but he also had direct contact with a number of these major Marine units.

But as far as any ships at sea are concerned - you mentioned Commander Seventh Fleet, for instance - no contact whatsoever really with people of that sort.

Q: Did you stay there the entire year? Did you go back to Pearl?

Merdinger: On one occasion I went back to Pearl.

Q: What was the occasion of that trip?

Merdinger: The buildup at that time was such that for us to do our job in public works, we needed a great many more people than we had. And my main purpose was simply to go back to convince them that we did need these additional people - oh, some 500 at the time, and as we projected the number ran into a few more thousand.

Q: Was this a difficult task, to convince them?

Merdinger: I don't think it was too difficult, because ultimately the numbers were approved. I think that we had a good logical case. Sometimes it's difficult to put this down precisely on paper and make it as convincing as you can in person. So I think that this was a very useful trip back. In addition, an interesting thing happened at that time. While I was in Pearl, I got a call from Washington telling me to report back to Admiral Aurand in the Pentagon. No particular mention was made,

Merdinger #5 - 275

as I recall, of the reason for reporting back there.

Q: There never is.

Merdinger: I might add that my wife had come out to meet me at this time, so we were having a little R and R in Hawaii, and here we were ordered right back to Washington where we were living. I was able to convince everybody that really I should stay those extra few days, rather than go directly back to Washington. But when I got back there I found that Admiral (Pete) Aurand had been President Eisenhower's naval aide, and that Eisenhower had asked Aurand to get me back there. It turned out that he, Eisenhower, and some others interested in the formation of Eisenhower College wanted to talk to me about being president of this college.

Q: How did General Eisenhower know about you? Had you met him before?

Merdinger: No, I'd never met him, but I think it came about through contacts at West Point. Abe Lincoln was head of the social sciences department, Colonel Abe Lincoln, retired as a general now - he had mentioned my name as a strong possibility, and on the strength of that I guess General Eisenhower thought he'd like to see me.

So the upshot of this was, I was helicoptered from the Pentagon up to Gettysburg, and there I met the General and his assistant, Kevin McCann, I must have spent maybe 45 minutes, a little longer, in company with the two of them. This was the first time that I'd ever met the General, and I found him a very warm wonderful human being. He seemed even finer than the public picture of him. At least that's my recollection. We talked about a number of things, about how he originally wanted to go to Annapolis but ended up at West Point. I had wanted to go to West Point and ended up at Annapolis. And he talked about his time in the Army, a little bit about his relations with Montgomery, and ranged over a wide variety of topics. He mentioned that surely some of the happiest days of his life were when he was president of Columbia University. Then the subject of the presidency of Eisenhower College came up, and we discussed the pros and cons of it, what they were looking for in a President and so on.

At the end of the interview, I don't recall the exact words but it was something along these lines. In shaking hands, I said, "It's been a great privilege to meet you, General," and he said, "Well, I'd consider it a privilege if you'd consider the job." Or words to that effect.

Then I was put on a plane. By this time my wife had joined me and we got on this plane that J. Earl McGrath, former U.S. Commissioner of Education, was on, and he spent some time talking about this and said if he were my age this is just the thing he'd like to do, to become president of a college like this and get started and shape it in the years to come and so on. So I got the feeling that there was quite a sales pitch going on.

Q: Earl McGrath was actively looking for somebody?

Merdinger: Well, yes, and he had the official title of chancellor, I believe, at that time. We finally landed close to the place at Seneca Falls and there my wife and I met a number of members of the committee.

We were taken out to the college, and found it in its very early stages. It was just coming out of the ground. There were very few staff members selected at this point, so the idea was that the new president would come in and to a large degree set up his own staff.

So we had a very interesting day. It was a fascinating prospect. And yet I wasn't quite ready, I guess, to make my decision. Of course, one never knows. I had the impression that had I said yes that day, perhaps that would have been it, because they told me I was the only candidate. Now, who knows?

The point is that I said I wanted to go back to Vietnam and reflect on it, and after some correspondence with Kevin McCann that extended over some period of time I finally said yes, I thought I'd like to go, but by this time they'd made other arrangements. So that was an opportunity - I'll never know whether it was good or bad - but I missed it.

Q: The selection of president was the initial step. They had to have somebody to take charge of it.

Merdinger: That's correct. And I must admit that I didn't make up my mind right there, and I have no way of knowing that I would have been selected had I made up my mind, but the impression I had was that it was there if I wanted it.

Q: That was a very unexpected interlude, wasn't it, fighting the war in Vietnam and suddenly being asked to head up a college.

Merdinger: Yes, it was quite a surprise, a pleasant surprise because, of course, as I think I've mentioned, from the time I was stationed at the Naval Academy, I was beginning to think along these lines and was looking forward to an opportunity of some sort in this area.

Q: How did Mrs. Merdinger react to this particular offer?

Merdinger: Oh, I think that had I jumped into it with both feet, I think she would have been just as enthusiastic. But I think both of us were a little startled with the suddenness of it and we wanted to reflect on it a little, so we just withheld our opinions on it.

Q: Well, that would certainly seem to be to the good. One can't just say yes to a totally unknown proposition of that sort.

Merdinger: Well, every now and then I've speculated, what if we had said yes? Nothing might have come of it anyway. But had we gone there I know we would have been in for a lot of hard work, because I know the college has had what one would expect in the way of growing pains for a new college, particularly from the financial angle.

Q: So you went back to Vietnam again.

Merdinger: Yes, back to Vietnam. Then I stayed there, of course, through my tour the end of March. Then I went home the other way. That is, I didn't come back across the Pacific, I think I must have been one of the last ones who was able to go to Europe, because I was stopped, a couple of stops along the way, and told the possibility of going east was no longer there, and that regulations were saying we had to go back the other way. As I say, I think I was about the last man through, and there were a couple of others who were in the same category.

Q: Why was it changed, economy?

Merdinger: It was never quite clear. Usually reasons for such decisions are given on the basis of economy. I'm not sure whether this was fact or not. But I had orders to board one of the embassy planes in Bangkok. I might say that I took a little bit of a vacation en route. I went from Saigon and then took the commercial flight down to Singapore and came back to Kuala Lampur and then went from there to Bangkok. It was in Bangkok that I was scheduled to pick up the official flight enroute to Spain. Well, I did catch that flight, but there was a certain amount of discussion about it in Bangkok and again in New Delhi, which was getting pretty late in the day. When I got to Torrejon, it was a short matter of getting a flight up to Germany, then one to England, and it was there that I was scheduled to meet my wife, who'd come over from the States. We met at Oxford. Our daughter was there doing some postgraduate work in archeology. So the three of us had a great reunion. This was my homecoming from Vietnam.

Then, of course, back to Washington, where I spent a couple of months, largely in pulling together some reports on my experiences in Vietnam - putting this official report together and sitting on a number of boards and other things that a stray captain is always useful for in Washington.

Q: Anything of particular interest for the record?

Merdinger: Nothing beyond the report that I recall at this point. I think an important part of that time was spent collecting a lot of information to put in this report that was available in various places but had not been put together. Hopefully the next time we have to assemble such a Public Works Department, this report will offer some guidelines.

Q: In addition to the written report, were you called upon for verbal reports from any quarter?

Merdinger: Oh, yes, consulting particularly with the people who were concerned with the logistics out there in the western Pacific. These would be basically Navy people in the Pentagon and, of course, our own people in the Facilities Engineering Command, who were concerned with public works matters.

Q: CincPac, when you were in Hawaii, was he interested in the project? Did you make a verbal report of any kind to him?

Merdinger: Not to CincPac --

Q: Admiral Sharp, was it?

Merdinger: Yes -- but I did report to ComServPac, Admiral Cooper, and he and his staff were certainly interested in what we were doing there.

Q: So, having cleared up this by writing your report, did you anticipate what kind of - what kind of assignment did you anticipate?

Merdinger: Well, I didn't really know, and I felt that it was going to be my last assignment. I think about the only thing I wanted it to be was a good interesting job, and in the United States, so that I would be available to look into job opportunities. Fortunately, I was assigned as the commanding officer of the Facilities Engineering Command, the Western Division, at San Bruno which is just outside of San Francisco. I'd say that this certainly was one of the choice duty assignments in the Civil Engineer Corps in the eyes of many, and I so regarded it. It was a big division. It has a lot of interesting work going on, and certainly offered sufficient professional challenge, and I think we were delighted too to have an opportunity to live in the San Francisco area.

Q: I would think so.

Merdinger: Well, it was good for a couple of years, but I don't think we'd care to stay there forever, particularly in San Bruno. We were right under the airplane pattern. We were right next to the airfield, five minutes from it, and this is the international field I'm talking about, so you've got planes taking off at very short intervals. So we had that noise above us. Now, we had a superhighway going on one side of us, another superhighway on a second side, a new road situation coming in on the third side, and on the fourth side they were building a supermarket, so we were completely surrounded by construction. I mentioned the planes overhead. And the moles were digging up from underneath. So we were attacked on all sides.

Q: It doesn't sound very restful.

Merdinger: It was a delightful little house, but it was certainly besieged I can tell you.

Q: Shaking the foundations. Tell me about the job itself and some of the interesting projects.

Merdinger: The Western Division was responsible for all of the design and construction for naval and air force programs in the northern half of California, Utah and Nevada. Now, most of these bases tended to be within reasonable range of the Bay Area. I think the furthest project was a couple of hundred miles away. We had some interesting construction projects, and these took place in industrial areas such as the shipyards at Hunters Point and Mare Island, and in countryside settings such as Naval Air Station Lemoore. One of the most interesting projects during my time there was the purchase of Port Chicago. You may recall that the ammunition dump at Port Chicago had a very horrible explosion some time in the period of World War II, and there were hundreds of people killed and many wounded. It had long been a desire of the Navy to buy up a safety zone around the ammunition depot there, and included in this was the little town of Port Chicago. This had gone for years, but finally Congress had appropriated the funds and given the authority to proceed. Our division then was assigned the responsibility to go in and condemn the town and buy up all the property.

Q: How many dwellings there?

Merdinger: I don't recall how many dwellings, but I've got a feeling maybe a couple of thousand people might have been involved. I do recall that the total cost of this approached about 20 million dollars in negotiated settlements. Everything considered, I think that we did a very fine job in processing this. Towards the end there was one lone holdout who was pictured in the paper with a shotgun. He wasn't going to let the sheriff take him out of his house, but ultimately this was all taken care of.

Q: Was there any attempt to hold the government up for high price?

Merdinger: Well, I suppose as in any human dealings you have a few, but by and large I think the negotiations went fairly, equitably. I don't think anybody made a great killing on it and I don't think the government gouged anybody. A lot of this was sentimental - as you can appreciate, some of these people had lived there for many many years and the idea of having to move their home was a very tough thing as far as they were concerned.

Q: Were you involved with resettlement problems too?

Merdinger: Not as such. There was one section of relatively new houses and there was a question of a mover coming in and moving them some place else. So we had a kind of indirect interest in that. But basically our problem was to negotiate with the owner, buy his property, then either get rid of it or let him get rid of it as the case might be, and then his resettlement became his own personal problem.

Q: None of them were employed there at the base?

Merdinger: I don't know specifically but I wouldn't be surprised if some were. It would have been a natural place for some.

Q: That's an interesting project.

Merdinger: Yes, that wasn't precisely in the line of construction.

Q: It wasn't an engineering assignment.

Merdinger: Yes - well, you see, real estate is part of Civil Engineer Corps responsibility. When you say civil engineering, I guess you normally don't think of automotive transportation either, but that's another responsibility that we have.

Well, that was one time that was a little off beat. There was another project. This was a construction project and nothing unique in itself, but it involved the first Turnkey operation for building family quarters in the Department of Defense; and we were elected as the division to carry out that experiment. Traditionally the government would hire an outside engineer or maybe do the design itself, would design a project and then simply let it out for bids. In a sense you have two stages. You've got your architect-engineer initially, your builder finally. The Turnkey concept lumps the two of these stages together, and goes out to companies and says, "We want you to build this kind of a development, give us your schemes," and then you evaluate it not on cold hard cash as you do under the other system. In other words, low bidder wins in the first system I described. You design something, that's it, and the money then decides who gets the bid, the low responsible bidder.

The turnkey concept gets a little trickier, because you're not only evaluating the money but you're also evaluating the concept, and so therefore you have to put a lot more time into evaluating your proposals.

Well, the interesting thing that came out of this was that the firm we finally picked turned out to have some minority groups in charge. We had a Chinese-American who was the architect, we had a black construction man and so on, so this gave rise to sudden inquiries as to whether future Turnkey projects given by the government would only go to minority, contractors. Well, we didn't even know they were minority before we'd selected them.

So this was a new step, administrative step if you will, in the whole business of government housing. The project was not completed before I left so I can't speak specifically about it, but the thing was certainly going well when I did leave. My impression was that it was a success. I suspect that this may be the way that a lot of future government housing is built.

Q: A prototype.

Merdinger: Correct. I might add that about the same time, Philadelphia was also in the picture, so there may be some argument as to which was first. I think we had the first assignment, but who got the houses occupied first, I'm not sure.

Q: Did you have any work at Point Mugu?

Merdinger: There was work at Point Mugu but that did not come under our office. It came under the San Diego office. I might add that this was another thing that came up during my time, and that is the Facilities Engineering Command decided to combine all its field offices. We had similar field offices to the Western Division, one up in Seattle and one down in San Diego. The decision was made to combine all these activities at San Francisco. So we were concerned with consolidation on top of doing all the things that were normally within our purview, and having the other two divisions continue their work. I might add that the Seattle division, for instance, ran its work all the way out into the Aleutians up in Alaska. So we had the problem of keeping that work going and yet working to consolidate these divisions. By the time I left, the consolidation had just about taken place, and this involved moving scores of civil servants from Seattle or from San Diego, many of whom had been in the place for years and years. It was quite an operation just for the people involved, let alone all the legal and technical problems incident to this kind of a shift.

Q: And expense.

Merdinger: Yes. Of course, it was felt that as the Navy cut down in size, these huge divisions would go down too and perhaps perform more efficiently if combined. Satellite offices obviously were still left in San Diego and Seattle, but certainly nothing of the size they'd had under the old system.

I might add that there was another responsibility the division had, and that was to look over all public works maintenance and operations in the various public works departments within our division, within our area. This was not a construction or design function but rather you might say a management function. So that occupied a good deal of our time too.

Q: Was China Lake within your program?

Merdinger: No. That would be the San Diego operation.

Q: What kinds of facilities in Nevada were you concerned with?

Merdinger: We had an auxiliary air station at Fallon, and there was always something going on there, whether it be an addition to the hangar or another few buildings of one sort or another. I'd been to Fallon a number of times before and was pleased to see its development. Also, as I recall, there were some National Guard areas that we also did a certain amount of paving for — repaired hangars, that kind of thing.

Q: Some of these operations I imagine put you in touch with state authorities, didn't they?

Merdinger: Yes, to a degree. Although I personally didn't deal with too many of them. Normally it would be the project engineer or somebody else who would deal with this — with his counterpart in the state. I recall specifically a number of times talking with state authorities about proposed bridges in the Bay Area and how they would involve naval property and so on. So there was that kind of continual discussion with these people. Also, we had discussions with a number of state and local people on the question of pollution, pollution of the Bay, and as a matter of fact, I do recall one interesting incident when Congressman Reuss and his committee came out -

Q: Wisconsin Reuss?

Merdinger: Yes - to look into the pollution of San Francisco Bay, and I as the head of the division was one of the navy Chief witnesses.

Q: Was the Navy the principal culprit?

Merdinger: No, the Navy wasn't the principal culprit at all. Again my figures are vague, but of all the effluent contributed to the Bay, perhaps the Navy contributed something around one percent. Yet the newspapers of course, would always make this out as something very significant, because they liked to use us as a whipping boy.

But let me give you some idea of scale here. Let's say that some 500 million gallons of effluent were going into the Bay from all sources. Some of this would be treated, others would not be treated. Maybe the Navy's total out of this would be about four million gallons. In other words, perhaps less than 1 percent.

Q: Certainly not a major part of the problem.

Merdinger: Yet when this sort of thing was reported the newspapers would merely say that the Navy was pouring millions of gallons into the Bay a day.

Q: I suppose the feeling that the federal government should be a model.

Merdinger: That is correct. I might say that by and large the Navy was a model. We were far in advance of many of the other communities in providing this kind of treatment. Of course, there were problems. Many times we didn't get as much as we knew we needed. It was a question of when this went into a military appropriations bill. Military hardware would tend to get a higher priority in dollars than items such as sewage which would be fairly far down the list. Now, with all this talk of ecology we've been getting recently, maybe some of these items receive a higher priority than they used to.

But the Navy's contribution to the pollution did not stem from ignorance. The Navy knew what its problem was. It knew how to solve it. It had plans to do this. It simply was never able to muster the funds to accomplish it.

Q: And it was before the great campaign.

Merdinger: Yes. Yes. And I might add that we were also in the same business on anti-smoke pollution. That was one of the projects we had while I was out in the Western Division, and that was to create a big smoke eater on Treasure Island. This is where they had the fire fighting school, and had it for a good long time. A number of ships' crews would come over and train with a simulated ship, and, of course, all kinds of black smoke would billow up from this device. Now, in terms of its actually polluting the air, I doubt that it was very significant, when you consider all the other industrial activities in the area. But on the other hand it was Navy and it was visible at a great distance. So as a result of the public hew and cry the Navy acted to develop what amounted to a smoke eater; there was still smoke coming out of it but you couldn't see it any more. In other words, all the blackness had been taken out. So this was I think a relatively successful first pass at that particular problem.

I would say that in all areas of pollution, the Navy was on its guard, not only because the public was pushing it but because it just seemed to us that the proper thing to do was to get on this anyway.

Q: What about Treansure Island itself, the naval facilities there?

Merdinger: Oh yes. We did a lot of construction there, and particularly some of the new barracks. I think that some of them have set a rather nice standard for what the modern barracks ought to look like. For instance, we didn't have the stairways. We had a winding spiral that gradually took you up to the next floor.

Q: An iron staircase?

Merdinger: No, it was concrete and then overlaid with carpet. As you looked into the center area, you looked through portholes and there was a little garden in the center, so this was certainly a far cry from the old barracks that people had traditionally known. Yes, we did a lot of construction there at Treasure Island, but I guess the barracks seem to stick out in my mind more than anything else.

Q: Now, what about the naval shipyard? Did you get involved there or is that within the purview of the shipyard itself?

Merdinger: No, no, anything that had to do with construction of facilities.

Now, of course, we had nothing to do with construction of ships. But anything to do with constructing a building or putting in a railroad line or utility system, anything along those lines would fall under our purview.

We did work at both Hunter's Point and Mare Island.

Q: What sort of a budget would you have for an operation like this?

Merdinger: At any given time we probably had about 60 million dollars worth of construction physically under way. I think it fair to say we probably had in design, well over 100 million worth of construction at any given time. That is, it was on line and would utimately be let for contract.

As I mentioned, while we had a bit of in-house capability to do design, most of the work we had designed by architect engineering firms who reported to us. I would say that we probably had 400 or more such companies who were on tap for us to call on. At any given time we'd perhaps have 100 of these companies under contract to us.

Q: Could you go out and put a company under contract, after investigating it, or did you have certain requirements which came on from Washington, to which they had to conform?

Merdinger: Well, there were some general guidelines from Washington, but basically the local division sets its own standards. It has selection procedures calling for a look into each company that has indicated an interest in designing in a certain area. For instance, some people are interested in designing electric utility systems. Not everybody is interested in that. Others are designing school houses or roads. In the Division when a project comes up, you look to the people who have the expertise in that area. A selection board weeds out a number, on the basis that they'd had a number of jobs with us and we want to spread it around, or perhaps they haven't performed as well as somebody else might, a number of factors - how busy they are and so on. Then ultimately you get down and finally negotiate with the one you've chosen. But it's not a procedure where they come in with a low bid as you would in construction. It's professional negotiation based on a number of factors.

Q: Do you want to focus for a moment on the subject of labor relations? You obviously got involved in this.

Merdinger: Yes, one of the interesting areas we got into while I was there was that of hiring minority workers and being sure that we had a proper number of minority workers on a given job. This specifically came up -

Q: - the Philadelphia Plan.

Merdinger: The Philadelphia Plan came into the picture. It specifically came up in connection with a huge building - about a four or five million dollar job - that we were doing for the Air Force at Moffett Field. I got some correspondence from a fellow representing one of the black organizations who complained that we didn't have enough minority workers on the job at Moffett Field and wanted me to do something about it. I checked into this situation and found that as a matter of fact, even the foreman on the job was minority. But it turned out that he was Chicano and not black, and, of course, this other fellow didn't mean minority, he meant black.

Well, he pursued the matter for a while with us. We explained to him that basically our instructions came from Washington on these contracts, that we had no authority to specify any certain number of ethnic groups on any particular job. He, of course, was referring to what ultimately became known as the Philadelphia Plan wherein the contractor is supposed to attempt to have a certain number of minority people in various trades.

Of course, what he was really trying to get was the unions. Most of the unions at least in that area were pretty restrictive. It wasn't only a question of being restricted to whites, but only certain whites. If your father had been a carpenter then maybe you could get in, but if you didn't have a friend or relative you might find it pretty difficult. At least this was the public image of the situation. I can't say quite honestly what it was.

The truth of the matter was that the unions were very exclusive and there were very few blacks in them. And with the system the way it was -- as a matter of fact sponsored by the federal government, wherein the contractor would basically have to hire his people through the union hall -- the contractor in a sense was at the mercy of the unions. Again, this was something that you might say had been forced at the Washington level years ago.

So we pointed out to him that really our hands were tied and that he should go back to Washington on this score, if he was going to break the hold of the unions - in connection with minority employment.

After having a couple of sessions with him, he faded from the picture and I never saw him again.

Q: He made his pitch.

Merdinger: Yes, he did, and I trust that he got to somebody higher up. Because there was nothing, as I say, that we could really do.

Q: Did you have any other labor problems?

Merdinger: Oh, nothing of any significance. I think that, everything considered, during the two years I was there, we had a relative period of labor peace. Still every now and then there would be some kind of a strike here and there, on one of our jobs, but I don't recall anything very significant that really closed us down.

Q: Did you have a labor relations man on your staff to deal with these?

Merdinger: Yes, we did, and, of course, he talked with a number of people here and there, hopefully before the event became explosive. So I don't think that there's anything of any significant nature really to record on labor relations, except that by and large they were smooth. Part of this had to do with the fact that many of the unions were on three year contracts, and that the renegotiations for some of these did not take place during this time. In other words, they were still operating under the old -

Q: - a turnover period.

Merdinger: Yes. That's right.

Q: Were all the workers union workers or did you have some non-union?

Merdinger: Oh, I suppose we had some non-union in some places. It was pretty difficult to follow all these jobs. The point was, the contractor had to pay a certain minimum wage. This he had to do by federal law, for each one of the jobs, I should say each one of the trades. I just couldn't tell you how many were union and how many were not, off hand. I suggest that the majority were union.

Q: ... an operation under way, it must have required a lot of vigilance on your part and a lot of traveling.

Merdinger: Yes, I did a lot of traveling. But, of course, as you can appreciate, an organization like this has a lot of satellite offices. For instance, at each one of the stations of any size at all, the public works officer had two duties. He was the public works officer and he was also our resident officer in charge of construction, and he then would have one, maybe two - depending on the size of the place - assistant officers in charge of construction who would be assigned right out of our office. To give you some idea of the structure, normally the public works officer would be ordered by the Bureau of Personnel to the station directly as the public works officer, and he had the responsibility for his department. But then he would get this additional duty which would place him on our staff, and as he was the senior civil engineer on the station, all these assistants who were coming out of our office would report to him. So they were not in any way on -- you might say -- the rolls of the station, but rather over on our payroll in San Bruno. But it is true that I did a lot of traveling to every one of our different sites, just to check from time to time as to how things were going, whether it be the design part of it or the construction part. But, of course, the basic work was being done in the field.

Q: So this wound up your naval career?

Merdinger: That's correct. That was my last tour of duty, and I think it was an exciting one, a very pleasant one, stimulating, and I left with a feeling that it's a job that was worth doing, and it wasn't just some kind of a pre-retirement slot, far from it. It was a very active kind of a job.

Q: Were you able, in spite of all this activity, to put out feelers for something in the educational world, where you wanted to go for a second career?

Merdinger: Yes, I wrote letters to a few friends and mentioned to them that I figured on being available in the summer of 1970, and that I was interested in something in education, if they knew of anything to let me know. In the course of this Washington College decided that they were interested in me, and ultimately I was selected as president. That selection, as I recall, came formally in January of 1970. I didn't officially leave the Navy until August 1st, 1970, but the last month on leave, from

July to August, was actually in the president's chair. I assumed the presidency on the 1st of July, 1970.

Q: Did you find it a very great wrench to leave the Navy and take up something so drastically different?

Merdinger: Not initially, because so many of the problems were similar. It was in some ways like being the commanding officer of the base. You've got your personnel problems and your budget problems, and all these other things that come together to make an organization. So in many ways, I didn't feel much of a change initially. As time went on of course, the disparity became more evident, as I got into problems, really academic problems or problems with the faculty and so on that were different basically from the day to day problems one has in the Navy organization.

Q: The military command idea doesn't prevail in the university.

Merdinger: No, as a matter of fact that's anathema. I think, if I could generalize, a good many faculties would prefer to live in a state of anarchy. They don't really want to be organized. They don't want anybody over them. So many things are done by committee and consensus, and there's usually resistance to anyone coming in and making any kind of unilateral decision without a multitude of discussions.

Q: Laissez-faire.

Merdinger: Yes. They become used to this kind of operation, doing everything - doing most things by committee and consensus, and it's very difficult really for an executive to come in and operate in the way an executive normally operates let's say in business or even in the Navy.

Q: Nevertheless there are assets in a career like this.

Merdinger: Oh yes. I think that having been subjected to the discipline in the Navy in approaches to organization, to budget, - relations with people and so on - all these are things one can use very handily when he moves into an academic administration spot. As a matter of fact, I have talked to a number of people in academic administration who had previously served in the armed forces, and almost universally they tend to regard their service in the armed forces as perhaps the most valuable single experience they had to prepare them for this administrative post.

I remember one superintendent of schools in Massachusetts telling me precisely that, that of all the postgraduate study he'd done the thing that benefited him most was his experience in the armed forces, in terms of doing his job as superintendent.

Q: I can see where it would be of immense value.

Merdinger: In some ways it can be a handicap too. At least in these last few years, as you know, there's been really a very anti-war, anti-military sentiment on a good many of the campuses. Yes, it's an emotional thing, and manifests itself in many ways. I certainly sensed it when I came on the job and haven't completely shaken it either. I would like to say that all is peaceful and quiet, but it's not. There are still certain reverberations and they stem in part I think from this military background.

Q: Well, I certainly do thank you for taking the trouble to give me these interviews, and I trust that when you get the manuscript you'll be pleased with the fact that it is a part of the record.

Merdinger: Thank you too, Jack. You have been a very adroit questioner and a patient listener. I have enjoyed this experience immensely, thanks to you.

Index

to

Series of Interviews

with

Captain Charles J. Merdinger,

U. S. Navy (Retired)

ADAK - Aleutian Islands: Merdinger goes there to command the 124th Seabee unit and to serve as Public Works officer, p 135 ff; caliber of the working force, p 137; problems involved in organizing and improving the force and operations, p 140-1; consolidation and centralization of buildings, p 141-2; entertainment, p 142-3; athletics, p 143-4; personal reactions and recommendations, p 145-7; expense of maintaining the base, p 147-9.

USS ALABAMA: Merdinger transfers to ship building at Norfolk, p 56; installation of new control equipment for guns, p 57; caliber of new recruits, p 58-59; preliminary training, p 60; equipped with radar, p 61; near collision off Newfoundland, p 61-2; discipline on board ship, p 64-67; to Scapa Flow with British Home Fleet, p 71-2; the Murmansk run, p 72; fake invasion of Norway, p 73-4; to the South Pacific, (mid 1943), p 74-5; comraderie with Royal Navy at Saipan, p 76-7; performance of her 16 inch guns, p 80.

ATOMIC BLAST SIMULATOR: a prototype design made at Pt. Hueneme, p 167.

AURAND, VADM Evan Peter (Pete): Calls Merdinger back to Washington to talk with General Eisenhower about possible appointment as President of Eisenhower College, p 275.

BUREAU OF YARDS AND DOCKS: Merdinger given assignment there after return from Oxford University, p 126; as program coordinator - illustration of his work, p 126-7.

CAMP TIEN SHA: A Navy Cantonment in the Danang area, p 258; Navy Public Works provide the water supply, p 258, 265.

Civil Engineer Corps: see entries under RENSSELAER POLYTECHNIC INSTITUTE. After two years at RPI Merdinger inducted into the Corps, p 91.

CIVIL ENGINEERING THROUGH THE AGES: title of book written by Merdinger at Oxford and published in 1963, p 117; how its chapters appeared initially, p 128-129.

Danag, Vietnam: Merdinger in charge of Public Works Department in 1967-8, p 252 ff; concern with real estate acquisitions, 255, 263-5; attack on the base (1967), p 256; Public Works becomes involved with new construction, p 258; diversified nature of workers, p 259; efforts at training for relief, p 259; success of training, p 261-2; p 265; employment in the base and graft among Vietnamese, p 266; no noticeable supply of drugs apparent, p 268; high morale of the Seabees, p 269; clarification of chain of command from Danang through Saigan to Pearl Harbor - and through the Marine commands in Vietnam, p 273; Merdinger makes trip to Pearl Harbor to ask for additional personnel, p 274-5; tour of duty ends in March, 1968, p 278-9.

DAVISVILLE, R.I.: Navy establishes school to deal with practical problems of the Civil Engineering Corps, p 92; now at Port

Hueneme, p 93-4.

Deck Officer: Duties of contrasted in North Atlantic and South Pacific, p 81.

Dietrich, RADM Neil K.: executive on the ALABAMA at time of her commissioning, p 60, 64-5.

EADES, Capt. James: p 103.

EISENHOWER, Gen. Dwight D.: Calls Merdinger to visit him in Gettysburg, Pa. - discuss possibility of presidency of the new Eisenhower College, p 275.

ENTHOVEN, Dr. Alain: p 234-6.

Farfan, Panama Canal Zone: p 95-96.

FIFTEENTH NAVAL DISTRICT HEADQUARTERS - PANAMA: Merdinger becomes the base maintenance officer, p 94; also resident officer in charge of construction - roads and houses at Farfan, p 95; contracts, discrimination, p 98-103.

FORRESTAL, The Hon. James: acts to get Navy permission established for Rhodes Scholarship applicants, p 106-7.

Harlem Globetrotters - p 133-4.

HISTORIOGRAPHY: Course at the Naval Academy for which Merdinger served as co-teacher, p 199, 202.

HOOPER, VADM Edwin B.: Commander, Service Force, Pearl Harbor (1968), p 273, 280.

KIMMEL, RADM Husband E.: p 48-50.

MARINE CORPS I: Vietnam: p 252 ff; p 257-8, p 261.

McCANN, Kevin: Assistant to General Eisenhower, p 275, 277.

McGrath, Dr. Earl J.: Accompanies Merdinger to Seneca Falls, New York to visit site of Eisenhower College, p 276.

Merdinger, Captain Charles J.: Personal history, p 1-4; selection for Naval Academy, p 4-7; marriage, p 89; birth of first daughter in Panama, p 103; wins a Rhodes scholarship, p 103; suggestions made that he seek a scholastic career after the Navy, p 222-4; personal reactions to a year of duty in Danang (1967-8), p 269; called to Washington for conversation with General Eisenhower about Eisenhower College, p 275-6; retirement from the Navy (Aug. 1, 1970), p 296.

Mills, Capt. Gloom: skipper of the NAS at Miramar, p 158-160.

Miramar - Naval Air Station: Merdinger transferred to air station from Adak, p 150; station just commissioned as a full fledged station, p 151; master jet station, p 152-3; problems in securing land, meeting objections, etc., p 153-4; rapid refueling of planes, p 155; planning for jet runways, p 156; consultation in Washington, p 156-7; building a dog house, p 158-164.

MOREELL, Adm. Ben.: p 226.

NABESHIMA, VADM Baron: Japanese Senior Staff Advisor to Merdinger at Yokosuka; p 177-8; characteristics of the Japanese worker, p 178, 180; his views on the background to Japanese involvement in WW II, p 180-182.

NAGAGAWA, VADM. Head of the maintenance shop, Yokosuka, p 179-180.

NAURU: Alabama bombards island in connection with Tawara landings, p 78-80.

U. S. Naval Academy: entrance and comments on the course of study, p 6-7 ff; training for leadership. p 9-10; athletics, p 10-12; curises, p 13-15, 18-20; career appeal of the Navy, p 17-18; pride in being regular navy, p 21; comments on importance of class standing, p 23-26; disinclination for aviation, p 27. Merdinger returns as head of the English, History and government department, p 197 ff; change in course emphasis, p 203-4-5; trend to specialization, p 205-6; discussion of faculty, p 208-9; p 219-220; The Academic Board, p 212-3; Public Speaking classes, p 213-4; disciplined education in a military set-up vs the freedom in a private institution of learning, p 214-5-6; citation of statistical table on Naval Academy men doing graduate work at MIT, p 217-8; faculty selection, p 220-222.

U. S. NAVAL ACADEMY - Foreign Affairs Conference: Merdinger acted as Chairman during his stay at the Academy, p 199-201.

NAVAL FACILITIES ENGINEERING COMMAND: Merdinger becomes Assistant Commander for Maintenance and Operations, p 225; the administrative set-up and the duties, p 227-231; cost analysis, p 232-3; p 236-7; the single executive idea, p 238-9; Merdinger writes a detailed report on his work at Danang, p 272; Merdinger (1968) becomes Commanding Officer, Western Division, at San Bruno, Cal. p 281.

U. S. Naval Reserves: comments on, p 21-2.

NAVAL REVIEW: Merdinger wrote an article (1970) entitled, "Seabees, Civil Engineers and Bases in Vietnam," p 272.

NAVAL SUPPORT ACTIVITY COMMAND: Evolution of this command in Viet Nam, p 253-5.

USS NEVADA: Merdinger's first duty after graduation (Feb. 1941), p 28-30; discussion of pre WWII philosophy as it pertained to the battleship, p 30-31; duties on NEVADA in days immediately preceding Pearl Harbor attack, p 32; also - see entry under PEARL HARBOR - Dec. 7, 1941; repairs at Bremerton, p 50-51; Merdinger stays with NEVADA until she is taken to Bremerton, p 55-56; near grounding before she goes into drydock, p 67; charges made by captain, p 69-71.

NIMITZ, FL. Adm. C.W.: comes aboard the ARIZONA to present awards after Pearl Harbor attack, p 54.

OXFORD UNIVERSITY - England: Postgraduate work at Oxford, p 12; see entries also under Rhodes Scholarships; p 119-120; method of awarding degrees, p 120-1; academic environment, p 122-126.

PARAVANES: use of on U. S. ships at Scapa Flow, p 75-6.

PEARL HARBOR - Dec. 7, 1941: story of the attack on the BB NEVADA, p 33-43; immediate reaction of junior officers to the Japanese attack on ships and installations, p 48-49; early recovery of order, p 52-3; hospital facilities, p 54-5.

PHILADELPHIA PLAN: as it pertained to the construction job at Moffett Field, p 292-3.

PHILCO-FORD contract: p 259; explanation, p 260-1.

POINT HUENEME: Naval Construction Battalion Center - Merdinger becomes the Commanding Officer and director of the Naval Civil Engeering Lab. p 164; formation of ice airfields, unit at Squaw Valley, p 165; designing of atomic blast shelters, p 166; work on designing gear for use in amphibious landings, p 168; desalinization of water, p 171; awareness of similar research efforts in other places, p 171-173; comments on productivity, p 174-6.

PORT CHICAGO - San Francisco Bay Area: Navy condemns the town property and purchases it to establish a safety zone about the ammunition dump, p 282-3.

PUBLIC WORKS DEPARTMENT - Puget Sound: p 130 ff; problems with labor unions, p 130-133; the Jim Creek Radio Station, p 130-1; atheltics, p 133; basket ball coach, p 133-5; transfer to Seabees unit at Adak, p 135.

QUA VIET: p 254; Public Works constructs a little village, p 258.

RADAR: early training in use of radar at time of Pearl Harbor attack, p 43-44.

Rensselaer Polytechnic Institute: Merdinger takes postgraduate work in civil engineering, p 8-9, 12; joins CEC and goes to RPI in Jan. 1944, p 83 ff; war-time speed-up course, p 84, 86-9, 91, 100, 107.

RHODES SCHOLARSHIPS: history of navy attitude towards, p 103-105; Merdinger makes application as a graduate of Rensselaer Polytechnical Institute, p 107-8; special interview arranged for Merdinger in Bogota, Colombia, p 109-112; reaction in BuPers to Merdinger appointment, p 112-3; financial arrangements, p 114; travel, p 115-116; Merdinger writes a history of Civil Engineering as his dissertation, p 116-7; Oxford life, p 118-126; background to Merdinger appointment in 1962 to head History Department at U. S. Naval Academy, p 198.

RICKOVER, ADM Hyman George: his criticism of education at the Naval Academy, p 198.

RMK - BRJ: Civilian engineering contract in Viet Nam, p 240-1, 245.

ROOSEVELT, President F. D.: p 49.

RUSSELL, Frank: member of Rhodes Scholar Association - encouraged the Navy to permit participation, p 105-6.

SALLIED SHIP: illustration of an ancient technique to get a ship off a sandbar, p 63-4.

SAN BRUNO - WESTERN DIVISION, FACILITIES ENGINEERING COMMAND: Merdinger sent there in 1968 as Commanding Officer, p 281-2;

Port Chicago project, p 282-3; TURNKEY Operation for building family quarters, p 284-5; consolidation of the Western Division, p 286; extraneous duties, p 286-7; pollution of San Francisco Bay, p 287-9; a "smoke eater" on Treasure Island, p 289-290; Treasure Island construction, p 290; Budgets and contracts, p 291-2; minority workers on construction jobs, p 292-4.

SEABEE Battalions and Teams - in Vietnam, p 241, 243-5; p 248, p 257-8; p 269. (See also - entries under ADAK, Aleutian Islands.)

TARAWA: 78-90.

Taylor, Dr. F. Sherwood: curator of Museum of History of Science, p 118.

TEREDO (Toredo): pile eating worm - problem dealt with at the Naval Civil Engineering Lab in Port Hueneme, p 165, 167.

BB TIRPITZ: German Battleship in North Sea, p 72-3, 75.

TOP SECRET: comments on the side effects of such a classification, p 43-45.

TREASURE ISLAND - San Francisco: p 290.

TURNER, VADM Stansfield: influential in getting Navy to permit men to apply for Rhodes Scholarships, p 106.

TURNKEY OPERATION: for building family quarters in Defense Department, p 284-5.

VIETNAM: p 239 ff. the Civil Engineer Corps, p 240 ff; training

of Vietnamese workers, p 243-3; use of Koreans, p 243. Jo
Joint Construction Agency - purpose to set construction
priorities throughout Vietnam, p 246. Aid program, p 244-5;
use of Seabees in villages, p 244-5. Hamlet program,
p 248-251. U. S. Correspondents in Vietnam, p 249-251.

Washington College: Merdinger selected as President in January, 1970, p 296-7.

Whiz Kids: p 234-5.

YOKOSUKA: Merdinger spends three years as Public Works Officer (1959-62), p 177 - 197; description of duties of Public Works Department, p 182-185; problems with supplies, p 186 ff; home defense attitudes, p 187-8; language problems, p 190-1; Japanese manners, hospitality, p 193-196.